TRADING FUTURES

filipe maia

A THEOLOGICAL CRITIQUE
OF FINANCIALIZED CAPITALISM

trading
futures

DUKE UNIVERSITY PRESS · DURHAM & LONDON · 2022

© 2022 DUKE UNIVERSITY PRESS *All rights reserved*
Printed in the United States of America on acid-free paper ∞
Designed by Aimee C. Harrison
Typeset in Minion Pro, Inknut Antiqua, and Vectora LT
by Westchester Publishing Services

Library of Congress Cataloging-in-Publication Data
Names: Maia, Filipe, [date] author.
Title: Trading futures : a theological critique of financialized
capitalism / Filipe Maia.
Description: Durham : Duke University Press, 2022. | Includes
bibliographical references and index.
Identifiers: LCCN 2021062186 (print) | LCCN 2021062187 (ebook)
ISBN 9781478016144 (hardcover)
ISBN 9781478018780 (paperback)
ISBN 9781478023425 (ebook)
Subjects: LCSH: Capitalism—Religious aspects—Christianity. |
Financialization—Religious aspects—Christianity. | Wealth—
Religious aspects—Christianity. | BISAC: RELIGION / General |
BUSINESS & ECONOMICS / Finance / General
Classification: LCC BR115.C3 M235 2022 (print) |
LCC BR115.C3 (ebook) | DDC 261.8/5—dc23/eng/20220608
LC record available at https://lccn.loc.gov/2021062186
LC ebook record available at https://lccn.loc.gov/2021062187

Cover art: Andrew Ellis Johnson, Detail of *Futures*, 2005-09.
Acrylic on five panels; 80 × 180 inches total. Courtesy the artist.

For my father, whose memory conjures up hope

CONTENTS

The work that led to this book is bookended by two global crises whose impact and lingering effects are connected and still unraveling. In the embryonic stage of this project, the world was hit by the financial meltdown of 2007–2008. If there's one moment when the thought of *Trading Futures* first became possible, it was when I was confronted by the pious calls to "save the banks." Although I was still early in my studies, my mentors in Latin American liberation theology had taught me well: this creeping in of theologically inflected vocabulary in the realm of capitalist economics was not just a matter of a secularized religious ethic. Capitalism ought to be investigated as a mode of enchanting reality according to its own principles. The calls to "save the banks" haunted me sufficiently that I entered a doctoral program in theology wanting to investigate financial capitalism.

The future, up to that point, was already at the center of my theological concerns. But what I learned surprised me: the future was also at the core of financialized capitalism. As I expose it in this book, in the age of banks, capitalism turns its energies toward projecting, predicting, and anticipating the future. I suggest that we have been thrown into this projecting spree of financialized capitalism. As I thought about this and investigated the critical literature on financialization, I realized that the work of theology, which to me was so centered around future-talk and the possibility of hope, could not remain the same after the advent of financialization.

Trading Futures thus attempts to offer a critical portrayal of financialized capitalism as a future-engendering social force. As this is a work of Christian liberation theology, I must begin in the calamity of the present and linger on the wreckage inflicted by this all-consuming mode of future-talk. But I also insist that the Christian eschatological imagination might afford different forms of constructing our collective sense of futurity. The futures predicted and promised by financialized capitalism are ubiquitous in social life. And yet the future remains fundamentally unpredictable, unpresent, and unpresentable. The future is a time that is not yet. The eschatology of liberation I offer in this book finds its edge—its theological vitality and political radicality— precisely in this "not yet."

As I was completing this project, the COVID-19 global pandemic hit, and a familiar narrative emerged. As the virus spread, we faced calls for "reopening" the economy at the expense of public health concerns. To me, the echoes with the demand to save the banks were transparent. Once again, hegemonic economic forces prioritized the need to keep the economy running, this time by exposing workers to the perils of a deadly virus. What may have been opaque for many was coming to light in full color: when choosing between the profit motive and social and planetary life, capitalism easily opts for the former. As readers will notice, the theological and political tradition that I follow in this book is not naive about the ties between neoliberalism and neofascism. Neoliberal policies, after all, were first tested under the dictatorial regime of General Augusto Pinochet in Chile in the 1970s. The weight of that tradition bears heavily on me when I confront our current global wave of neofascist regimes and the multifaceted pandemics we now face. This death-dealing logic of capitalism and the demand to keep the economy always in operation continues to enclose the future of millions.

The economy must remain open; banks must be saved. The two crises that envelop my work in *Trading Futures* harbor the apt motto of neoliberalism: there is no alternative. In this context I have understood my task and vocation as a theologian in the Christian heritage as necessarily saying a resounding no to the alternative-less predicament imposed by neoliberalism. I have found my way into this position through critical engagement with the vocabulary of Christian eschatology. I sustain that the language of hope is, prior to anything else, a way of persisting in saying that what will come cannot be conflated with what is. This book is my theological statement that there must be a way, that the future may come with something other, that the future offers a ringing "not yet" to hegemonic claims about what simply "is."

In this book I insist that, faced with all-encompassing crises and oppressive systems, the vocabulary of Christian hope offers no easy solutions, no panacea of a world that will be just fine in some there and then. Rather, I have come to believe that learning to cope with pain and learning to work for justice entail a certain ability to say "not yet." In other words, the work of mourning and the work for justice engender and require hope. They engender and demand some form of future-talk. In this sense, the contrast that I trace between the futures of financialized capitalism and the Christian eschatological imagination fundamentally points to different modes of socially producing future-talk. I insist that the language of hope that springs forth from bodies and communities in pain cannot be confused with the drive to predict the future for the sake of profit. My hope is that the future that this book tries to summon bears witness to the cries and the demands that we have heard in this crisis-ridden period of ours.

. . . . .

Though punctuated by these crises, the work that now culminates in this book was accompanied by a multitude who made this path joyful and fulfilling. Mayra Rivera's mentorship and careful reading of my work accompanied me since the conception and early iterations of this text. My gratitude to her is boundless. Amy Hollywood and Joerg Rieger were also careful readers of an early version of this manuscript, and I'm very grateful for that. Julie Meadows encountered this project at a juncture where I thought the manuscript had run its course, but her generous spirit and editorial gifts allowed this text to flourish into what it has become.

Several other colleagues read portions of this manuscript. Jung Mo Sung read chapter 2 and offered substantial commentary on chapter 4. My studies of Franz Hinkelammert's work are in large part the fruit of his influence at the very beginning of my academic journey in Brazil. I'm grateful for the members of the research group Capitalism as Religion, representing various Brazilian universities and social movements, for lively conversation and feedback about chapter 2. The short-lived but successful Bay Area Theologians workgroup also offered insightful comments on my introduction, and I'm especially grateful for Jessica Coblentz's suggestions. My former colleagues at the Pacific School of Religion also were introduced to portions of this text and encouraged me in the process of revising the manuscript.

I especially thank Inese Radzins for commenting on a previous version of chapter 3. Years before Susan Abraham joined the Pacific School of Religion as dean, she nourished my budding eschatological proclivities and witnessed my first writings on Hinkelammert. For these serendipitous encounters, I'm thankful.

I thank Dean Mary Elizabeth Moore for granting me a course release during my transition to Boston University School of Theology and for generously supporting me with funds for editorial work. My gratitude also goes to Dean Sujin Pak and to Academic Dean Bryan Stone for their encouragement and support for my work. I'm grateful for Hyebin Hong, who offered bibliographic support to my research, and Miranda Mason for invaluable support with formatting my endnotes and bibliography. Shelly Rambo offered helpful feedback on chapter 6 in addition to being an incredible mentor. A very honorable mention to my outstanding colleagues Jonathan Calvillo, Becky Copeland, Nicolette Manglos-Weber, Luis Menéndez-Antuña, and Shively Smith, all of whom read my introduction and helped me better frame my goals for this project. Their friendship and collegiality mean the world to me.

I extend my gratitude to the students who joined the seminars in which I shared material included in this manuscript. Thanks to the members of the God and Capital seminar offered at the Pacific School of Religion and the Graduate Theological Union in Spring 2017 and Spring 2019 and to the members of my Readings in Marx seminar, offered at Boston University School of Theology in Fall 2020. Portions of this text were also delivered at the Gould Lectures Series at Eastern Nazarene College in Spring 2021, and I'm honored by the invitation and the hospitality extended to me by Philip LaFountain.

The anonymous readers who commented on my manuscript offered incisive, generous critique. I hope they will notice their presence in this book. Thanks are also due to my editors at Duke University Press, Miriam Angress and Annie Lubinsky.

Writing can be an isolating process, and this has been the case for me. Yet I was always surrounded by an affective infrastructure that sustained and enlivened me while writing this book. My friends Rafael Ferreira, Louise Junker, and Yohana Junker were a wellspring of pure joy. Daniel Souza: *eu vivo e morro sendo amigo seu.* My mother, brothers, parents-in-law, brother- and sisters-in-law, nieces, and nephews: your love and care nourished me into who I am, and I can only be as long as you are fully alive. Juliana, my friend and wife, is the one with whom I learned that hope is the name we give for our love for the future. The chance of loving what is yet to come alongside her is the greatest gift life has given me.

As this project comes to a close, I remember that it started in mourning. In what had been projected as my first month of dedicated time for writing, my life came to a halt as my father crossed to the other margin of the river as an ancestor. His passing was painful, and the work of mourning was long. And yet, somehow, in his ancestrality he communes with me in hope. This book is dedicated to his memory.

introduction
of edges and hedges

The future is the theme of this book. Readers in the Christian theological tradition may recall Augustine's confessions and know that this book is therefore about something that does not exist. "Who therefore can deny that the future does not yet exist?"[1] Apparently, no one can. To offer a book about the future, I therefore must confront the brief caveat that Augustine's text opens up: the future does not *yet* exist. And so I may clarify the purpose of this book: that which is not yet is what I hope to write about. More precisely, I want to reflect on the pause one makes when saying that the future is not—yet. I approach this pause as an invocation of something to come. The moment we gather our breath to speak of the future is a time when something comes to pass. In this book I propose that future-talk *summons*. The future may not be yet, but it can make things become.

The Christian imagination of the future finds its breathing room in the pause of the not—yet.[2] It functions through negation and expectation, resistance and invocation, all the while conjuring up a multiplicity of senses.[3] *Sense, sentido, sens*—these are words that mean, on

> How does the future, which does not yet exist, diminish or become consumed?
> —AUGUSTINE, *Confessions*

> [In] finance we worry about money and we worry about the future.
> —PAMELA PETERSON DRAKE & FRANK J. FABOZZI, *The Basics of Finance*

the one hand, something akin to "meaning" or "understanding." As I argue throughout this book, discourse about the future functions to create meaning, to provide a narrative about history, to indicate one's expectation about something to come, to predict and prevent, to engender hope and despair. On the other hand, if I may write with an accent, *sense* can also identify a *direction* or a *trajectory*. In which *sentido* are you walking?, one could ask in certain languages. Language about the future functions thus too: it indicates a direction. In some instances it might create one where none exists. Future-talk unveils a direction, not a destination or assurances of arrival. As I will show, in the theological traditions committed to liberation, the future offers an escape route used to run away from the ties that bind us to an unjust present.

With the weight of this semantic multiplicity, this book proposes that future-talk makes sense. It offers meaning and signals directions. We soon shall see that these meanings and these directions are not one. Multiple forces take hold of the pause implied when saying that the future is not—yet. *Future-talk*, as I present it in this book, names the diverse ways of construing a time that is to come, the forces at work in shaping our expectations for the future, and the manifold embodiments of hope. More than mere speculation, discourse about the future signals something about the world, its suffering and expectations. This book portrays future-talk as mirroring something back to all who proclaim a word about the future. Underneath the voice that speaks of the future, there is always a voice addressing the present.

In theological discourse, eschatology occupies the space created by this not—yet. Catherine Keller reminds us that the eschatological imagination takes us to the *edges*—of time, of the world, and of ourselves. *Eschatos* means "edge," among other things.[4] Jacques Derrida enlarges the list of possible definitions: the *eschaton* is "the extreme, the limit, the term, the last, what comes *in extremis* to close a history, a genealogy, or very simply a countable series."[5] This book seeks to move its reader to these edges, to the limits of time. In these extreme moments, I show how theologians committed to liberation have encountered the hopes and dreams of those who have been pushed to the margins.

The edges of Christian eschatology have long been punctuated by the future-talk of the marginalized. Liberation theologians have embraced this heritage, showing that on the margins of society, future-talk functions not simply as the extreme of a "countable series" but as a demand that one indeed moves on to a new story. Addressing a Latin American context marked by colonial domination and economic exploitation, liberationists suggested that the Christian eschatological vocabulary enlivens resistance to oppression.

2

Hope in this register offers marginalized communities a world-shifting perspective. It represents the reality of the status quo from its underside, and its statements about the future defy the forces of oppression. Future-talk, in this *sense*, summons the twist from a present of injustice into the possibility of a story of liberation.

But not only that. Other modes of future-talk also inhabit this pause engendered by the recurrence of this not—yet. Future-talk is also a key weapon to validate and expand nefarious projects. In our times, Keller posits, the "codes" of the Christian eschatological vocabulary "have been smoothly integrated into a military-industrial-infomedia empire with the power to fulfill much so-called prophecy."[6] Perhaps unnamed in Keller's list of sites where the "explosive" futurism of the Christian tradition persists is exactly what this book seeks to address. And that is the empire of finance. I propose in this book that financial discourse has hegemonic power over future-talk.

So, yes, the theme of this book is the future, the future that places us on the edges of time. But also the future that makes us *hedge*. *Trading Futures* probes the tension between an edge and a hedge. The latter, I submit, marks a dominant mode of future-talk in contemporary times. We have come to think of the edges of future-talk with the definitive accent of the hedge, of the bet, of the risk, of the maneuver that seeks to make a profit out of something that is not—yet. This pause offers the breathing room for financial profit.

With attention to the hedge, this book leads us to the realm of finance. I invite the reader to contemplate the ubiquitous concern that financial discourse has with predicting and managing the future as the secret of a profitable business. Social ethicist Nimi Wariboko identifies this future-bound ethos as integral to capitalism and its "split" economy, a term he uses to name the fundamental schism between finance and the economy. While making provisions for the future is a central task for any economic system, in capitalism the split harnesses a present of deprivation while finance keeps pushing the economy toward the future.[7] In a naming that is far from coincidental, a futures contract, one must remember, is a commodity that can be bought and sold in financial markets. As we shall see in more detail in the next chapter, a futures contract is a type of financial transaction that "requires a party to the agreement either to buy or sell something at a designated future date at a predetermined price." Economists Frank Fabozzi and Franco Modigliani clarify that the function of futures markets is to allow "market participants to hedge against the risk of adverse price movements."[8]

I argue that in the current iteration of global capitalism, these financial gadgets do more than manage risk. The hegemony of finance over our global economy has allowed it to construct the future in its own image and like-ness. Our very sense of time and our aspirations for the future have been shaped by financialized capitalism. Sociologist Elena Esposito has explored the hedges made in financial markets to similarly argue that they in fact produce our collective futures in their attempt to anticipate market move-ments. When one trades a futures contract, "one generates a constraint that influences the course of time and contributes to the creation of what will become true in the future."[9]

In finance, future-talk is the site for profit making. Our very sense of time and our perception of what remains possible in the future have been de-termined by financialized capitalism. Admittedly confused but nevertheless intrigued by the technical jargon of financial textbooks and corporations, I could not help but notice how central the future is in financial discourse. Finance, as specialists in the field define it, is "the application of economic principles to decision-making that involves the allocation of money under conditions of uncertainty."[10] This uncertainty is pervasive in the grammar of finance. Financial institutions have intensely pursued accurate ways of predicting and anticipating movements in financial markets as a means of generating money. Gathering data in order to forecast market movements propels the global economy toward the future. As a textbook in the field confesses, somewhat inadvertently, "in finance we worry about money and we worry about the future."[11]

Indeed, we worry. At the hands of financial institutions, the global econ-omy entered a spiral of crises that has plagued us for the past decades and whose effects continue to be felt.[12] In the United States alone, the mort-gage crisis of 2007–2008 caused $19.2 trillion to evaporate from American households.[13] Americans' 401(k) retirement funds, an old promise that ac-cess to financial markets could be democratized, suffered precipitous losses during the recession.[14] As I will suggest, an economic landscape of stagnant wages and diminished labor rights expanded the power of financial corpora-tions into every aspect of social life. But when banks and financial juggernauts crashed, the price of the crisis was paid in full by the most vulnerable and impoverished sectors of society. On a global scale, a crisis first experienced on the level of private capital soon made itself known in public finance in the fiscal crises experienced by countries in the Eurozone and from there spread to several other parts of the world.[15]

For a minute portion of the world, however, the economic landscape of the past decade brought stellar prosperity. Since the financial crisis, we have grown accustomed to reports about staggering levels of income inequality.

By 2017 eight men owned as much wealth as the world's poorest half, and the wealth of the top percentile of the global population surpassed the wealth of the other 99 percent.[16] The world's 2,153 billionaires own as much wealth as 60 percent of the global population, or 4.6 billion people.[17] In the aftermath of the Great Recession, between 2010 and 2016, the wealth of the world's bottom half—3.6 billion people—decreased by $1 trillion (a fall of 38 percent), while the wealth of the richest sixty-two individuals increased by more than half a trillion dollars (an increase of 45 percent).[18] The numbers give a somber verification of David Harvey's apt description of capitalist progress as a process of "accumulation by dispossession."[19] Financialization has turned "bare life" into the very source of profit, says the economist Christian Marazzi.[20] If in finance "we" worry about money and "we" worry about the future, it appears that our concerns for the future are not evenly distributed.

The concern for the future in financial discourse has led me to interrogate the stakes of this massive process of financialization of future-talk. This book asks, What happens to our worries about the future when they are framed as a concern for money? What mode of future-talk is constructed in the context of this overwhelming search for financial profit? What underlying assumptions are at play when *futures* has become the name of commodities furiously exchanged in financial markets? What are we to hope for in these financialized times?

This book probes these questions to indicate that financial discourse produces a particular mode of future-talk, one that hides deeply rooted injustices. In the words of the political scientist Ivan Ascher, the society engendered by financialization is one where capitalists have appropriated the means of *prediction*.[21] Similar to the control over the means of production, the means to predict and anticipate the future do not benefit us equally. Literary theorist Annie McClanahan points out that the risks associated with the hedges of financial markets have been summarily transferred onto the "most vulnerable economic subjects."[22] For multitudes, the future-bound spiral of financialized capitalism introduced what a *New York Times* report ably called a "chronic crisis over the clock."[23] This chronic crisis unveils a true disparity in what may be termed the social distribution of expectations. Today access to financial power dictates a class divide that materializes in disparate levels of hope for the future.

Economists and social theorists have employed the term *financialization* to describe the dynamic whereby the center of gravity of capitalist profit making shifts from industrial production to financial transactions and speculation.[24] This turn is entangled in the rise of neoliberalism. Neoliberalism is an economic and political theory about the functioning of markets and their ability, when unimpeded, to lead societies into prosperity.[25] Neoliberal economists advocated that giving free rein to financial markets would propel the economy toward a future where we would be unhindered by oppressive government forces and where the lifting tide of a booming economy would benefit us all.[26] As will become clear in my exposition, the stories of neoliberalism and financialization overlap to the point of becoming indistinguishable. "The neoliberal era is one of finance," say the French economists Gérard Duménil and Dominique Lévy.[27]

The renowned sociologist Anthony Giddens once portrayed capitalism as a system that "actively tries to break away from its past" in an intense pursuit to "colonize" the future.[28] I suggest in this book that the movement to explore unknown territories with the desire to control them is a good metaphor for capitalist temporality. If explorers navigated west in their pursuit of riches, capitalism pushes toward the future in its pursuit of profit. For the political theologian Adam Kotsko, in the late modern period, when it appears as if capitalism has exhausted its search for new places to colonize, neoliberalism has engendered a new form of "temporal colonialism" and sought to explore the uncharted territory of tomorrow's land.[29] As we probe financialized capitalism, I will narrate this conquest of the future.

This book engages finance as a major social and political force, not just a branch of economics or a sector of the economy. As I construe it here, finance is a mode of discourse that shapes our collective life and our very hopes and aspirations for the future. Under financialization, forecasting and anticipating the future has turned into a very profitable business for those who assume control over the means of prediction. For the rest of us, it has wrought a society of economic disparities where access to the future—in the form of a pension fund, a mortgage, a university education—must be mediated by financial markets. Anthropologist David Graeber has suggested that the rise of finance to the center stage of the global economy has set a new trajectory for how we imagine the future: "It could be well said that the last thirty years have seen the construction of a vast bureaucratic apparatus for the creation and maintenance of hopelessness, a giant machine designed, first and foremost, to destroy any sense of possible alternative futures."[30] More and more, our expectations for the future have been diminished by a financialized capitalism that consumes our very ability to hope.

I propose in this book that a liberating account of future-talk is needed to address this massive destruction of an alternative sense of the future. This book insists that hope for the future is more than a disposition to see the cup as half full, as the saying goes. Instead, I investigate the social means by which future-talk is produced. Critiquing pie-in-the-sky imaginaries is less my concern than questioning the social forces that projected the pie in the sky in the first place. What social agents and forces benefit from such ethereal hope? In what follows, I propose that the colonization of the future advanced by financialized capitalism creates material conditions in which our senses—our meaning-making energies and our directions—are diminished and exploited for the sake of profit. Yet, and herein lies the liberationist maneuver I seek to weave into my argument, the future that financial discourse so confidently seeks to predict and anticipate is also that which is not—yet. In this pause the drive to colonize the future encounters its moment of instability: that which is projected as the possibility of profit is also what cannot be controlled.

The future, as that which is to come, escapes the managing aspirations of financialized capitalism. This escape, I argue, is the site of a liberating hope that gains control over the means of production of future-talk. For this reason this book attends to the ways in which future-talk offers a safe haven for many to whom the present is simply too stifling. For multitudes, the fact that the future is not—*yet* offers a pause to conspire different world becomings. Hope-filled words about the future are enmeshed in our material conditions, and when they are uttered under precarious and oppressive conditions, they are more than speculation about what might come. They function as a summons of a time that is not—yet but that must become. In this mode of socially producing future-talk, we are conjured by hope as a tactic to maneuver around and escape an all-consuming present.

Hope in Financial Times

In the current iteration of global capitalism, our worries about money and the future have expanded to the level of ultimate concern. I propose we confront our economic predicament under financialization by bringing financial discourse into the maze of the eschatological imagination. My goal is to think of the edges of Christian eschatology with an eye toward the hedges performed in the world of finance. Whether as a bet on a horse or as a prophetic announcement, the future is always at stake in financial and theological discourse.

The future-oriented dimension of finance triggers the theological analysis this book seeks to offer. The theological maneuver here is warranted, I argue, because financial discourse privatizes the discursive means of future-talk. Theologian Joerg Rieger suggests that hope is "tied to images of what is ultimate and on which we can depend." Financial crises therefore impose a "long-term crisis of hope" as they expose the flaws of economic structures that we tend to think of as reliable and ultimate.[31] Kathryn Tanner's recent incursion into financial discourse offers a perceptive theological reading of the crisis of hope engendered by financialization. Tanner tracks the "new spirit of capitalism," arguing that financialized capitalism disciplines subjects to an "unbearable continuity ... between past, present, and future."[32] Tanner argues that the push to forecast and anticipate the future has the effect of eliminating the surprising quality of the future and of circumscribing our imagination of what may come. Under the constraints imposed by financialization, one "learns to hope for nothing more from the future than what the given world's present limits allow."[33] Financial discourse has given the dominant shape to our future-talk by binding us all to hope for nothing else than continuance.[34]

Our inability to expect anything of the future but continuance is connected to the economy of debt imposed by financialization. I demonstrate that shifts in global capitalism have made the majority of the world's population dependent on the financial sector for services like housing, education, health care, and other basic necessities of life. Financialization engenders an economic predicament in which debt is massively socialized, subjecting poor and working-class people to their creditors. Drawing from critical theorists and continental philosophers, I represent debt as a socioeconomic mechanism that shapes our subjectivity. Under financialized capitalism, indebted subjects have their expectations for the future bound to the power of their creditors.

Philosophical theologian Philip Goodchild goes so far as to suggest that "[debt] takes over the role of religion in economic life."[35] In *Theology of Money*, Goodchild inveighs against the power of monetary promises to capture our attention, demand our devotion, and consume our time.[36] He claims that modern economics creates a "heavenly future" that promises the end of all constraints on human development but identifies money as the sole path to attaining this future.[37] But as the economy continues to launch itself farther and farther into its concern for money and for the future, it continuously consolidates the power of money over our lives. The anticipation of the promised future "introduces a distortion into emancipatory practice, producing ignorance and slavery."[38] As Goodchild implies, behind the promises of future wealth offered by capitalism lies a perverse logic that entraps people in a present state of debt.

8

My theological response to the debt economy imposed by financialization is to retrieve and expand the tradition of Latin American liberation theology. In this heritage I identify a twofold insight that goes to the core of financial discourse: first, that future-talk in the hands of the powerful functions to justify and validate systems of oppression; and, second, that future-talk makes different senses when uttered by marginalized communities. These alternative senses of future-talk afford a prophetic and poietic rendering of reality with the power to subvert the order of things.

Latin American liberation theologians have explored the vocabulary of Christian theology to conjure forms of hope that resist hegemonic imaginaries about the future. In fact, the preferential option for the poor, the cornerstone of the tradition, puts theology at the crossroads between economic exploitation and temporal deprivation. Gustavo Gutiérrez famously traced the project of liberation theology back to the incessant search for riches that marked the invasion and colonization of the Americas.[39] The genealogy of liberation that Gutiérrez sketches remembers the testimony of the Dominican priest Bartolomé de Las Casas, who, at the dawn of the colonial age, cried out against the lust for gold, an ambition that "stripped [Amerindians] of their lives before the time."[40] For Las Casas, the death of Indigenous populations is folded into the desire for wealth. Gutiérrez concluded: economic exploitation materializes in the premature death of the poor. In language that I explore further in this book, economic injustice ends up "devouring" the future of multitudes.[41]

For liberation theologians, theological reflection begins when one confronts this moment when life is taken before its time. At the dawn of the neoliberal era, under the dictatorial regime of Augusto Pinochet in Chile, liberation theologian and economist Franz Hinkelammert began to suspect that the incessant drive for profit making harbors capitalism's own way of enchanting reality.[42] Hinkelammert detects the capitalist force operating at the subliminal layers of social life to shape our hopes and aspirations for the future, only to then subject us to its own power. Hinkelammert suggests that capitalism produces an insidious imagination of the future that authorizes and validates current power differentials and injustices. The pursuit of financial profit, much like the thirst for gold in the colonial era, consumes the lives and expectations of a large portion of the world's population. In retrieving Hinkelammert's work, *Trading Futures* sets out to offer a theological critique of the capitalist mode of future-talk enshrined by financialization.

Liberationists have a deep appreciation for the vocabulary of Christian eschatology and have often embraced it to articulate their critique of oppressive systems. With a nod to Karl Marx, liberation theologian and poet Rubem Alves contends that Christian hope gains different shapes when we attend to the "sighs of the oppressed creature."[43] In Alves's theology, I argue, the sighs and groans of bodies in pain are signs pointing to the possibility of different futures. For him, constructing different modes of social organization is tied to different modes of imagining and speaking about the future. Alves offers a poetic and prophetic account of Christian eschatology that unearths the subversive force that hope has in twisting the timelines of oppressive systems. Hope is not immaterial daydreaming nor wishful thinking. For Alves, hope matters, it gains flesh, and it embodies resistance.

The poietic energies harbored by future-talk carry the theological work this book offers. By combining God-talk with this future orientation, the theological task entails the formation of alternative imaginaries about the future that may confront the future-devouring forces of financialized capitalism. Though our context is rather distinct from the decades in which liberation theology was first formulated, my gesture follows a discernible pattern. In the early years of its formation, liberation theologians followed Gutiérrez's famous definition of the theological task as "critical reflection" on praxis in light of the Word of God.[44] Hope for Gutiérrez was historically bound to human action in history and to God's encounter with the people in the event of liberation. A similar argument was developed by Alves in his 1969 book *A Theology of Human Hope*, a publication based on his doctoral dissertation, entitled "Towards a Theology of Liberation."[45] As these titles suggest, liberationists were prone to relating their theological impulse to a critical engagement with future-talk. For liberation theology, hope has functioned as an interruptive force against dominant discourses. It is therefore telling that in his later writings Gutiérrez spoke of the work of theology as a "hermeneutics of hope."[46]

In this book I combine Gutiérrez's definitions to suggest that theology is *critical reflection on hope*. This gesture binds the critical impetus of liberation theology to the ultimate reality to which hope directs us. It also ties theological discourse to the ubiquitous concern for the future in financial discourse. Attending to the centrality of future-talk in theological imaginaries affords a perspective on the ways financialization has shaped our very ideas of ultimate reality. As this book shows, our common hopes and aspirations for the future are too often bound to the futures traded in financial markets.

I suggest that the work of theology, as critical reflection on hope, is even more urgent in the context of the dominant future-talk constructed by financial discourse. Financialization shapes our hopes for the future, our

10

subjectivity, and encloses possibilities for the future. Addressing this context theologically entails the exposure of this future-shaping, hope-enclosing force of financialized capitalism. This is the task I embrace in the first part of this book. Furthermore, I maintain that theological work can identify and explore alternative sources of hope if properly inflected by the tensions that pile up on the margins of society.[47] In the second part of the book, I argue that escaping the imposed debt economy of financialized capitalism embodies a tactic to occupy the means of prediction. Future-talk, as I approach it in this book, may afford routes to escape financialization. *Trading Futures* suggests that the pause needed to say that the future is not—yet is a capacious moment for the invocation of a different world into becoming. An eschatology of liberation constructed from the edges of the social body invokes us to escape the pull of the hedges of finance. Therein we are summoned into alternative future becomings.

Futures Denied

My concern for the future and appreciation for the language of hope meet an intellectual and political environment in which future-talk is a contested territory. Eschatology, while gaining prominence at the start of the twentieth century, remains a space of sharp divisions—and majestic dismissals. The latter attitude has in fact been embraced by major figures in progressive thought. Portraying the future as a moment of easy resolutions and as a shorthand for conservative agendas is a common trope in contemporary theory and theology. For good reasons, obviously. Admittedly, Christian images of the future have informed social and political imaginaries that serve the purposes of reactionary programs. For many, future-talk and the Christian eschatological imagination are escapist and offer bad news for those to whom the present is stifling. These progressive thinkers address the problem of futurity from different standpoints, but they concur that the language of hope is regressive. In the following paragraphs, I offer a brief catalog of arguments for the disavowal of future-talk.

Writers concerned about progressive causes tend to represent future-talk as a form of obscuring the operations of hegemonic forces. Mark C. Taylor's 1984 book *Erring* offers a model argument for the dismissal of eschatology. The book responds to crises in religious sentiment in a postmodern context that has grown suspicious of grand narratives. Taylor sets out to deconstruct theological paradigms of historical progress and propose a notion of history as "erring," a term he coins to name a disposition to inhabit reality without recourse to teleological justifications.[48] Taylor criticizes theological narratives for their tendency to totalize history and eliminate its "loose ends."[49] For Taylor, disavowing future-talk is liberating: it alleviates the need for teleological reasoning for one's actions, it frees the subject to adventure into endless wandering, and it "liberates the drifter from obsessive preoccupation with the past and future."[50] Taylor's understanding of the postmodern condition thus invites the full embrace of the present moment.

Such a rejection of the future is similarly adopted by queer theorist Lee Edelman, who suggests that future-talk operates in a heteronormative framework that associates hope and positive expectation with the ability—and desire—to produce children. For Edelman, a social obsession with the figure of the Child engenders a "reproductive futurism" that ultimately preserves heteronormativity.[51] Across the political spectrum, the image of the Child regulates queer loves by launching a "fantasy of the future" that cannot fathom any real political possibilities apart from the Child.[52] There can be no space for queers in the future precisely because the queer is socially construed as the one who denies the coming of the Child. Edelman argues, "That future is nothing but kid stuff, reborn each day to screen out that grave that gapes from within the lifeless letter."[53] In theorist Lauren Berlant's work, this is known as "cruel optimism," an affect or an attachment to something that actually interrupts our flourishing.[54] Edelman demands we get rid of such an attachment to futuristic projections.

Addressing anti-Black racism, theologian Anthony Pinn has rebuked the task of projecting futures, suggesting it assumes an epistemological location "outside and external to circumstances from which the theological hermeneutic operates."[55] For him, discourse about the future assumes a "Gnostic" and "esoteric" position that empties theology of its grounding in material, immanent reality. As an arrogant claim to knowledge, future-talk cannot exist without neglecting the actual circumstances of any given historical moment. "Abandon hope," Pinn recommends, "and reject the projection of futures as theological categories."[56] What he dubs "moralist theology" disavows speculation on the future as futile in order to attend to the urgent needs of the present.[57] Theology wastes time when it labors to project futures, whether these are within the realm of possibility or not. For Pinn, what is left for us to do is simply to embrace reality with all its troubles and work toward its transformation.

The denial of future-talk for the sake of justice is conclusively articulated in the work of liberative ethicist Miguel De La Torre. In *Embracing*

Hopelessness, he claims that the problem with the language of hope is its impetus to supplement a scene of injustice and oppression with "quick and easy fixes."[58] Hope can exist only under privileged circumstances.[59] For the oppressed, "eschatological visions of utopia" function in alienating ways and veer them away from rebellion and revolutionary praxis.[60] De La Torre maintains that narratives that try to harmonize present suffering with future resolutions are stratagems of oppressive forces. He insightfully argues that the construction of history is never innocent and that the projection of future scenarios "serves to justify and mask atrocities and injustices today as a necessary evil required to usher in some future salvation history."[61] In contrast, justice as a historical fact is born out of attitudes that confront tragedy and oppression without maneuvering into future solutions. Against hope, the Christian position is to remain steadfast in the pursuit of justice in the present while dismissing any promise of future reward. "The hopelessness I advocate," De La Torre explains, "is a methodology propelling the marginalized toward liberative praxis."[62] By disavowing hope, he says, we can fully embrace a stance of faithfulness, perseverance, and discipleship.

In this book I embrace the critique of future-talk, and I support the claim that Christian eschatology has validated and in fact motivated conservative, sexist, heteronormative, racist, and otherwise oppressive movements. I fundamentally agree with arguments that criticize the deployment of the language of hope as both a justification for present injustice and an excuse for the lack of historical engagement. But as readers will soon notice, this book does not treat hope and justice, future-talk and present action, as antagonists. While the critique of future-talk interests me in this book, it must be said that this concern presumes the plurivocity of the language of hope. The assumption that future-talk functions in one single way is oversimplified. As I will argue, the voice that speaks of the future also responds to the present, even if opaquely. It is far from certain that the imagination of the future—even when it entails some traditional Christian narrative—forms a timeline that abolishes the "loose ends" of history, as Taylor claims. It is doubtful that liberative action can be satisfied by a commitment to a present without remainder, as De La Torre pleads.[63] As I approach it in this book, hope need not be a statement about easy guarantees that everything will be all right. It remains historically true and theologically salient that future-talk has been one of the defining tactics and survival techniques of those whose very futures are being cut short. In fact, for those whose futures are colonized by time-consuming economic forces, hope may offer the respite necessary for survival.

13

No doubt, escapism is a true problem—including when it is manifested as an attempt to evade the question of the future. As presented in this book, the struggle for liberation is a wellspring of liberating hope, not its antagonist. My position is not an attempt to safeguard Christian hope against its critics. More fundamentally, I'm interested in the subversive spirit that remains possible in future imaginaries. I suggest that future-talk is in fact a mode of critique, a critical disposition against all that presents itself as ultimately conservable. Liberative movements and action escape the hold of the present and spill over to the future in the form of hope. The hope that I seek to conjure derails the claim on eternity made by hegemonic forces and the firm grip on the now wielded by oppressive powers.

Most critics of future-talk often neglect that the very possibility of saying a word about the future implies—perhaps even *summons*—a rupture with the present moment. To every political and theological system that claims ultimacy and completion, future-talk intervenes by saying "not—yet." Theological work committed to liberation cannot disavow this pause, this interruption, this invocation. In the disavowal of future-talk, we encounter a well-justified and well-articulated critique of futurity as that which can save us from the aporia of history. These critiques put us on the verge of abandoning future-talk, perhaps even crossing that edge and sublimating Christian eschatology altogether. But as Keller quips, Christian theology cannot easily "delete" its apocalyptic passion for the future without "committing" it.[64] Likewise, *Trading Futures* maintains that Christian theology cannot disavow future-talk without conceding the victory to the forces of financialized capitalism. As financialization strives to colonize the future for the sake of profit, this book remains within the influence of Christian eschatology to plot hope-filled escape routes that elude the all-consuming temporality of financialized capitalism.

Constructing Futures

Embedded in the commitments of liberation theology and inflected by the spirit of constructive theology, *Trading Futures* remains within the eschatological imagination to witness to alternative embodiments of hope that insist on interrupting the straight lines that financialization projects onto the future. This book attends to the interruptions and pauses that the Christian eschatological imagination can foster against the inexorable timelines of financialized capitalism. In doing that, I attend to a vein within queer theory and constructive theology that wants to locate subversive possibilities in the pause engendered by future-talk.

With queer theorist José Esteban Muñoz, I should like to meet recommendations to abandon hope with a more colorful position. For him, "we are not queer yet."[65] The force of this not—yet gains the queerest contours in Muñoz's *Cruising Utopia*. Queer time disrupts the ontology of "straight time" and its claim over the present. The strangeness, the displacement, and the displacing summoned by futurity cannot coexist with a "here and now."[66] The impossible moment of realization of queerness is there and then—in the radical no-place called utopia. What is at stake in the appeal to utopian thinking for Muñoz is a different ontology of time and a different politics of present possibilities. The present, as Muñoz construes it, is never simply what "is" now but is always entangled in the perception of past and future worlds.[67] The perception of present reality and the imaging of what may come in the future are mixed together in a complex nexus of affects, aspirations, and desires. Perceiving reality while attending to its future possibilities is Muñoz's manner of resisting and interrupting "the temporal stranglehold" of "straight time."[68] Similar to the thesis that I develop in this book, Muñoz suggests that hope is not a naive attitude but rather an attitude of resistance against the "stultifying temporal logic of a broken-down present."[69] The queer cannot "be" in the present. They must displace the present, and this interruption opens up a new and queer horizon.

The straight line toward the future is a direct line tying heteronormativity with ableist ideology. Both heteronormative and normalized bodies gain flesh in the concern for a straight timeline. Here, too, we require an interruptive moment. In Sharon Betcher's theological work on the interstices of disability studies and postcolonial theory, the normalized, able body is constructed against the backdrop of eschatological projections of wholeness and perfection, which in turn are built on the repressive gaze on the Crip body.[70] Classical visions of history's end not only offer closure to erring, as Taylor would submit, but indeed exclude bodies that do not conform to the ideal of wholeness contained in those eschatological projections.[71] Betcher is clear that every theology of the end involves a politics of the middle.[72] Calibrated by the critique of normalizing theologies, Betcher notices the dire effects of theological future-talk in performing the role of this "agent of final perfection, as salvific solvent erasing the material effects of cosmic devolution."[73] With her focus on disability studies and experiences, Betcher's work exposes future imaginaries that expect and hence demand bodily perfection.

Thankfully, the Crip body interrupts the promise of wholeness. In Betcher's terms: "We refuse to be resolved, saved, made whole, thereby invalid/ating eschatological idealism."[74] Against this ethereal hope, disabled bodies offer the medicine to face and affirm life in "less-than-ideal" situations.[75] For Betcher, any potential "cure" for the eschatological normalization of the body needs to issue an "exit visa from globalizing capitalism," an economic system that so deeply relies on the construction of a "productive," able body.[76] Interrupting the eschatological promise of wholeness liberates us to face ourselves in light of our own mortality and finitude.[77]

This does not configure as despair or hopelessness but rather conjures a different cartography for future-talk. "The Crip turns out to be a map of hope," Betcher submits.[78] This affords a fragile, yet trustworthy, gesture of "sympathy for Spirit." Trust, contrary to triumphalism or capitulation to despair, "is a way of abiding with our own mortality, where sentience not only confirms the registration of pain, but bedews the body, baptizes it unto life."[79] Betcher acknowledges her interest in a "religious hope that recognizes that finitude and mortality and transience are conditions for the everlastingness of the world."[80] The force of her careful nod to future-talk emerges from the incapacity of traditional views of the eschaton to embrace the lack of wholeness socially projected onto disabled bodies. But it goes further than that: it also questions the politics of this Kingdom of Ableness as the illusion of a stabilizing gaze that constructs the ideal on the backs of the Crip.

Trauma functions as a similar stumbling block for triumphant modes of future-talk in Shelly Rambo's theology. The experience of trauma interrupts the expectation of the coming of future resolutions insofar as trauma is that which refuses to go away.[81] Traditional narratives of redemption easily "elide" or "gloss over" the experience of trauma in favor of a "quest for redemptive ending."[82] But, like Betcher's Crip bodies, trauma attests to the ongoing reappearance of pain. The iterative character of trauma bears witness to a narrative that simply cannot be told as the progression from problem to resolution, from death to life, from present suffering to future bliss.

Rambo proposes a theology of "remaining" that relocates redemption from the "end" to the "middle," a theme she theorizes as the space of Holy Saturday.[83] Therein, even the witness of resurrection is tainted by the reminders of fleshly pain. The "temporality of trauma" cannot afford linear narratives where the future resolves past suffering. "Trauma tells us that death returns, haunting the life that follows," Rambo claims. Standing in the middle, "any interpretation of redemption must acknowledge that death and life are inextricably bound, in such a way that theologians must account for death's remainder, death's haunting."[84] The cross, as the paradigmatic Christian symbol of redemption, must be looked at from the perspective of its "wake," in its "excess, in its transmission and witness."[85] For Rambo, witnessing requires a capacious imagination to "imagine beyond an ending" and to attend to the trauma that remains.[86]

In my work I overhear this witness to the remainders of history in the claims made about the future. Future-talk is never *just* about the future. Hopeful projections and the forebodings of a time to come are also witnesses to the suffering that remains with us. I approach future-talk as a companion to the flows of history that does not eschew trauma or injustice. As Betcher suggests, the critique of oppressive idealisms is insufficient if one does not offer instead "capacious imaginaries for the flourishing of life," without which we "may not at this time be able to pose an interruptive variable to empire."[87]

My contention is that the eschatological imagination is necessary for this interruptive variable. What happens when the eschaton is not the normalizing projection of the powerful but the destabilizing maneuver of the disempowered? What if the eschatological move is in fact one made in order to see the present differently, not to foresee its closure? And what if future-talk is not an attempt to solve the riddle of history but a way of wrestling with it? In the context of financialized capitalism, what senses might future-talk produce for indebted people who remain bound to financial corporations to meet their basic life needs? When futures turn into commodities traded in financial markets, what are we to make of the future-talk that irrupts from the experience of those living in the underside of financialization?

Muñoz adds this tantalizing conclusion: "We must vacate the here and now for a then and there. . . . What we need to know is that queerness is not yet here but it approaches like a crashing wave of potentiality. And we must give in to its propulsion, its status as a destination."[88] In this book I invite readers to conspire—to breathe together—with the pulse of a hope that vacates hegemonic forces in the present and propels us in the direction of a just future.

The mode of future-talk that I embrace suggests that one cannot remain faithful to the here and now without attending to a certain *sense* of a there and then. Future-talk makes sense. An eschatology of liberation will insist on the material conditions under which meaning and directions are produced. Against the push to predict and profit from the future, this work will marvel at the radical strangeness of the future, a time that cannot be made present. The not-yet-ness of the future instead derails any attempts at crafting straight lines between now and then. As I will show, attentiveness to the "sighs" of the oppressed creature signals that something must come, that justice cannot be satisfied in the present. Liberation exceeds the hold of the present; it spills over to the future. Something about our very perception of reality, especially the confrontation with the pain of the world, triggers a disposition toward the future. I maintain that this disposition instigates a displacement. It displaces us from the stranglehold of a present of injustice by summoning something that is not—yet. In the eschatology of liberation that I offer in this book, I suggest that we face this pause as the summoning of something that must become.

A sensory perception that something is disjointed engenders the need to say a word about the future. In the process of writing this work, I have often reminded myself of an old proverb: *O futuro a Deus pertence*. The future belongs to God. Like much of popular wisdom, saying that the future belongs to God has many senses. It most clearly resounds as a form of resignation: I leave what I cannot control, the future, to God. End of story. It might also sound like an admonition: make your future God's, for the future is God's, not yours. Period. Yet, even as the voices of resignation and admonition speak, it is possible to overhear the stifled sound of a voice that utters a petition and a disposition. The mood of the utterance speaks to the indefiniteness proper of a situation of anxiety, when times are difficult, disjointed, dishonored, unjust. Cultural protocols suggest that the sentence ought to be pronounced in such times. One says that the future belongs to God in times of anxiety, doubt, and inde*fin*iteness. When ends—*fins*—are difficult to trace, one utters that the future belongs to God.

A-Deus, to God, belongs a time that is not—yet. Saying a word about the future summons this necessary pause. Not yet. In this pause liberation theologians have found the courage to say a word about a God who does not conform to the procedures of the status quo. God is not the god of the present age. And so, as I prepare myself to say a word about the future in the age of finance, this pause is necessary and refreshing. It is an interruption that Christian theology cannot neglect, lest it submit itself entirely to the consuming force of financialization. To say that the future belongs to God in these times is to insist on the open-endedness of the future. It is to protest the impetus to make a profit out of something that is not yet. The hope this book seeks to engender is persistent in its rejoinder: the inexistence of the future makes it uncontrollable, despite the policing efforts of financialization.

18

In the all-consuming temporality of financialized capitalism, we may find rest in the things that are not. Yet.

Structure of the Book

This book unfolds following the protocols of liberation theology. Chapters 1 through 3 perform a reading of the "signs of the times," which is the necessary first step before one can begin to understand God's liberating activity in history. These chapters offer a critical lens to observe the reality of financialized capitalism, its drive toward constructing our collective futures, and the injustice it harbors. Schematically put, these three chapters respectively address financialization as a future-shaping, subject-forming, and death-dealing mechanism.

Chapter 1 describes financialization as a watershed moment in the history of the global economy. In my analysis I stress how financialized capitalism is fundamentally concerned with predicting, anticipating, and managing the future. At the same time, and not by chance, the rise of finance has been accompanied by a widespread increase in economic inequality and the socialization of debt. This, I show, is a symptom of a mode of future-talk that promises wealth only to then police people's hopes and expectations through the massive burden of debt.

Chapter 2 investigates the category of the promise as an entry point to my analysis of capitalism's way of shaping subjects according to its vision for the future. A promissory note, as both a sign of a debt and a token that serves as cash, inscribes the future in the modern way of thinking about money. I trace this back to Adam Smith's work, locating it in the context of the rise of the modern banking system in eighteenth-century Britain and the widespread distribution of promissory notes as a new instrument for trade. I then follow Friedrich Nietzsche's work on the ambivalence of the concept of a promise as it triggers the production of a docile, predictable subject bound to its creditor. I maintain that the subprime mortgage industry unveils the material conditions in which this promising subject is formed and the racialized and gendered dimension of the indebted person.

The third chapter argues that Karl Marx's critique of capitalism can be read as an analysis of the death-dealing temporality conjured by capitalist social relations of production. With Marx, I set out to investigate the material dimension of capitalist temporality. I argue that the future—often associated with lofty speculations and apocalyptic nonsense—matters. My argument engages in a close reading of Gayatri Chakravorty Spivak's approach to the Marxian corpus to suggest that even as financial transactions occur at speeds that challenge our ideas about the passage of time, Marx's specter forever demands that our economic imagination be rooted in the lives—concrete, embodied, material, social—of those who sustain the production of capital. This time, the time of workers, the time of those living in debt, haunts financial discourse and is the lever that can turn the economy around.

The book's second act is the moment of theology, as liberationists suggest. In this section I strive to occupy the means of production of future-talk. The final three chapters introduce an eschatology of liberation that represents future-talk as a mode of critique, as an invocation of absences, and as an escape tactic. Chapter 4 offers a critique of the capitalist mode of future-talk through a reading of Franz Hinkelammert's corpus. I show how he was able to capture the theological intricacies of capitalist economics while indicating that the Christian eschatological imagination may interrupt the senses engendered by capitalist future-talk.

Chapter 5 offers a reflection on an alternative mode of hope. In dialogue with Rubem Alves's theological and poetic work, I offer an eschatology in which the sighs of the oppressed creatures summon new worlds into becoming. I posit that liberation theology approaches the pause of the not—yet nature of the future with a resolute theological and political spirit. As Alves was fond of saying, for Christian theology, the not—yet is the time in which one encounters God.[89] In naming this absence, future-talk summons different times and demands that justice come. I insist that the poetic nature of Alves's theological work offers a path of resistance to the hegemonic mode of future-talk engendered by financial discourse and its drive to colonize the future.

Trading Futures closes with the unveiling of a fugitive future. In dialogue with Catherine Keller's work on apocalypse and philosopher Fred Moten's contributions to Black study, I suggest that future-talk discloses paths for circumventing a reality of oppression. The fugitive runs (away), escaping a present reality that cannot possibly harbor the demands of liberation. While the escape offers no assurances, fugitivity itself harnesses a passion and a commitment for the future. Like the fugitive, one cannot contain the future, not within the bounds of the present. It escapes us, and we, runaways from the stranglehold of financialized capitalism, shall continue to run with it.

It is worth reiterating: the theme of this book is the future, that which takes us to the edges of time and also that which makes us hedge. By confronting futurity in the context of financialized capitalism, my work here emphasizes that financial discourse constructs the hegemonic sense of futurity of our time. We are subjects to the futures produced by financial mechanisms, and our very ability to hope has been inflected toward the futures traded in financial markets. The mode of future-talk I adopt recognizes this force while insisting that hope might be produced differently. Future-talk summons. That which may come might be the companion we need in our struggle against that which is the mark of our time—a system to which there is no alternative. The future, the unpredictable time that is not—yet. My work here is to attend to the liberating force that persists in this pause.

futures devoured

1

Financial markets propel the global economy toward the future while promising that this maneuver can turn uncertainty itself into a profit. In the epigraph above, we are introduced to the financial mechanism that makes this possible. A futures contract suggests that the future holds something valuable. It is a contract that designates a future date and predetermines the price of a transaction, hedging that something profitable may come. Under the current landscape of global capitalism, these hedges drive our economy's quest for money in an endless projection of future scenarios. These are not simply bets. As we shall see in this chapter, future-talk makes its appearance in financial discourse as more than just speculation. The hedges made in financial markets situate contemporary financialized capitalism along the edges of future-talk. In the times of financialized capitalism, we rush after these futures. But in the voracious pursuit of predicting the future, something more fundamental happens: financial instruments in fact constitute our collective futures.

In this chapter I wrestle with the metaphor of a "future devoured." The expression comes from Thomas Piketty's

A futures contract is an agreement that requires a party to the agreement either to buy or sell something at a designated future date at a predetermined price.
—FRANK FABOZZI & FRANCO MODIGLIANI, *Capital Markets*

Capital in the Twenty-First Century, the commanding contemporary study on economic inequality.[1] For Piketty, the twenty-first century has begun with a reprise of the socioeconomic scenario of early nineteenth-century western Europe. His work substantiates this claim with extensive economic data from advanced capitalist economies over the past three centuries. As the numbers show, capitalism has an endemic disposition to move past wealth into the hands of a minority of individuals and then foreclose the possibility of fairer distribution levels.[2] Occasionally in the book Piketty's prose lets go of the codes of economic calculation to refer to this economic scenario with the intriguing image of a future-devouring past. Wealth accumulated in the past grows faster than wealth produced in the present. And the future? In the quasi-aristocratic context of contemporary capitalism, wealth and power harnessed from the past launches itself toward the future in a growing spree devouring all within sight.[3] What is to come, *l'avenir*, is devoured.

I should like to supplement Piketty's forceful claim by asking, *Whose* future is being devoured?

A 2014 piece in the *New York Times* tells the story of Jannette Navarro, a barista working at Starbucks in New York City. The work schedule of Ms. Navarro, a poor, Latina worker, was managed by technology that can anticipate work influx and send out requests for employees so that they come to work at any given moment. The *Times* reports, with some poetic license, "Along with virtually every major retail and restaurant chain, Starbucks relies on software that choreographs workers in precise, intricate ballets, using sales patterns and other data to determine which of its 130,000 baristas are needed in its thousands of locations and exactly when."[4] As she reflected on her situation, Ms. Navarro confessed that the scheduling of her work hours dictated the pace of her entire life—from the hours of her son's sleep to the type of groceries she could afford at the end of the month. For Ms. Navarro, life had turned into a "chronic crisis over the clock." Quite appropriately, the company that provides the work-scheduling software is named Kronos. As the god of time, Kronos met Ms. Navarro with a future-devouring force. When she started her job at Starbucks, she dreamed of completing an associate's degree in business, moving on to a master's degree, passing a driving test, and buying a car. A month into her job, "she had downgraded her ambitions," the *Times* reports. "[The] best she now hoped for was to be promoted to become shift supervisor." Working in the shadow of Kronos had devoured her aspirations and future possibilities.

What future can indeed survive this devouring appetite that turns every single minute into a profitable moment? In what follows, I trace the historical development of what scholars refer to as the *financialization* of capitalism in order to expose the mechanisms that shape this future-devouring economy. I survey the incessant drive to predict and anticipate the future for the sake of profit to show that the push toward the future is a hallmark of financialization and a signature of the hegemonic temporality engendered by financialized capitalism. If, on the one hand, financialization established the future as a central concern for profit making, the appetite for future profits elides a perverse logic that binds people to the present. As the focus of capitalist profit making turns to financial speculation, the future of multitudes is devoured to appease the hunger of a small minority. Financial discourse speaks with impunity about predicting and anticipating the future, but under its prognoses lie the perverse logic that foreclosures future possibilities different from the ones projected by financiers. Like Ms. Navarro's, our aspirations are consumed by the demands of life under financialization. An economy of debt is the underside of the futures traded in financial markets.

25

In this chapter I offer an account of the financialization of capitalism over the past decades. Driving this push toward the future are financial institutions whose hegemony in the global economy coalesces to form a peculiar mode of future-talk. I pay particular attention to financial derivatives and futures contracts as a pathway to uncover the future orientation of financialization. These instruments reveal to us the mechanisms finance deploys to turn unknown futures into profit.

Financialization has engendered the dominant mode of future-talk of our epoch. In its drive for profit, financialized capitalism has constructed social patterns that conjure up a new form of imagining the future. Futures contracts and other financial innovations produce an economy that makes profit out of uncertainty while consuming what may come for the vast majority of the world's population. As I will suggest, the devouring of possibilities for what is to come is inscribed in our economy's own passions for the future. The futures contracted in financial markets place our paths and images of the future in the tracks of a future-devouring power. This, I show, is a symptom of a mode of future-talk that promises wealth only to foreclose hope through the imposition of a massive burden of debt.

Economies of Debt

The historical process that brought financial markets to the center of the global economy is aptly referred to as *financialization*. The term designates processes in which the center of economic activity moves away from industrial

FUTURES DEVOURED

production to the financial sector. This dynamic is well exemplified by shifts within automobile corporations, whose profits over the past decades have come primarily from their financial branches and not directly from auto sales.[5] To contextualize the scale and speed of the financialization process, notice that in 1990 the ten largest financial corporations in the United States represented 10 percent of the total financial assets in the country. In 2008 this percentage had grown to over 60 percent. Globally, the ten largest banks accounted for 59 percent of the world's financial assets in 2006, whereas in 2009 that figure had risen to upward of 70 percent.[6] Economist Christian Marazzi suggests that financialization represents a historical period in which finance is *cosubstantial* with all aspects of production and services.[7]

I approach this impressive takeover of the global economy by the financial sector by following closely the work of Marxist economists writing for the *Monthly Review*. Their analyses indicate that financialization allowed consumption levels to remain high at a time of decreasing wages and stagnant economic growth. In fact, Paul Sweezy, Paul Baran, and Harry Magdoff are among the first economists to take into account the rise in consumer debt among the working class during the 1970s. For workers, acquiring debt became a necessary step to meet basic necessities like food, health, housing, and education. The Marxist lens adopted by the *Monthly Review* economists directs our attention to the social and material conditions under which financialization appeared in the global economy.[8] Such attentiveness will reveal for us the untold story of financialization, namely, the massive distribution and socialization of debt among the working class. My account of financialized capitalism in this section substantiates *whose* futures are devoured by the future-consuming force of financialized capitalism.

The abridged version of the financialization of capitalism runs like this: During the Great Depression of the 1930s, the global economy suffered an irreparable hit whose effects could be ameliorated, ironically, only by the boom in military spending during World War II and the financing of Europe's reconstruction after the war. As economic historian John Kenneth Galbraith put it, the Great Depression never ended but merely converted into a war economy.[9] The postwar economy witnessed a staggering growth in productive capabilities and an unparalleled expansion of public spending in the mode envisioned by John Maynard Keynes, whose towering presence in economic theory and policies was unmistakable during the 1940s and 1950s. This period was marked by significant gains in compensation for labor, labor rights, and social security networks throughout advanced economies.

With time, however, the expansionist policies of the postwar period began to lose steam, and the specter of depression haunted the world's economy. Consumption rates plummeted, causing paralysis in industrial production and investment. Already in the mid-1970s, political theorist Daniel Bell foresaw the coming of what he called the postindustrial society.[10] As social tensions increased and economic crises mounted, Keynesian policies came under attack, and an emerging neoliberal paradigm gained ground with its prescriptions of deregulation of the financial sector, decreases in government spending, and tax incentives for large corporations.[11]

Sociologist Greta Krippner links this economic shift to the social and political tensions experienced in the 1960s and 1970s in the United States. For her, financialization provided a way out of the social turbulence of the period by depoliticizing economic discourse and thus "deferring" questions related to social and political accountability in the context of a "fading prosperity."[12] What social agents and institutions would bear the burden of allocating diminishing resources in a society overloaded with tensions? Government was forced to deal with a growing suspicion that political agents had no ability to understand and manage the dynamics of a complex economy. At the same time, policymakers realized that their involvement in economic issues often hampered their political ambitions. Obviously, in a context such as this, economic theories that insisted that market forces alone could steer the economy back to prosperity turned out to be very appealing.

For Krippner, financialization conveniently depoliticized economics and "[allowed] policymakers to escape a zero-sum political calculus where directing capital to one use meant denying it for another."[13] But the weakening of political oversight over the economy had an unmistakable role in politicizing the private sector, particularly financial organizations. Under the guise of the efficiency of markets, the private sector took on the mantle of providing social goods previously thought of as a government responsibility. Feminist theorist Miranda Joseph speaks of a shift in the "locus of responsibility for social welfare provision."[14] Financialization and its inseparable ally, neoliberalism, gained political and social acceptance insofar as they enshrined the free market as an autonomous and legitimate force to guide a society's economy.

The perceived autonomy of market forces has, however, its social costs. For Marxist economists, the era of financialized capitalism wrought a new economy of *debt*. Sweezy, Baran, and Magdoff suggest that the economic crisis of the 1970s was a symptom of a *surplus absorption problem*, a term used in Marxist literature to describe dynamics in which growth in production is not matched by an equivalent growth in consumption.[15] This is an endemic problem in capitalism: "Expanding industrial capacity," Magdoff and Sweezy write, "always ends up creating *over*capacity," which turns out to be a problem if capital generated by the industrial sector fails to find new markets for its continuing growth.[16] A first sign of the crisis in surplus absorption is the formation of large corporate monopolies that temporarily remedy the lack of market expansion by diminishing competition among businesses.[17] While monopolies offer a short-term response to economic crises, they cannot solve the surplus absorption problem.[18]

The stage for financialization is thus set. On the one hand, capitalist production must exceed immediate demand so that the margin of profit can grow. On the other hand, for real demand to grow, consumers need to have the means to purchase surplus production.[19] In the context of stagnant wages, such as we start to witness in the 1970s, this economic arrangement can only lead to "divergence," as economists like to say. Financialization hence emerges as a way of "absorbing the investible surplus that inundated the sphere of production by channeling it to the realm of finance."[20] Instead of being reinvested in production, surplus capital is redirected to banks.[21] In short, the material conditions for financialization are tied to the funneling of capital into financial institutions and away from further investment in production. In the context of stagnant economic growth, highly capitalized banks start to extend credit lines to households, industries, and nation-states that are growing significantly cash poor.

Broadly speaking, this is the origin of the external debt of poor countries in the Global South. As David Graeber narrates, during the oil crises of the 1970s, the countries in the Organization of Petroleum Exporting Countries (OPEC) were sitting on piles of money that they themselves could not absorb back into their own oil businesses.[22] In the terms used by the *Monthly Review* theorists, this is productive capital that cannot be reinvested in production. Eventually, this surplus capital found a new home as money started to flood the accounts of New York investment banks. Capitalized, these banks extended massive credit streams to poor countries, most of which were ruled by dictatorial regimes. Unsurprisingly, financial credit came with strings attached. The availability of credit to developing nations created the need for them to establish a "financial architecture" that ultimately made them dependent on the political centers of financial capital. China and India, both countries that have witnessed significant economic growth over the past decades, are still trapped in what economist John Bellamy Foster calls "imperial systems of foreign exchange and financial control."[23] Dependency on

28

this imperial financial system culminated in the vast debt crisis of the 1980s and the ensuing power exercised by the International Monetary Fund in poor countries.

Magdoff observed that "the slowdown of industrial investment" in the postwar period made the financial sector intensify its search for alternative customers.[24] He perceived the trend taking shape in the form of a rapid increase of both government and personal debt.[25] Magdoff went on to argue that the extension of new credit lines by financial institutions opened up a new horizon for investments that could absorb the money paralyzed in the productive sector. In the following decades, this tendency would be consolidated: by 1985, he and Sweezy concluded that debt was already a major force in the US economy as the country's outstanding debt was then twice as big as the nation's gross domestic product (GDP).[26] As multiple studies confirm, the trend continued to gain momentum in the 1990s and 2000s. By 2013 American public debt was calculated at $16.7 trillion (100 percent of the GDP).[27] Household debt followed a similar pattern, growing by a margin of $1 trillion in 2021, the largest increase in one single year since 2007.[28] For the *Monthly Review* analysts, this is a symptom of the expansion of credit that functioned to counterbalance economic stagnation. Politically, it was the decisive mechanism to preserve the interests of the capitalist class.[29]

In his study of financialization, Marxist economist Costas Lapavitsas reflects on the growth of the subprime mortgage industry in the years preceding the financial crisis of 2008. For him, the very existence of this business represents a significant milestone in the development of capitalism. He observes how mortgage lending to the poorest of workers tied their fates to the mechanisms of financial capital. "It is hard to exaggerate what an extraordinary fact this is," Lapavitsas ponders. "Under conditions of classical, nineteenth-century capitalism it would have been unthinkable for a global disruption of accumulation to materialize because of debts incurred by workers, including the poorest."[30] The penetration of the financial sector into household economies was a major social event. What Lapavitsas refers to as the "financialization of personal revenue" turns all aspects of social life dependent on the financial sector—from housing to education, from pension funds to health insurance, from the purchase of basic goods to leisure activities.[31]

Finance has become ubiquitous in everyday life.[32] The mechanism amounts to a true whirlwind: cash is sent to banks in the form of deposits for loans, pension funds, mortgages, credit card debt, and so on. These moneys then flow into the coffers of financial institutions, which bundle together the expected streams of future repayments for any given underlying asset (a house, a car, a college tuition), securitize them, and launch them into financial markets as tradable commodities.[33] Through this financial maneuvering, everyday payments are integrated into the global flow of capital. The dissemination of debt into the realm of everyday life is, in Marazzi's words, what allowed financialized capitalism to sustain itself on a global scale.[34] As payments flow into this financial machine, payers soon are themselves pushed into becoming their own financial managers. As we saw, neoliberal theory emphasizes personal responsibility and entrepreneurship over state intervention in the economy. In this way the task of investing and speculating on the future is introduced into the practices of everyday life. Though cushioned in the language of entrepreneurship, financialization cannot hide the underside of this hunger for future investments: as everyday life is financialized, debt becomes a "structural necessity," in the words of critic Fiona Allon.[35]

The massive growth and socialization of debt is the economic outcome of capitalist financialization. Its social cost is the increasing dependence of households and impoverished nations on the financial sector. Its human cost is the subjection of human relations to the vicious logic of debt, a theme that I develop at length in chapter 2 as I investigate the formation of the indebted subject under financialized capitalism. What remains to be investigated is how financialization has shaped our very understanding of the future. In what follows, I demonstrate that the futures traded in financial markets have been constituting our collective imaginary about what is to come.

Trading Futures

In the process of establishing futures as financial contracts, financialized capitalism ushered in a new form of future-talk. The economic path for financialization was paved by the creation of new financial commodities that turned the volatility and unpredictability proper to future scenarios into the very thing that makes financial markets viable. The story of financialization is thus the story of the commodification of the future. My goal in this section is to investigate the formation and expansion of derivatives, a financial artifact that made possible the turning of future risk and unpredictability into the stuff of financial profit. Financial discourse must portray the future as predictable in order to render it profitable. In doing so, derivatives and other financial mechanisms have dictated and policed the tempo of our aspirations for the future. In dialogue with theorists associated with the Cultures of Finance Workgroup, I will show that the commodification of the future has implications that transcend the confines of finance.[36] Financialization has in fact engendered a shift in our sociocultural understanding of the future, our aspirations, and our capacity to envision the future.

In an essay dated just a few months after President Richard Nixon unpegged the dollar from the gold standard, neoliberal economist Milton Friedman announced the dawn of a new era—the era of speculation. This new epoch in the history of capitalism would seek ways of capitalizing on speculative activity. As we shall see in the following pages, this mode of thinking about financial commodities and transactions produced its own mode of future-talk.

In the fall of 1971, Friedman was asked by the chairman of the Chicago Mercantile Exchange, Leo Melamed, about the possibility of a futures market in foreign currency. Until then, futures were primarily, if not exclusively, traded in agricultural contexts as hedges against the possibility of future crop losses. Friedman nevertheless envisioned a more expansive role for futures markets. His now-famous "feasibility" paper, "The Need for Futures Markets in Currencies," might very well be the shortest and most influential paper in economic theory.[37] It argued that creating the conditions for monetary volatility would establish a new financial atmosphere where speculative action could reduce market instability. Extolling the gift of flexible currency markets, Friedman predicted that foreign trade would expand, and economic prosperity ensue, with the rise of risk-taking. "The larger the volume of speculative activity," he averred, "the better the market and the easier it will be for persons involved in foreign trade and investment to hedge at low costs."[38] In this new financial sphere, the value of a currency is guaranteed neither by the state nor by gold but simply by market mechanisms.

With Friedman's theoretical innovation came a revamped financial commodity—derivatives. A derivative is a financial contract that derives its value from a different underlying asset, stock, or market index whose value is by contract set to a fixed date in the future. Derivatives are often portrayed as insurance instruments that function to ameliorate or transfer risk. But derivatives are much more than just insurance against the unpredictability of the future. In financialized capitalism, derivatives "make it possible to buy [or sell] *the risk* of possessing an asset without buying the asset itself."[39]

Financial textbooks invite us to imagine the following situation. Consider that you buy tables from me, but instead of agreeing on a price for your order, we agree that the value of our transaction will be based on the price of the wood needed to produce the tables. In our transaction the wood is the underlying asset that ultimately will determine the value of our transaction. For me, the deal functions as an insurance policy that guarantees that I will not lose money if there is a sudden rise in the price of wood. For you, the indetermination of the price might mean you will save some money if the price of wood drops. For both of us, the transaction involves some risk. Derivative contracts such as this vary wildly in shape and scope, but they all essentially function, in Lapavitsas's wording, as "a punt on the future direction of the price of the underlying asset."[40] Profit, in this context, is tied to uncertain—yet contractually fixed—variations in the future value of an asset.

Closely aligned with derivatives is the commodity called *futures*. It names financial contracts that stipulate a time in the future when a transaction shall come to its conclusion. A futures contract offers a delayed transaction while leaving a margin for variables to influence its final price. Fundamentally, futures contracts establish transactions in which nothing is bought or sold at the moment at which the contract is signed. What takes place is a commitment in which two parties "agree to buy or sell a specific amount of a specific item at a specified future date."[41] The textbook in finance gives a new imaginary situation. Suppose "Bert" signs a futures contract with "Ernie" stipulating that the former will buy an asset from the latter three months from now. They agree to complete the exchange at that time with Bert paying $100 for Ernie's asset, a stock from the company xyz. This futures price is a projection, roughly based on the present value of the underlying asset being exchanged. Still, the nature of a futures contract is such that the parties bet on fluctuations in this price. If the market price of the asset increases, Bert makes a profit; if the asset's price decreases, Ernie gains.[42] Ernie and Bert thus have different expectations for the future, and one of them will be merrier than the other when his projection proves to be the right one.

Futures transactions such as Ernie and Bert's are not a new invention. Their history can be traced to agricultural societies where the vicissitudes in the production of food demanded a different approach to business. Farmers, for example, may want to fix the price for corn during seeding season so as to secure against a potential bad harvest.[43] Owing to this agricultural backstory, the center of futures trading is the American Midwest—Chicago, to be precise. Since the mid-1850s, commodity futures such as pork bellies and corn have been traded in Chicago. But, with Friedman's theoretical support, traders would soon be capable of trading futures whose underlying assets were not just pork bellies or corn. Starting in 1972, a year after Friedman's feasibility paper, futures contracts started to be traded in the currency market. These innovations were soon transplanted to other financial markets

32

CHAPTER ONE

and would eventually dominate the global economy.[44] For economist Jakob Arnoldi, derivatives are by far the "most successful financial innovation within the last three decades, creating new high-liquidity markets of truly staggering dimensions."[45]

For theorists of financialization, this colossal shift in financial markets required a new approach to the future. Arnoldi attributes the rise of derivatives to a *"type of knowledge that is able to conceptualize risk, contingency, and open futures."*[46] But conceptualizing risk and contingency is not simply a matter of picturing the future as open. More fundamentally, financialized capitalism construes the openness of the future as a site for profit making. Knowledge of the future is thus rendered as a mode of control over the future, as the ability to measure and predict that which is to come.

The confidence that reliable knowledge of future risk can be obtained is a watershed moment for capitalism. The futurology of financial discourse is founded on an entire apparatus of financial models built to assess and predict the future profitability of any given asset or transaction. In the case of derivative trading, the Black-Scholes model is the gold standard. First proposed in 1973, it offered a way to calculate the price of certain derivatives by assessing not their underlying assets but their volatility. The purpose of the model itself is to reliably predict risks so that a financial transaction can involve the least possible risk.[47] As anthropologist Benjamin Lee points out, Black-Scholes is based on a "brilliantly simple" idea: to measure risk as a way of avoiding risk.[48] The consequence of such an idea was to transform risk, until then a factor to be guarded against, into a financial commodity in its own right. Former derivative trader Elie Ayache claims that Black-Scholes made the indeterminacy of the future tradable.[49] Or, more aphoristically, derivatives are the *"un-knowledge* of the future, made market."[50]

We will need to linger on claims such as this in the chapters to come. In a work committed to a critical reflection on future-talk, this morphing of the unknowable into market is at the crux of my theological concerns. In chapter 4 I return to this motif to suggest that by commodifying the future, financialized capitalism encloses the very possibility of a just future. Trading on indeterminate futures means more than claiming knowledge of what is to come. Construing the unknowability of the future as a marketable commodity is the source of the power of the futures trader. The power to predict and anticipate market trends summons a future in the image and likeness of the hedges performed by players in financial markets. But as we may conclude from Ayache's suggestions, turning indeterminacy into a tradable commodity implies the policing of future indeterminacies. By bringing the future

33

into the protocols of calculability, financialized capitalism confines our collective future to its own divinations.

The hegemony of finance in contemporary capitalism implicates all of our futures in the financial machine. For the scholars associated with the Cultures of Finance Workgroup, derivatives and other financial mechanisms direct our entire social reality toward the future projected by financial discourse. Approaching finance from an interdisciplinary and critical lens, these theorists portray market agents as *creators* of markets, not simply cogs in an already existing reality.[51] As performers working with a given script, financiers shape social reality when they venture into their speculations about future reality. In this process they produce a reality that mirrors the speculative action that takes place in financial markets. Derivatives, in this sense, are not simply financial "tools" but rather residues of a particular social relation between creditors and debtors. Derivatives and other financial innovations shape social life through their forecasts for the future and the social relations they engender.[52]

Derivatives are therefore artifacts that embody the social relations proper of financialized capitalism. The creditor-debtor relation is construed on the basis of the assessment of the risks involved between these parties as well as on the profitability predicted as the outcome of the transaction. It is a social relation built on future calculations. Cultural anthropologist Arjun Appadurai indicates that derivatives represent a "new form of mediation" that integrates a multitude of social agents by bridging the distance between material goods in the present and their potential for future profit.[53] A mortgage, for example, is constructed on the social evaluation of the reliability of the person asking for the loan and on the expectation of future monetary reward. This is "a bet on a relationship and a tango with time," in the words of anthropologist Edward LiPuma.[54] The financial instruments introduced by financialization offer mechanisms to gauge the prospects of future profit and shape social relations in accordance with these projections.

Financial models like Black-Scholes and instruments like derivatives do more than assess and predict price volatility. For sociologist Donald MacKenzie, the influence of financial models in fact created the market that they first sought to analyze.[55] They steered the market in the direction of derivative trading and constructed a global economy that mirrored the futures these models predicted. Black-Scholes's success is that it "created a self-referential feedback loop that pushes options prices in the direction predicted by the model and closes the spread between theoretical and market prices."[56] Financial commodities carry no value as physical things nor as paper certificates. What makes them valuable are the claims they embody about the "future states of the world."[57] Financial discourse seeks to predict and anticipate market movements, but its discursive and social force turns out to "coconstitute" the future by means of its projections.[58] Financialization builds itself on the assurance that something about the future is marketable and indeed profitable. Derivative trading confirms this commitment to turn what is not—yet into something profitable now. But through the incessant pursuit of knowledge of the future, financialization has engendered its own modality of future-talk. It is one where the future is rendered as predictable for the sake of profit.

Profitable Unknowns

I have been arguing that financialization brings future-talk to the center of capitalist discourse and binds us to the futures anticipated by financial mechanisms. As I already indicated, economists refer to finance as "the application of economic principles to decision-making that involves the allocation of money under conditions of uncertainty."[59] This uncertainty is ubiquitous in financial discourse, and its management is the key to a profitable financial enterprise. Financial discourse portrays this uncertainty as somewhat manageable and definitely profitable. As we shall see, the wrestling with uncertainty engenders the spirit of financialized capitalism, similar to the way Max Weber identified that capitalism is connected to the Protestant anxiety about the state of one's salvation. The new spirit of capitalism sets it in a forward motion that wants to make a profit out of unknown futures. In financial discourse, future uncertainty is construed as the condition for a profitable business.

The proclivity toward the uncertain is a founding concern of contemporary financialized capitalism.[60] Economist Frank Knight set the tone of the debate in 1921 by offering a distinction between uncertainty and risk and suggesting that the latter is a "measurable uncertainty."[61] For Knight, the *uncertainty* of the future is the condition of possibility for the existence of financial markets. The *measurement* of risk is the condition of possibility for financial profit. Profit, he stated, "arises out of the inherent, absolute unpredictability of things, out of the sheer, brute fact that the results of human activity cannot be anticipated and then only in so far as even a probability calculation in regard to them is impossible and meaningless."[62] Knight places the unpredictable nature of the future at the center of his theorization about finance. Players in financial markets ought to position themselves before unknown futures and therein make decisions that will turn the unpredictable into profit.

Following the basic intuition of Knight's work, economist Fischer Black, one of the authors of the famous Black-Scholes model, distinguished between "noise" and "information." Noise, he explained, is everything that appears random and irrelevant to a particular financial transaction. It is a consequence of the fact that financiers play on the unpredictable terrain of the future. Noise is to be distinguished from information as that which affords reliable data relevant to a financial transaction. Black did not advocate that noise should or could be abandoned. He acknowledged that financial markets cannot exist without the interference of noise that continuously threatens to disrupt profit making. Finance is therefore set up in this double bind: "Noise makes financial markets possible, but also makes them imperfect."[63] This is the enduring enigma of financial markets: the uncertainty of the future makes financial markets both possible and imperfect.

This obsession with the uncertainty of the future is not a deficiency that financialized capitalism seeks to address. To the contrary, it is its defining feature. Uncertainty and indetermination are critical to the operation of contemporary finance for this is precisely where it exercises its power. Political economist Martijn Konings argues that neoliberalism "embraces a speculative orientation toward the future" as its own "organizing principle." The neoliberal "logic of governance" portrays finance not simply as a site to assess future probability but more fundamentally as one that seeks to "construct an unknown future."[64] From its handling of indetermination, neoliberalism derives techniques of governance that historicize and concretize its orientation toward the future. Konings has pointed to the tension between the necessity to speculate and the urgency to actualize speculative activity as the temporal conundrum of financialized capitalism.[65] The necessity to speculate at all moments combined with the need to manage levels of uncertainty dictates the tempo of neoliberal capitalism.

Konings calls this the "paradoxes of preemptive temporalities."[66] This refers to the tendency in neoliberal reason to produce a unique kind of certainty out of situations of dire uncertainty. Konings therefore challenges the understanding that neoliberal economists portray finance as equipped to transcend risk in its attempt to manage uncertainty. Financialized capitalism does not presume sovereign knowledge of the future nor claim to be outside the vicissitudes of uncertain temporalities. Rather, financial discourse establishes the protocols of governance in the face of risk. Building on Michel

Foucault's work, Konings affirms that neoliberal reason affirms its power precisely in the confrontation with uncertainty. What is at stake is not the "ability to act on accurate knowledge of the future, but a definite certainty as to what needs to be done in the absence of such knowledge."[67] The financial crisis of 2007–2008 offers the prime entry point to this logic: standing before both future indetermination and the imminent effects of the crisis, neoliberalism had a ready answer: submit to the logic of financialized capitalism and assure the viability of the banking system. Konings points out that bailing out banks represented the "absence of meaningful choice." The "intense uncertainty" generated by the financial crisis "[coincided] with a compelling certainty as to what needs to be done."[68] For financialized capitalism, more than an unsolvable paradox, this predicament is a source of power: at the moment of indecision about future outcomes, the temporal logic of neoliberalism quickens the conservation of the status quo.

Friedrich von Hayek serves as Konings's exemplary figure for this paradigm. For the neoliberal economist, perfect knowledge of the future is impossible and irrelevant for the logic of finance. What is needed is an understanding and acceptance of the self-organizing forces of the market.[69] For Hayek, the goal is not to control the future but to submit oneself to the forces that produce the future. For this reason, the paradigmatic figure of neoliberal governance is not the entrepreneur who shapes the future but the debtors who are obliged to submit to repaying their debts.[70] The debtor's relation to the future, Konings insists, is *preemptive*. The futures presented by financialized capitalism offer no real open possibilities, just the call for submission.

In the next chapter, I investigate in greater depth this subjection. At this point, my interest lies in the mode of futurity established by financial discourse and its established protocol for action in the face of future indetermination. For Appadurai, the combination of apprehension toward and fascination with the uncertainty of the future informs the new "spirit" of capitalism.[71] He compares the uncertainty of financial gain to the uncertainty of one's salvation that Weber identified as the birthing spirit of capitalism.[72] Puritan Calvinists, in Weber's study, wrestled with the uncertainty of their election while striving to live as if they were chosen by God for salvation. In time, Weber observed, this attitude toward the unknown shaped an ethic of work and asceticism that would prove beneficial for the birth of capitalism.[73] While knowledge of God's providence remained impossible, Puritans started to understand financial success as a sign of their election. For Weber, that intuition was pivotal for the formation of the spirit of capitalism.

Appadurai observes that players in financial markets are similarly fascinated by the unknown and that their actions follow a discernible protocol of acting as if their actions could anticipate future realities. As we have been observing, what is at stake here is not asserting dominion over the future but establishing the correct course of action when confronting uncertainty. Players in financial markets arrogate to themselves no special dispensation of knowledge of what is to come. The successful trader has "a different strategy of divination, of reading the signs, charts, trends, flows, patterns, and shifts in the market."[74] True to the spirit of capitalism, financial discourse does not presume knowledge of the future itself, but acts as if the anticipation of what is to come is akin to the sign of one's election. The future remains uncertain, but one's profit signals that one correctly submitted to the protocols of the governing forces behind financial markets.

But financialized capitalism does not distribute its favors evenly. While some may hedge against future unpredictability and profit beautifully, the majority of the world finds itself bearing the cost of speculative activity. Edward LiPuma shows that the compulsion to predict and anticipate the future leads to an actual constraint in the possibilities the future can bring about. He posits that derivatives offer a bet on the future based on a particular perception of the present but that, eventually, the "implied future . . . defines a forthcoming that transforms the present . . . across the interval stretching between now and a derivative's expiration date."[75] Differently put, the leap toward the future disguises a project to conserve the present or, perhaps, to effectively devour future possibilities. The maneuver onto the future under financialized capitalism brings about the continuance of the social power held by financial institutions.

Financial instruments like derivatives and futures contracts present themselves as tools of prediction that can turn a profit out of uncertain future realities. But their deployment under financialized capitalism makes them more than tools of analysis of market trends. They produce futures. Under the hegemonic force of financialized capitalism, future uncertainty is ordered according to the present state of affairs. Future uncertainty is affirmed by financialized capitalism in order to establish what ought to be done when one stands before the moment of indetermination. Financialization founds itself on the basis of a relation to the future that must be predicted and anticipated for the sake of profit. This mode of futurity nevertheless conjures a vision for the future whose existence can only confirm what the present already is or is projected to be. It preempts possibility while demanding subjection to the forces of financialization.

Divining futures, anticipating futures, trading futures: these activities constitute a reality that consolidates the power of those who can straddle the hedges of financial discourse. What trades as futures in financial markets is devouring the future possibilities afforded to us. In its own mode of inhabiting the edges of future-talk, financial discourse is shaping what is to come in its own image. The commodity that the future has become under financialized capitalism turns unknowns into profits, indeterminacies into marketable commodities. But the price of such commodification of the future is hefty. Financialization has imposed a regime of temporality in which the futures projected and anticipated by financial markets have become the irresistible future of our planetary life. In the age of finance, the future of workers and the future of the poor have been consumed by the incessant drive for profit. Our very sense of the future and the material conditions for the production of alternative forms of future-talk is diminished by this all-consuming economy. The financial gadgets for divining the future constitute the sense of our times, its meaning and its direction. In financial discourse, what becomes of the future is that which leads to profit. And no more.

promissory notes 2

Neoliberalism is an
economy turned toward
the future, since finance
is a promise of future
wealth. . . . From this
perspective, all financial
innovations have but one
sole purpose: possessing
the future in advance by
objectivizing it.
—MAURIZIO LAZZARATO,
*The Making of the Indebted
Man*

Financial discourse is based on the promise and lure of future wealth. But to make wealth a matter of the future, neoliberalism needed to produce a particular mode of future-talk. As the epigraph from Maurizio Lazzarato points out, financialized capitalism must objectivize that which it seeks to possess and profit from. In the previous chapter, we tracked how future-talk in financialized capitalism conjures up our contemporary sense of time, its own temporality, and our common hopes and expectations for the future. I have insisted that future-talk under the regime of finance offers no real alternatives or possibilities for the future—only subjection. Debt is the social and economic outcome of financialization. In this chapter I argue that as financialization objectifies what is to come, it likewise subjects persons and populations to the logic of its promises of future wealth. We shall come to this by tracing the formation of a promissory subject, a mode of being human imbricated in the promissory notes issued by financial institutions.

The future announced by the promise of future wealth is what intrigues me in the pages to come. Wealth in the future is a peculiar thing as, at first sight, it does not function as wealth proper: it does not acquire goods nor services, it does not mediate transactions, and, as a matter of fact, it does not make one wealthy now. Yet this promise of future wealth does have effects. It summons a promising subject, a subject whose very future is bound to the promise of future wealth. This subjectivity is constructed in the power interplay between debtors and their creditors. The indebted subject is obliged to assure that its future will be exactly what the creditors expect and demand it to be. In financialized capitalism, debt renders subjects bound to a promise of repayment that entraps them in the present.

In what follows, I juxtapose the circulation of promissory notes with the formation of a promising subject. More specifically, I portray the expansion of the financial sector in the modern period as setting the historical and material conditions for the shaping of a mass of indebted subjects, whose futures remain in the hands of their creditors. Promissory notes are monetary tokens that carry an inscription that launches the economy toward the promise of future wealth.[1] As carriers of a promise of future repayment, these notes are artifacts that bear the capitalist mode of future-talk. They in fact turn debt into money. As I will show, Adam Smith approached promissory notes and the burgeoning banking industry of his days with surprising ambivalence. I suggest that even as Smith attempted to ground his political economy on the solid—and present—foundation of a country's gold reserves, his vision of economic progress nevertheless launched the economy toward the future.

And so *we* are launched into the future. I go on to probe the formation of a promissory subject by exploring Friedrich Nietzsche's considerations of debt as a subject-forming, future-conjuring reality. For Nietzsche and some of his contemporary interpreters, economic forces render indebted subjects and their futures as necessary and docile. The creditor-debtor relationship, which has become ubiquitous under financialization, makes every debtor bound to their creditors. I will indicate that this indebted person is gendered and racialized in ways that expose the "predatory inclusion" sponsored by financialized capitalism.[2] At the conclusion of the chapter, I show that the mortgage industry is a material site to observe the formation of people and populations under the regime of indebtedness created by financialization.

These encounters with indebted subjects allow us to perceive the subjecting force of financialization and its deadly ethos. I claim in this chapter that the futures inscribed in the promissory notes that sustain the financial system are material reminders that debtors must repay their debts. Bearers of money carry with them a debt load that subjects them to the power of financialization. The neoliberal promise of future wealth shapes gendered and racialized subjects whose futures are thrown into the future-consuming and subject-forming machine of financial markets.

To Tender a Promise

In this section I offer a historical account of promissory notes as a financial mechanism that allows debt to be treated as money. I follow insights emerging from the credit theory of money that treat money as a development of debt tabulations. Moreover, I investigate the use and circulation of promissory notes in the context of the emergence of the modern banking system as my entry point to an analysis of the centrality of debt in finance. As the British Parliament defined them after a long century of legal debates, promissory notes fix a determinable future in which a certain transaction will be finalized: "A promissory note is an unconditional promise in writing made by one person to another signed by the maker, engaging to pay, on demand or at a fixed or determinable future time, a sum certain of money, to, or to the order of a specified person or to the bearer."[3] In these promissory notes, this "fixed or determinable future" inscribes a specific temporality in economic discourse, as if minting the future in our monetary system.

David Graeber's sweeping investigation in *Debt: The First 5,000 Years* suggests that debt is an ancient social factor. In fact, he traces the origin of paper money to promises of future repayment and shows that credit systems that treat money as a tally of debts precede the advent of money itself.[4] Graeber follows economist Alfred Mitchell Innes's credit theory of money to indicate that money is first and foremost a measure of debt. Whereas conventional wisdom indicates that a banknote is a promise of repayment in kind, the credit theory of money argues that a "banknote is simply the promise to pay *something* of the same value as an ounce of gold."[5] The emphasis here is on the promise of repayment, not on the medium in which the repayment must occur. Currency does not measure the value of objects but rather gauges the level of public trust in individuals.[6] Coinage, banknotes, and cash are registries that account for public confidence.

The Bank of England, founded in 1694, offers a typical example of this. The bank was created after a group of English bankers loaned £1,200,000 to the king, who needed the money to pay for his army's war against France.[7] In return, the monarch granted these bankers the monopoly on issuing banknotes. With royal approval and the formation of the Bank of England, bankers became capable of transforming royal debt into money, a move that elevated the social power of banks to unprecedented heights. Graeber explains the implications of this arrangement: "What this meant in practice was that [bankers] had the right to advance IOUs for a portion of the money the king now owed them to any inhabitant of the kingdom willing to borrow from them, or willing to deposit their own money in the bank—in effect, to circulate or 'monetize' the newly created royal debt."[8] With the backing and the confidence of the sovereign, the modern financial system came into being through its capacity of creating money.[9]

43

But with the commercial and industrial explosion that marked the eighteenth century, tracking and regulating commerce proved to be an arduous task for legislators and judges. In that period British courts staged intense and controversial debates about the nature, legality, and negotiability of promissory notes—a financial technique employed extensively in commercial transactions in Britain and beyond. As the mechanism came to be defined, promissory notes were "a promise or engagement in writing" in which one party promised to pay a "specified sum of money" at a specified moment in the future.[10] Although the British Parliament legalized them in 1704, there was still a great level of confusion in the ensuing decades with respect to the nature of these notes and their function in commercial relations.[11]

The central question in these disputes was the degree to which promissory notes were negotiable. Insofar as they were written promises of future payment, how could they be utilized to purchase goods and services in the *present*? Some critics pointed out that treating a commitment of payment—technically a debt—as an asset in commercial activities was a legal anathema. Some argued that the laws that favored the use of promissory notes were a sign of the power of merchants, whose audacity lay in placing the laws of Lombard Street, the center of commerce in London, above the laws of Westminster Hall, the center of government.[12]

Despite criticism, promissory notes became a regular mechanism for commercial exchanges. In 1758, for example, an important court decision sought to end the legal controversy by stating, unequivocally, that promissory notes were to be "treated as money, as cash, in the ordinary course and transaction of business, by the general consent of mankind."[13] The crucial turn was the understanding that written contracts such as promissory notes could be used to settle third-party debts. As sociologist Nigel Dodd suggests, "[These] were the paper bills that subsequently became money."[14] This is not only a promise that determines a future date of repayment. It is a promise of a future that turns itself into money.

The treatment of money as debt is a key insight from the credit theory of money, normally attributed to economist Alfred Mitchell Innes, who developed his theory in the first decades of the twentieth century.[15] In sum, the theory suggests that credit precedes money. For Mitchell Innes, money is "credit and nothing but credit." More precisely, a monetary system is a form of circulating debts that can be repurposed and deployed as cash. Mitchell Innes illustrates this scenario in a crude way: "A's money is B's debt to him, and when B pays his debt, A's money disappears. This is the whole theory of money."[16] In Dodd's concise formulation, money "is not a promise to hand over a material thing such as gold, but the *opportunity to cancel a debt.*"[17] In this view, promises of future repayment establish the territory on which economies and societies are built.[18]

Admittedly, this is a counterintuitive claim. Promissory notes are, on the surface, just that: a promise of future repayment. But, ambiguously, they function and ought to be "treated as money, as cash."[19] Promissory notes are, on the one hand, a legal tender, a substitute for metal coinage. On the other hand, these bills function as bonds, serving as documents signaling a deferred transaction that, at present, cannot exist because the state cannot actualize the amount represented by the bill. For religious studies scholar Devin Singh, promissory notes make transactions "widely transferable and anonymized" as they join the creditworthiness of the original lender with "the backing of the power structure that makes such tokens efficacious."[20] In social and political terms, Singh concludes, the circulation of promissory notes "[tells] the tale of an authoritative, governing apparatus" that puts all of society into a "structural relation" with debt.[21]

As the case of the Bank of England demonstrates, the formation of the modern banking system exposes the paradoxical nature of promissory notes and the tensions between paper money and debt. As a credit instrument, a banknote signals a deferred payment in the future, but as a legal tender, it demands redemption in the present. According to philosopher Joseph Vogl, this ambiguity signals the temporal paradox of financial transactions. We are faced with the tension between the value that promissory notes need to fulfill in the present and the fact that they remain a promise of repayment that must be deferred continuously. Promissory notes must occupy a time that constantly doubles itself between present and deferred value. For Vogl, the paradox can be solved only by a "temporalization" of the financial

44

system. The only possible way that an absent form of value can circulate is by means of the monetization—legally, socially, and imaginatively—of an "endless deferral." Monetary value is here assessed by measuring the temporal gap created by a promise of future repayment. "Chains of payment had now become chains of payment promises: every operation seems to anticipate an open future and break up a formerly closed circle of reciprocity."[22] In this system, payment deferral is not a glitch in the system or an exception that derails the economic equilibrium. Rather, deferral is a "constitutive disequilibrium in the system," making time "a productive factor" in financial profit. This is a system that took up the "risky transformation of assets into chimeras and shadows" and "functionalized" them as a cog in the financial machinery.[23] The "pledges" and promises of finance are as binding as they are untenable.

The indeterminate nature of financial value puts the modern banking system into an endless cycle of monetary value and its stubborn deferral. As we observed in the previous chapter, the pursuit of financial profit puts the economy in a future-bound trajectory. Promissory notes follow the same pattern, always seeking to valorize themselves in this forward-looking movement. The problem, as Vogl identifies, is that the value of promises lies not in their realization but in their deferral. "Interminability" is tapped into the core of the modern financial system and the widespread circulation of promissory notes.[24] Theorist Lisa Adkins puts it thus: "The promise to pay . . . operates via a double movement in regard to time: it defers the present but does so by counting on (and counting) the future."[25] This constant deferral is crucial for the temporality of financialized capitalism. By counting on the future, finance continuously binds us to the promise of future repayment. The moment of deferral is the moment when the debt cycle is renewed and the indebted subject is once again asked to commit to repayment.

The promissory note inscribes the future into modern economic discourse. Consider the dollar bill: "This note is legal tender for all debts," it says. For the credit theory of money, this innocent artifact of everyday life is a "material memory" of a promise of future repayment.[26] Banknotes hold a hidden promissory note and make their bearers accountable to fulfill their promises of future repayment. They bind us all to a debt economy.

The inscription of debt into paper money offers an entryway into the neoliberal promise of future wealth and the subjects it engenders. As these promissory notes circulate in the economy, they stir in the subject a certain disposition toward the future. As bearers of money, we are made into bearers of the promises of wealth that launch the economy toward the future. In the cash flow of money as promises, we encounter the promissory subject, subjected to these futures.

A "Wagon-Way through the Air"

Adam Smith understood that these promissory notes were a "new wheel" in the movement of commodity circulation.[27] As such, they were an extremely important instrument to enhance the wealth and well-being of a nation. More important, he insisted that insofar as they contribute to the flourishing of commercial societies, promissory notes contribute to the general advancement of humanity. For Smith, historical progress is indivisible from the human urge to improve and grow. Such desire "comes with us from the womb, and never leaves us till we go into the grave."[28] Progress, in this sense, is the consequence of "a certain propensity in human nature . . . to truck, barter, and exchange one thing for another."[29] True to the spirit of the Enlightenment theory of progress, Smith was interested in understanding the implicit law that governs human and societal development.[30]

For Smith, the circulation of commodities plays a pivotal role in this drive toward progress. In fact, many of Smith's economic convictions stemmed from his disagreement with mercantilist political economists who argued that the wealth of a nation amounts to its reserves of gold and silver.[31] Smith was convinced that a nation's money reserves should be put into circulation as a means of increasing commercial activity and production and that circulation was necessary for a society's improvement. Smith compared gold and silver to the "utensils" and the "furniture" one holds in the kitchen. That is to say: one does not have more food on the table by hoarding forks and knives. Quite the opposite: the need for utensils grows in accordance with the number of mouths to be fed and the quantity of food in the household.[32] The wealth of a nation is therefore not in its gold and silver reserves—it is in its ability to produce and circulate goods that contain value.

The focus on the importance of circulation led Smith to pay considerable attention to financial institutions and mechanisms that were gaining shape during his lifetime. He was especially intrigued by the printing of paper money, particularly the development of promissory notes. Smith described paper money issued by banks as a "new wheel" of commerce and treated it as an important tool for the more rapid and efficacious circulation of goods and services.[33]

46

Smith's account of the banking system begins with a conjecture. Suppose a bank advances money to its customers by printing promissory notes totaling one hundred thousand pounds. Gold and silver in the same amount are kept in the bank's coffers, with a portion of it, stipulated at twenty thousand pounds, reserved for occasional demands. In the meantime, the promissory notes issued by the bank circulate in the economy and often return to the bank in the form of payment of a particular loan granted by the bank, along with the interest accrued on it. "By this operation," Smith concluded, "twenty thousand pounds of gold and silver perform all the functions which a hundred thousand could otherwise have performed. . . . Eighty thousand pounds of gold and silver, therefore, can . . . be spared from the circulation of the country."[34] Promissory notes therefore function in the economy in the same manner as gold and silver, with the difference that they are much safer and more convenient. For the nation, this is doubly important as it makes commerce more fluid while also permitting banks to employ their gold and silver reserves for new investments.

Smith describes the circulation of commodities made possible by the banking system with a mild sense of wonder:

> The banks, when their customers apply to them for money, generally advance it to them in their own promissory notes. These the merchants pay away to the manufacturers for goods, the manufacturers to the farmers for materials and provisions, the farmers to their landlords for rent; the landlords repay them to the merchants for the conveniences and luxuries with which they supply them, and the merchants again return them to the banks, in order to balance their cash accounts, or to replace what they may have borrowed of them; and thus almost the whole money business of the country is transacted by means of them. Hence the great trade of those companies.[35]

Smith saw promissory notes as a socially integrative element that opened up a pathway for greater commercial activity. Latent in the passage is his broader vision of a just society: an advanced commercial society standing at the summit of historical progress. Smith colorfully described the "judicious operations of banking" as a "wagon-way through the air" that provides the means for a country to develop its "highways into good pastures and corn-fields."[36]

In *The Wealth of Nations*, however, this midair highway receives an ambiguous treatment. As if perceiving the risks contained in an economy that circulates in midair, Smith was quick to voice his suspicions about promissory notes and the commercial dynamic they create. To make his case, he introduced the practice of drawing and redrawing bank notes. This was a growing practice in eighteenth-century Britain in which traders sought to gain a profit through the circulation of money.[37] The mechanism was ingenious: a person would borrow a certain amount of money from the bank and utilize the value inscribed in the promissory note to advance a new loan to a third party with the condition that the repayment of this second note came prior to the repayment date of the first. Let us return to our imaginary friends in chapter 1, Bert and Ernie. Imagine Bert borrows $100 from the bank, promising to repay it within six months. Bert then uses the promissory note to extend a loan to Ernie for the same amount of $100, demanding repayment in three months. At this time, Bert would receive back the $100, plus interest and a stipulated fee for the transaction, before repaying the original loan to the bank. Bert has mastered a way of making a profit out of a trick with future dates.

Smith is concerned with the fallacy of a mechanism that tries to raise money merely by putting money into circulation. He described these "projectors"—in short, people trying to profit from a debt—as extravagant dreamers whose illusions were not only false but detrimental to the economy. For Smith, the practice was "altogether fictitious."[38]

Even if fictitious, the practice remains economically efficient. It is certainly driven by the same attention to self-interest that Smith deemed the basis of societal progress. After all, is not the "projector" driven by the same desire of "augmentation of fortune" that Smith identifies as the major engine of a society's progress?[39] Even if poorly guided, was not the projector's regard to his self-interest supposed to function for the "greater good of society"?[40] As if betrayed by his own depiction of the practice of drawing and redrawing, Smith could not deny that fictitious money still functioned as money. While attacking the projectors and the process as immoral, Smith remained aware that this ingenious mechanism was somehow a latent possibility opened up by banking activity. The practice, while spurious, did not contradict Smith's theory of economic progress.[41]

Michel Foucault suggests that Smith's ambiguous treatment of the use and exchange of promissory notes might have been less an oversight than a sign of a definitive epistemic rupture in the "order of things," of which the birth of modern economics is a result.[42] As Smith acknowledged, one of the basic features of commercial societies is the circulation of money in the form of promissory notes—a pledge, in Foucault's terms. This pledge is accepted as an exchangeable token in commercial transactions. For Foucault, the reality of this "fiction" turns money into "a material memory, a self-duplicating representation, a deferred exchange."[43] What Smith identified as "altogether fictitious" cannot be expunged from commercial societies, Foucault insists. He rather identifies in Smith's economic writings the *acceptance* of the fictitious nature of money as a necessary condition for the existence of a commercial society.

For Foucault, the acceptance of the fiction of money is the symptom of a rupture in the epistemic and temporal scaffolding of reality. On the epistemic level, modern economics was the result of a shift from the study of wealth to the study of *value*. Money, in this context, moved from being a measure of the worth of commodities with regard to a material reality (e.g., gold) to a representation of something external to it, namely, labor.[44] Smith is the key figure in this epistemic revolution. His analysis created a distinction between the reasons for exchange (the basic human need for trading goods and services) and the nature of what is exchanged. Through his theory of value, Smith introduced labor and time as the true elements that determine the value of a commodity. This suggested that the value of the commodity is represented by something external to it. As Foucault sees it, Smith "formulates a principle of order that is irreducible to the analysis of representation: he unearths labour, that is, toil and time, the working-day that at once patterns and uses up [human] life."[45]

Humans trade *because* they experience needs and desires, but they "are *able* to exchange and to *order* these exchanges because they are subjected to time."[46] Foucault's conclusion points to an implicit and ambivalent connection between time and capital in Smith's work: "From Smith onward, the time of economics is no longer to be the cyclical time of alternating impoverishment and wealth; nor the linear increase achieved by astute policies, constantly introducing slight increases in the amount of circulating specie so that they accelerated production at a faster rate than they raised prices; it was to be the interior time of an organic structure which grows in accordance with its own necessity and develops in accordance with autochthonous laws—the time of capital and production."[47] For Foucault, Smith's economic theory is tied to and contributes to a rupture in the experience of time. The time of the Smithian economy is neither cyclical nor simply linear. Rather, it is a temporality regimented by laws that render historical progress *necessary*.[48] The Enlightenment theory of progress that Smith embraced follows the "autochthonous" laws of time and capital and therefore construes the development of capitalist economies as a historical necessity.

Promissory notes circulating as money conjured for Smith a vision of a bright future of progress, equality, and prosperity. It was a "wagon-way through the air" that would pave the way for a wealthy and just economy. But Smith's vision for the future betrayed his hopes as the fulfillment of the promise ignited a crisis of speculation and fictitious money. The temporality of Smith's economy will forever vacillate between an economy fixed on the present and one that pushes people toward speculative, fictitious future arenas. This trepidation is embedded in the future-talk of the modern financial system.

Financial transactions, as we saw in the previous chapter, are constructed around the projection of a knowledge of the future that is not simply a prediction but also a call to subjection to a future unknown. In Martijn Konings's terms, there is a "constitutive duality in the way moderns think about economy, simultaneously asserting the contingency of the future and the possibility of objectively discounting this future."[49] This is evident in Smith's account of the modern banking system. On the one hand, "the most judicious operations of banking can increase the industry of a country," while, on the other hand, left to the "autochthonous laws" of capital and production, financial institutions seem destined to render fictitious mechanisms real—and profitable. The crucial problem here is that the "autochthonous" laws Smith inscribed in the emerging discipline of economics enclose the possibility of the collapse of the entire system.

Again we find ourselves in limbo, suspended in midair: "The commerce and industry of the country . . . cannot be altogether so secure when they are thus, as it were, suspended upon the Dædalian wings of paper money as when they travel upon the solid ground of gold and silver."[50] Smith is concerned about the directions promissory notes might take when they circulate as money. As they stand suspended in the air, they risk cutting their ties to the foundations of the economy—gold and silver. But how close to the sun must one be before these wings of wax start to melt? Smith did not speculate on that. Instead, he wanted to spin a thread tying the midair circulation of promissory notes to the solid foundation of a nation's gold and silver reserves. As he sees it, the circulation of notes in airy spheres must assure that earthly goods can be properly produced and exchanged.

But herein lies the danger that Smith's text perceived but could only try to foreclose. The Dædalian wings that Smith feared would cause the financial system to steer away from the materiality of gold and silver were already inscribed in the promissory notes issued and circulated by a rising financial system. They are the wagon-way that elevates the economy into midair. As pledges, they contain the promise of future wealth as well as the foreboding of the melting of finance's promissory notes.

The "time of capital and production," in Foucault's terms, had already pushed money away from its metallic foundation and projected it further into the temporality of credit and fictitious money.[51] By wanting to maintain paper money and promissory notes grounded in solid coinage, Smith desired what his economic theory had already overcome—the very idea that paper money is somehow a measure of the materiality of gold and silver. What Smith saw but could not name was how the impetus to fly toward the spellbinding heat that melts Daedalus's wings was already implicit in the future inscribed in the promissory note. These notes are the material memory inscribing debt as the source of financial value, as the very basis of the modern banking system that Smith dreaded.

Promissory Subjects

If modern finance is built around the circulation of promissory notes, its hegemonic force grows when the bearers of these notes become themselves subjects of the promise. The promise of future wealth, introduced by Lazzarato as the basis of the neoliberal economy, indeed has a subject-forming power. Financialization has rendered us subjects of its futures. In finance, future-talk gains form through the social relations between creditors and debtors, between one who appears credible enough to fulfill the promise of future repayment and one who is prepared to wait until the repayment comes. Finance occurs in this temporal space "where the promise and the waiting can meet at a point in time."[52]

Not only does this social relation shape the economy; it also shapes life and regulates human hopes and expectations. Kathryn Tanner notes that the debtor-creditor relationship forces debtors into shaping an entire life around the promise of future repayment. That is because the debtor-creditor relationship transcends the length of a financial transaction to, in fact, shape the subjectivity of a person.[53] Debt is here encountered as a mechanism of social formation that subjects people to a particular regime of temporality. With its demarcations of future time and its promises of future repayment, financialized capitalism engenders a promissory subject. The subject under financialized capitalism is one subjected to the promise of future wealth.

Friedrich Nietzsche—the philosopher so often portrayed as antipolitical and self-consciously ignorant of political economy—has been a prominent figure in contemporary conversations around debt, the future, and financialization.[54] In Nietzsche's second essay in *On the Genealogy of Morality*, he ascribed interesting contours to the relation between the future and the economy. He opened the essay by posing the question, "To breed an animal with the prerogative to *promise*—is that not precisely the paradoxical task which nature has set herself with regard to humankind?"[55] Nietzsche suggested that the formation of a promising subject demands an ability to exert control over the future and "to view the future as the present and anticipate it."[56] Envisioning the future in these terms is nevertheless a costly endeavor for the subject. Before the future can become knowable to people, the subject must become "*reliable, regular, necessary*" so as to become responsible for its own future.[57] A promise is therefore always accompanied by a memory that reinforces it—a "memory of the future," as it were. For Nietzsche, economic relations are the fundamental sphere where this takes place.

Exchange relations, particularly the relationship between creditors and debtors, are at the roots of human sociability and culture, according to Nietzsche. This fundamental social relation requires a peculiar form of temporality, one that shapes a memory that does not preserve a past moment but that launches itself toward the future to project a reminder to debtors that they are answerable to a future in which they actually pay their debts.[58] For Nietzsche, "mnemonic" devices emerge from this so that the memory of the future can function effectively. These "devices" pierce the body of the promising subject and inflict pain on the flesh, to the extent that only what hurts stays in the memory.[59]

In this site where promises are made, the promissory subject must assure the creditor that the repayment will occur. The promise thus involves offering the creditor a collateral, something that can be taken from the debtor in case the promise is not met. Nietzsche's list of potential collaterals is revealing: the debtor's body, a spouse, the debtor's freedom, or their life.[60] The memory of a past promise thus pinches the body of the debtor and binds the subject to be responsible for the future. As that future approaches, the pressure on the debtor's body tightens, making their body a fleshly clock that ticks in the direction of the coming of the day of reckoning. What is to come binds the indebted subject to the creditor who awaits repayment.

By fixing his gaze on the body, Nietzsche was positioned to make his definitive claim: underneath every promise launched toward the future lies, concealed, a punishment that can cut through the body of the promisor. For Nietzsche, the bare truth of the creditor-debtor relationship is the violence inherent and yet concealed in it. The social relation between creditor and debtor was at the crux of the moral dilemma Nietzsche sought to unravel: "Precisely here, *promises are made*; precisely here, the person making the promise has to have a memory *made* for him: precisely here, we may suppose, is a repository of hard, cruel, painful things."[61] Offering credit, buying and selling, bartering—these are social interactions that put a subject in the position of measuring their value against another person's value, of calculating their own worth in relation to others' worth, or lack thereof.[62] For Nietzsche, the lines connecting these subjects are shot through with violence and domination.[63]

Eventually, assessing the worth of others and one's self-worth became the breeding ground for a self that learned to impose itself on others. Nietzsche insisted that exchange relations are at the core of all social relations and that these commercial interactions are at the root of human morality. Semantics reminds us of what the "genealogists of morality" have long forgotten: that the moral sense of guilt (*Schuld*) is derived from the contractual relation around debt (*Schuld*).[64] In this sense, to omit the economic dimension of our moral sense of guilt and shame was, for Nietzsche, a tragedy that modern times have wrought. Nietzsche approached debt with an ambivalence that he described in gendered terms: like the sickness that often accompanies pregnancy, debts must be assumed courageously— even when they inflict profound pain on one's body—so that new life can be generated.[65]

Translating this to the realm of larger social relations, Nietzsche implies that this sense of indebtedness grows in direct proportion to the power a given society attributes to ancestral forces to which that society owes an unpayable debt.[66] This creates an interesting power relationship whereby the greater a society's power, the greater its sense of indebtedness. We have already witnessed an analogous ambivalence in Smith's theorization about the financial system: the greater a bank becomes, the more imminent its collapse looms. The more promissory notes circulate in the economy, the more chances that these notes will wreck the economy by derailing it from its metallic foundations. Similarly, Nietzsche observed how the creditor-debtor relationship is in constant danger of being erased by that which makes it possible. That is because the power of the creditor lies not in demanding that debts be paid but precisely in *forgiving* debts. For Simon Wortham, "To overlook debt—to ignore the transgressor's 'default' or their un-repaid indebtedness—is to demonstrate that one is powerful enough to survive the 'loss' without needing recompense in the (economic) form of a substitution: punishment for debt."[67] In the forgiveness of a debt, the power of the creditor takes hold of the entire life of the debtor. We no longer speak here of a monetary debt but of an existential dependency on the creditor.

Philosopher Maurizio Lazzarato takes his cue from Nietzsche's thought in his account of contemporary finance in his intriguing book *The Making of the Indebted Man*. Following insights from *On the Genealogy of Morality*, Lazzarato observes how economic relations based on debt ultimately shape subjectivities that reflect the credit-debt relation and that the indebted person is forged as the promissory subject. Lazzarato sees in this the greatest achievement of Nietzsche's work on debt, that is, the tracking down of the "temporality and the 'ethico-political' subjectivation" underlying the creditor-debtor relationship.[68] Echoing Foucault's terminology, Lazzarato believes this to be a crucial insight to account for our present-day debt economy.

Neoliberalism, I have shown, puts us in this forward motion toward the future, only to then remind us to repay our debts. Lazzarato stresses that the neoliberal economy is in fact an economy of debt. Under these circumstances Nietzsche's work on debt and subjectivity is instructive insofar as it unveils debt as more than an "economic mechanism." Rather, debt exposes a "security-state technique of government aimed at reducing the uncertainty of the behavior of the governed."[69] Lazzarato insists that the shaping of a promissory subject grants capitalism power over the future "since debt obligations allow one to foresee, calculate, measure, and establish equivalences between current and future behavior."[70] For Lazzarato, the debt economy engendered by financialization features debt as the mechanism that ties subjects to a strict temporal regime.

This "economy of time" promises a future of wealth while piercing the social body with the sharp presence of debt. A debt economy "exploits" time by actualizing the future, stripping it of its mystery and unfinished status. All that remains of the future is the necessity to repay one's debts. Short of its indetermination, the future is normalized. The debt economy encloses the future into its own present: "[Debt] neutralizes time, time as the creation of new possibilities . . . , the raw material of all political, social, or esthetic change."[71] The promissory subject is likewise normalized, as they become a reliable and predictable subject. By "mortgaging" the indeterminacy of the future, in Lazzarato's apt phrasing, financial discourse promises a future that can only reproduce and reinforce present power relations.[72]

The indebted subjects of financialized capitalism are indebted to the promise of future wealth. As financial theory teaches us, financial transactions exist in the *"shared space of promising and waiting."*[73] But between the promise of the debtor and the patience of the creditor exists a social chasm

54

of power. The space between the promising and the waiting is not so much shared as it is occupied by the power of the creditor. In the moment of expectation, when the indebted subject promises something and the creditor awaits, capitalist temporality takes hold of the indebted subject.

Dead Pledges

In our times the "memory of the future" of which Nietzsche speaks is eerily close to home. The mnemonic device urging debtors to repay their debts is the very abode one inhabits. In the context of financialization, domestic space has become a prime site for the formation of the indebted subject. At the center of the financial collapse of 2007–2008 were subprime mortgages, loans extended to the poorest of workers with the attached promise of homeownership, a sign of upward mobility. Through advanced forms of mortgage securitization, the house becomes a financial asset, an object one invests in to leverage future consumption, retirement plans, and investment possibilities.[74] But I show that the mortgage industry produces something beyond homeowners. The house inhabited by the indebted subject is the ticking clock that reminds them that they must pay their debts. As financialization turns houses into financial commodities, it engenders unhomely subjects. This section attends to the material conditions that constitute this indebted subject while teasing out the gendered and racialized contours of financialization. To offer credit to individuals and populations, financialized capitalism musters old tropes and stereotypes to bait a population into the financial system. Debt acquired in the form of a mortgage situates the subject within the protocols of gender hierarchies and racial stereotypes. The mortgage industry will serve as our primary example of this tactic as domestic space serves as the primary site for the formation of the indebted subject. The mortgage haunts the subject with a death-dealing pledge of future repayment. *Mortgage*, etymology teaches us, derives from the French, *mort gage*. A dead pledge.[75] The promises we shall encounter here are indeed deadly.

How creditworthy is the promising subject under the regime of financialization? That is indeed a question that interests financialized capitalism. Assessing someone's worth is a necessary step for the financial analyst who decides whether or not to offer credit to a person. This evaluation occurs within intricate systems of value formation. Literary critic Annie McClanahan draws a parallel between practices of evaluation of a person's creditworthiness and literary typifications that represent "social class on the basis of its individual representatives" so as to produce "socially legible characters."[76] For McClanahan, the narratives of credit reports rely on similar typifications. While information about the financial background and moral standing of borrowers is always limited, creditors need to find ways to confidently judge the personal attributes of a mass of strangers. For McClanahan, the realist novel of the nineteenth century offered an appealing narrative technique to address that need. It "showed economic actors how to deduce the intrinsic character of the strangers."[77] Characters in the realist novel are not simply individuals but stand metonymically for a whole social group. Understanding one character allows a reader to enter into the mindset of an entire group of people—a technique with a vast appeal to lenders.

While narratives about creditworthiness are still paramount in contemporary financial discourse, McClanahan suggests that their form has changed under financialization. Exit subjective narratives of a person's moral standing, enter FICO scores. "Much as the credit narrative offered a social rendering of a personal detail, today the credit score represents a social rendering of a person's data."[78] Under financialized capitalism, intricate algorithms paint a picture of a person's creditworthiness. Algorithmic calculations are deployed to measure the creditworthiness of populations and individuals, whose existence is abstracted into social categories and ranks.[79] These calculations mediate the force field between creditors and debtors and gauge the probability of the latter fulfilling their promises.[80]

McClanahan situates the indebted subject within the power architectonics of financialized capitalism. She insists that credit scoring techniques do not represent the person as an individual but as a group—a neighborhood, a class, and especially a race.[81] Credit scores function doubly, as techniques of racialization that peg economic categories to racial stereotypes and, simultaneously, as maneuvers that rely on racialization. "Stereotype," McClanahan concludes, "is the form of characterization appropriate to an economy in which a large group of borrowers are rendered economically vulnerable not through their exclusion but through their inclusion, an inclusion that depends in turn on their reductive constitution as a risky population."[82] The subjectivity built around massive debt is a social category greater than any individual person. At the same time, massive indebtedness cannot exist without forcing itself into the minutest particles of the social body.

As many scholars and pundits have pointed out, the mortgage industry in the United States has a "preferential option" for racial minorities, especially African American women. This dynamic has led many to suggest that finance is a destructive force in the life of poor and minority communities as it depersonalizes its individuals by treating them merely as particular examples of larger social and racial stereotypes. Feminist theorist Miranda Joseph recognizes the "emotional appeal" of these claims but points out that it is precisely the attention to these particulars that *enabled* the expansion of technologies of mortgage lending.[83] Joseph claims that the subprime mortgage and, broadly speaking, the financialization of capitalism must be treated as a generative process of social formation. Financialization engenders a new type of biocapitalism whereby capitalist production reaches the depths of human subject formation.[84] Joseph insists that predatory lending and the massive indebtedness ensuing from financialization are not depersonalizing forces but indicate a "financial structure that . . . depends on a *disrespectful regard* for particular borrowers."[85] Attending to particularities of race, gender, ethnicity, and class enabled financial corporations to presume intimacy with minoritized communities and women. Such intimacy, however, is based on racist and misogynist tropes that are repurposed and expanded by the subprime mortgage industry. In financialization, gender, race, ethnicity, and class are constituted through social relations around credit offers and debt acquisition.

Feminist critics have insisted that financialization is a deeply gendered process. In particular, the centrality of the mortgage industry to contemporary capitalism has led many to consider how financialization is reshaping the very idea of a household. Fiona Allon has termed this the "feminization of finance."[86] This refers to various strategies designed to "integrate" women into the network of global finance while also financializing aspects of social life rendered as "feminine." The subprime mortgage market exemplifies the integration of the biopolitical formation of subjectivity into a global matrix of "macro-financial" structures.[87] For Allon, this integration between biopolitics and macrofinance has engendered a chasm in the traditional narrative of economics as that which is untethered from the household economy. The social identity of the home, in such a narrative, is that of being the private and safe space where women devote care and attention to reproduce a male labor force that will leave the household to build the nation's economy.[88] Financialization did more than erase this split between the household and the social sphere of production. By "including" women in the grasp of lending practices and in the mortgage industry, financialization has unsettled patriarchal structures while also creating "new kinds of subject-formation and new sites of value creation."[89]

Keeanga-Yamahtta Taylor insightfully describes this as "predatory inclusion."[90] She demonstrates how the mortgage business thrives within the parameters of an inclusive housing policy, while the patterns of this inclusion put homeowners in the powerful hands of the financial sector. Taylor demonstrates how the real estate and banking industries joined forces during the 1960s and 1970s to sell the dream of homeownership to African American communities and turn it into a widely profitable enterprise. Rebuilding the "inner city" drew significant economic interests to the center of urban landscapes in the United States: "Far from being a static site of dilapidation and ruin, the urban core was . . . a new frontier of economic investment and extraction for the real estate and banking industries."[91] For banks and real estate agencies, profit was abundant. For African American communities, on the other hand, "shattered credit and ruined neighborhoods" were the real consequences of the promise of homeownership.[92]

Taylor insists that the mortgage industry was particularly interested in including poor Black women in low-income homeownership programs. This was hardly a concern for just housing policies or reparations. Quite the contrary: poor Black women were targeted precisely because of the likelihood they would default on their loan payments and be forced into foreclosure. With incentives coming from the federal government, lenders "were able to parlay foreclosures into profits as the homes went back onto the market and the process was repeated over and over again."[93] For white populations, the housing boom that shaped the urban environment with the invention of suburban areas in the 1950s became a "bedrock of middle-class prosperity." The underside of the story was "the urban homeownership programs of the 1960s and 1970s [that] reinforced the optics of urban crisis while simultaneously appearing to confirm the role of African Americans in perpetuating it."[94]

Racism was not so much camouflaged under the guise of housing policies that favored African American homeownership. Rather, racism remained flagrant, only now under the signature of a mortgage contract. These contracts policed African Americans into segregated landscapes while subjecting Black communities to the mortgage industry. The inclusive policies for homeownership "[were] only allowable by maintaining other forms of exclusion." Taylor continues, "Credit inclusion became possible by holding the line on neighborhood exclusion."[95] Here we see a practice that renders Black subjects "free" to buy their own houses but in turn coerces them into the force field of lending institutions. With a single stroke, financialization manages to explore the neoliberal emphasis on freedom of choice, entrepreneurship, and ownership while binding people—particularly women of color—to the stifling logic of debt.

58

In the cruel logic of financialization, promises made by debtors summon their own demise. The promising subject must surrender their livelihood, their home, and their entire selves to their creditors. Neoliberalism insists that subjects are free to make those promises while eliding the social constraints that offer them no option other than submitting to the hegemonic forces of the debt economy. For the political theologian Adam Kotsko, the socialization of debt under neoliberalism offers an avenue to "responsibilize" more and more areas of social life.[96] In this scheme the more "responsible" people are for their own lives, the more blameworthy they shall be for their perceived failings.

In Kotsko's view, there is a demonic logic in these social arrangements. The demonic shadow of neoliberalism refers to its ability to demonize entire populations, that is, "to set up someone to fall" while providing subjects the "barest sliver of agency necessary to render them blameworthy."[97] The demon, in Kotsko's political theological account, is the figure that is destined to fall while also being culpable for its own demise. This "logic of culpability" treats subjects as entirely depraved *and* entirely blameworthy. A demon can do nothing else than evil, and yet it is blamed for doing so. Kotsko observes that student loans follow this logic. If borrowers do not get the "full benefit" of a college education and translate it into higher incomes, "that is their fault, and their personal failure does not cancel their obligation to make good on the lender's investment."[98] The indebted subject cannot escape debt because this has become the defining feature of their subjectivity. At the same time, they must be blamed for their recklessness, for their drive toward debt, for their lack of financial acumen. The demonic logic Kotsko identifies in student loan programs equally applies to the mortgage industry that I have been investigating. The mortgage owner is at once someone who has no other option than to make a dead pledge and, simultaneously, someone who is blameworthy for making such a deadly promise. Indebted subjects are at once fallen and guilty.

As I have been suggesting since the previous chapter, this guilt is not merely a personal matter afflicting the subject but a social affect engendered by the debt economy. The material and historical realities that I have named so far must be understood in conjunction with the subject-shaping force of financialization.[99] The indebted subject is shaped by the material forces of financialization. McClanahan is therefore correct in claiming that the guilt the indebted person feels cannot be dissociated from the very real threats of punishment for those whom financial institutions deem to be no longer creditworthy.[100]

The case of the mortgage industry is again illuminating. A mortgage, it bears repeating, etymologically presumes a dead pledge. The social relation established between lenders and borrowers makes the house of the indebted person an alienating entity that at any point can be taken from the home's "owner." McClanahan reminds us that for thinkers like Sigmund Freud, Friedrich Nietzsche, Karl Marx, and Theodor Adorno, the feeling of being a stranger in one's own house is the pathway to the *uncanny* (*das Unheimliche*). In the case of a mortgage, this is not just a matter of feeling unhomely with oneself but the very concrete possibility that one might become unhoused. McClanahan concludes, "Even before we are evicted or foreclosed upon, debt has already unsettled our relationship to domestic property."[101] The pledge one launches into the future to buy a house renders that house a zombie-like entity: "neither living nor dead," the mortgaged home is that commodity that may come alive and haunt its indwellers. That which one dreams about, owning a space for living, resting, and feeling at home, quickly turns into a constant reminder of the requirement to pay one's debts.[102] One's home is turned into a liability that may doom the indebted person. The property gains life, and the life it gains is stolen from its inhabitants.

The house inhabited by the indebted subject comes back at them with the inexorable demand—thou shalt pay your debts. The indebted subject condenses in their body the story of finance—from the enticing promise of future wealth to the inscription of this future in the promissory note. The subject no longer knows what is to come from the future but is forced to remember that they are bound to fulfill the promise of future repayment. Pledging allegiance to the futures of financialized capitalism quickens a present of subjection. This subject is the one who becomes what they promise to be: indebted to their creditors.

We have now a fuller picture of the devouring of the future of which I spoke in the previous chapter. Financialized capitalism may praise its supposed power to predict and control the future, but its real power lies in governing the futures of the mass of indebted subjects that it produces. Lazzarato states that the future imagined by the debt economy "[subordinates] all possibility of choice and decision which the future holds" while appropriating "each person's future as well as the future of society as a whole."[103] The debt economy touches all aspects of social life with its demand that debtors submit their futures to their creditors. If future-talk makes sense, financialization submits that the only possible sense the future makes is to bind debtors to their creditors. We have become bound to these death-dealing pledges.

The pause one makes when suggesting that the future is not—yet is occupied by financial discourse with a force that pulls what is to come to the center of its power. In the chapters ahead, I invoke the wisdom of liberation theologians who inhabited this pause as a form of summoning liberating social relations instead of relations of submission. For now, however, as my attention continues to be on reading the "signs of the times," I must insist on the social force of financialization. For the future promised by financialization, this pause offers no respite, only submission.

The future orientation of financialized capitalism has engendered subjects whose promises bind them to the spinning wheel of the financial machine. The debt economy has turned the future into the canniest of things by measuring it, predicting it, and charting pathways to a profitable future trade. But the untold story of this drive toward the future is the foreclosure of future possibilities for the indebted subjects of the debt economy. The indebted subject must submit to the fact that debts ought to be repaid. As lines in a bank's spreadsheet, our sense and expectation for the future are shadowed by the financial apparatus. In the all-consuming force of the debt economy, all that remains for indebted subjects is to offer dead pledges.

times that matter

3

Augustine, in his magnificent reflection on time in the *Confessions*, lamented how each "drop of time" dripped away from him.[1] He stated that these drops of time are precious, only later to confess that he could not measure their value: "So, my God, I measure, and do not know what I am measuring."[2] What indeed does one measure when one counts moments, hours, days, and years? Augustine is right to ask, "How does this future, which does not yet exist, diminish or become consumed?"[3] How does one measure a time that is not—yet? What could consume an expectation? How could future time be reduced or perhaps *taken*?

This chapter investigates the precious drops of time that constitute profit. I take my cue from Karl Marx, who, like Augustine, wrestled with the problem of measuring time. Marx in fact learned from reports about the labor conditions of nineteenth-century British factories that moments are the elements of profit. Each drop of time is indeed precious or, in his vocabulary, *valuable*. Marx believed that capitalism ultimately "extends the worker's production-time . . . by shortening his life."[4]

Through a reading of Marx's *Capital*, I argue that class power enforces a certain regime of temporality. Building on insights already established in the previous two chapters, I suggest here that if indeed moments are the elements of profit, it is necessary to identify *whose* moments constitute profit. The first chapter showed that financialization renders the future an objective reality that can be managed for the sake of profit, all the while consuming our expectations. Chapter 2 investigated the power of financialized capitalism in creating the indebted subject. The task now is to probe the material conditions under which capitalism produces its futures.

With his characteristic obliqueness, Jacques Derrida has suggested that the possession of time by "certain persons or certain social classes" is "the most crucial stake of political economy."[5] Derrida is careful to mention that it is "certainly not time *itself*" that certain persons or classes possess, for time is not something one can have.[6] But while it remains impossible to possess time, I insist that the exercise of power over people's time remains profitable. In fact, I argue that control of other people's time is the signature move of capitalist production. Class power as I depict it here is a mode of social control over people's time.

This chapter bears witness to the consumption of the future in production time. My aim is to show how the search for profit shapes a particular temporality around the working day and how labor time is materially tied to relations of production and class power. The reading I offer of Marx's *Capital* portrays time as materially constituted through social relations established in the "hidden abode of production."[7] In this context class differentials established in the realm of production give flesh to disparate experiences of time and differing expectations for the future.

After a close look at *Capital*, this chapter investigates present dynamics in the organization of labor time. I track contemporary transformations in the constitution of the working day to discuss how class power gains shape in financialization. As I alluded to in previous chapters, with deteriorating working conditions and plummeting wages, workers are forced to rely more and more on financial corporations. In such a context, exploitation transcends the abode of production and creeps into the abode of *prediction*, in the words of political theorist Ivan Ascher. His work will help us bridge from Marx's theory of capitalist exploitation to financialized capitalism to argue that capitalism privatizes the means of prediction and protection.[8] For Ascher, financialization shapes society in such a way that the possibilities and expectations of workers become a site for capitalist exploitation.

63

In conclusion, we revisit the Marxian theory of value with the lenses provided by literary critic Gayatri Chakravorty Spivak, who suggests that financialized capitalism does not release but only effaces the material grounding of the economy. Against those who stress the obsoleteness of Marx's work, Spivak shows that the labor theory of value brings to the surface the concrete, embodied realities that financial discourse elides. Modulated by Spivak's analysis, Marx's account of value exposes how financial profit consumes future expectations and possibilities. The material conditions of capitalist production and speculation are tied to the consumption of the worker's future.

Capital Moments

Marx's labor theory of value presents the capitalist mode of production as a process that constitutes a particular temporality. As I approach it here, Marx's theory provides an account of the entanglement between time and profit, labor time and exploitation, lifetime and economic expropriation. Marx's *Capital* offers an account of the material and social forces at work in shaping a lived experience of time.

The stated aim of *Capital* is to analyze the capitalist mode of production and its central goal—the production of surplus value, or profit.[9] To that end, Marx develops a rich vocabulary that surrounds the central concept of *value*, a term that appears under many guises in *Capital*. Among these are the concepts of use value, exchange value, and surplus value. In the early pages of *Capital*, Marx defines *value* as "socially necessary labor-time," already indicating the prominent role that time will have in his analysis.[10] In light of this definition, what is the value of a commodity, and how does one measure it?

The fundamental premise of the labor theory of value is that the value of any given commodity is determined and measured according to the duration of labor time employed in its production. More time spent in production yields greater value; less productive time yields lesser value. What makes this equation complex for Marx is the fact that the production of commodities and their evaluation, exchange, and consumption take place in a complex network of social relations. To wit, value is *socially* necessary labor time. As David Harvey posits, Marx's emphasis on the social distinguishes his economic thought from that of bourgeois political economists.[11] For the purposes of the reading of *Capital* that I offer, this attention to the social is critical, for it constantly draws Marx's attention to the work of others, *fremde Arbeit*—the alien, strange, and disjointed labor.

The story of time in *Capital* begins with the commodity. Marx devotes the first pages of the book to disentangling the double facet of commodities: they contain what he calls use value insofar as they meet human needs (e.g., a soda addresses my thirst), and they contain exchange value insofar as they can be exchanged for a different commodity (e.g., I can exchange my soda for a bottle of water). Value appears out of this entanglement between use and exchange.

The initial question raised by *Capital* could be summarized thus: What could make commodities with radically different use values—such as a Bible and linen, in Marx's later example—be exchanged as equivalents?[12] Assuming, for the moment, that one Bible equals twenty yards of linen, Marx poses the question, What makes this equality possible? Importing a basic intuition from bourgeois political economy, Marx argues that what makes *qualitatively* different commodities *quantitatively* exchangeable is an invisible "third thing": *labor*, the "value-forming substance."[13]

Commodities may be valued and exchanged with other commodities because they contain "abstract human labour" materialized in them. Marx illustrates: "The value of the linen as a congealed mass of human labour can be expressed only as an 'objectivity' [*Gegenständlichkeit*], a thing that is materially different from the linen itself and yet common to the linen and all other commodities."[14] That common thing, I repeat, is labor. As for the quantitative dimension of a commodity's value (i.e., *one* Bible is equivalent to *twenty* yards of linen), Marx posits: the "quantity is measured by its duration, and the labour-time itself is measured on the particular scale of hours, days etc. . . . [The] magnitude of the value of any article is . . . the amount of labor socially necessary, or labor-time socially necessary for its production."[15] The conclusion follows: the value of commodities is in direct relation to the time necessary, under certain social and historical conditions, to produce them.

Put this way, the relation between value and labor time seems straightforward: more labor time, more value. But as I already said, the transparency of the equation soon becomes opaque thanks to the social nature of the valorization process—value is *socially* necessary labor time. As Marx points out in a famous passage, value "does not have its description branded on its forehead; it rather transforms every product of labour into a social hieroglyphic."[16] To decipher the enigma and determine the value of commodities, it is insufficient to observe the circulation and exchange of Bibles and yards of linen. This is, for Marx, the basic mistake of "bourgeois economics": it confuses the *price* of commodities with their value.

Instead, to account for the magnitude of a commodity's value, one must look for "a secret hidden under the apparent movements in the relative values of commodities."[17] Marx wants to lead the readers of *Capital* through the realm of circulation and beyond the price tag of commodities to encounter there, in the "hidden abode of production," the roots of value.[18] And in this abode the relation is no longer between Bibles and yards of linen but between sellers of *labor power* and their buyers.

The concept of labor power appears at a dramatic moment in *Capital* when Marx is seeking to understand the production of surplus value, that is, the mystery of the transformation of money into capital. Marx revisits his general formula of capital: M–C–M, where money (M) is exchanged for a commodity (C) and then this commodity is exchanged for money to close the process. The goal of the capitalist is to end the cycle with more money— surplus value. The paradox, however, is that profit cannot be generated by a mere circulation process. Simply put, one cannot generate profit merely by circulating money, a mystery that already confronted Adam Smith, as we saw in the previous chapter.

Marx lifts the veil of the mystery: in the marketplace there is one peculiar commodity whose use value (its "utility") is to create value. Its very consumption is, in fact, productive.[19] The name Marx gives to this commodity is *labor power*. Like all other commodities, it contains both use value and exchange value. Unlike other commodities, however, labor power is the one commodity whose use in fact is not a mere consumption but also a creation: "[Labor power] differs from the ordinary crowd of commodities in that its use creates value, and a greater value than it costs itself."[20] Whereas regular commodities are used up as they are consumed, labor power *creates* something as it is consumed. Think again of my soda: its use value, addressing my thirst, is abolished once I am done drinking it. It is not so with labor power, a commodity whose use value is that of creating value, a value greater than the cost of its consumption.[21]

The political impetus of *Capital* as well as its ethical force is to claim that under capitalism the human ability to produce is appropriated and exploited in the pursuit of profit. As Marx grounds the formation of the worker's subjectivity in the materiality of the productive process, he centers time in the material forces of production. Time matters in *Capital*. This form of materialism is not a simple affirmation of the concreteness of matter, one normally juxtaposed to "idealism" or some variation thereof. The materialism that surfaces in Marx's work is one that accounts for the materiality of social relations. What matters is what happens in relation. Time in *Capital* is constituted by social relations of production, that is, by embodied forms of relation taking shape in a context of power differentials. These social relations inform a particular experience of the passage of time. In the tensions of the productive process, Marx identifies a true struggle over time whereby capitalists command the time of the proletariat.

In line with the argument that I have been developing, these tensions conjure a distinct form of imaging the future. As capitalists project the extraction of surplus value from the exploitation of labor time, laborers find their future hopes and expectations being consumed. Marx offers the following invitation to his readers: "Let us . . . in company with the owner of money and the owner of labour-power, leave this noisy place, where everything takes place on the surface and in full view of everyone, and follow them into the hidden abode of production."[22] Here, in the production context, we reach what I take to be *Capital*'s crucial account of time—the chapter "The Working Day."

Marx opens the chapter with the statement "We began with the assumption that labour-power is bought and sold at its value."[23] There are enough reasons in the previous chapters to make the reader suspicious of this assumption. Nothing in *Capital* is as simple as it seems. Wary, we learn that something is out of joint about the working day. It contains two competing temporalities running within it: there is a *constant* and a *variable* quantity of time. The constant facet of the day refers to the quantity of labor time necessary for the "reproduction of labour-power of the worker."[24] This portion of the working day is a hedge: How much work can the worker offer *today* so that they can still be alive and productive *tomorrow*? Marx thinks of the constant quantity of working time as a necessity but warns that under the capitalist mode of production this can only be a portion of the working day.

There must be something else to this day, a period Marx calls *variable*. During this time of the working day, workers do not work for their subsistence but offer their work entirely to the owner of labor power, the capitalist. Marx calls this portion of the working day *surplus labor*. These are therefore the two times of the working day, the two sides of the time clock counting the hours of labor time: on the one side is the work that guarantees the future life of the worker; on the other side is the excess of time that drips from the worker's sweat into the capitalist's pocket. As constant and variable times coalesce to form the working day, the temporality of the working day swirls with indetermination: "The length of the working day therefore fluctuates within boundaries both physical and social."[25]

Marx proceeds with an account of the social relations taking shape within the working day. In one of the characteristic shifts in genre that mark *Capital*, Marx increases the pace of his narrative, theorizing the working day with shorter and shorter sentences, as if his own hours were being cut short by the demands of a production process that pushes him to go faster and faster.[26] We hold our breath as *Capital* explores the temporal dynamics that undergird production. The capitalist purchases labor power for his use for a working day.[27] "But what is a working day?" asks Marx. "At all events, it is less than a natural day. How much less? The capitalist has his own views of this point of no return, the necessary limit of the working day."[28] That is: the goal is to make the working day as long as possible, even if that coincides with the long "natural" hours of the day.

This incessant need to extend the productive hours of the working day is not personally driven but is rather a social force greater than the behavior of individuals. Marx states that a capitalist is a social personification of capital: "His soul is the soul of capital." The *ruah* of capital "has one sole driving force, the drive to valorize itself, to create surplus-value."[29] Marx employs strong imagery, hinting at the deadly consequences of the temporality of the working day: "Capital is dead labour which, vampire-like, lives by sucking living labour, and lives the more, the more labour it sucks."[30] With the metaphor of a life-sucking beast in mind, we come back to the temporality of the working day: "The time during which the worker works is the time during which the capitalist consumes the labour-power he has bought from him."[31] Soon, we shall see, Marx realizes that what is being consumed is the worker's future.

Marx reproduces in a footnote the following commentary from a certain *Essay on Trade and Commerce*: "An hour's labour lost in a day is a prodigious injury to a commercial State."[32] That is because "[if] the worker consumes his disposable time for himself, he robs the capitalist."[33] Another voice speaks in the footnote, suggesting that the worker is a thief if they even take some time to rest: "If the free worker rests for an instant, the base and petty management which watches over him with wary eyes claims he is stealing from it."[34]

The tensions increase in the pages of *Capital* as the scene juxtaposes the worker's need for rest and the manager's watchful attention to every single instant of the working day. The capitalist character resorts to the law of commodity exchange to justify his actions: since he purchased the labor power of the worker, he has the right to demand "the maximum possible benefit from the use-value of his commodity."[35] We recall that the use value of the

68

commodity called labor power is precisely to produce value, surplus value. The capitalist fixes his gaze on this.

It is then that a voice bursts onto the scene in *Capital*, a sound that hitherto had been stifled in the text as much as in the "fury of the production process."[36] This is the voice of the worker yelling at the capitalist:

> The commodity I have sold you differs from the ordinary crowd of commodities in that its use creates value, a greater value than it costs. That is why you bought it. What appears on your side as the valorization of capital is on my side an excess expenditure of labour-power. . . . [By] means of the price you pay for [my labor power] every day, I must be able to reproduce it every day, thus allowing myself to sell it again. . . . I must be able to work tomorrow with the same normal amount of strength, health and freshness as today.[37]

The future of the worker is at stake here, we notice. Marx sets the stage for his labor theory of value in the context of a rally, and the worker gains voice to critique the exploitation they experience in the hidden abode of production. Unpaid labor today puts the future life of the worker in peril. These moments are precious, but their value is taken from the worker. The worker continues to cry out, now calculating their own life expectations:

> What you gain in labour, I lose in the substance of labour. . . . If the average length of time an average worker can live . . . is 30 years, the value of my labour-power, which you pay me from day to day, is $1/365 \times 30$ . . . its total value. But if you consume [my labor power] in 10 years . . . [you pay me] only one-third of its daily value, and you therefore rob me every day of two-thirds of the value of my commodity. You pay me for one day's labour-power, while you use three days of it.[38]

Once again, the worker notices that their future is being cut short every working day. Increasingly, work encroaches on personal time, consuming future possibilities. Of the thirty years' worth of working days, twenty remain unpaid and are transferred to someone else.

Tensions between workers and their managers constitute the temporality of the working day, and the moments that make up profit soon take their toll on the future life of workers. Working his theory of value through the voice of the worker, Marx believes that the math of the expropriation of surplus labor is simply unhealthy. By extending the hours of the working day, capitalists use up "a quantity of labour-power greater than [what the worker] can restore in three."[39] As the worker gets acquainted with the secret that surplus value is formed out of their extra unpaid labor, revolt erupts: "You are constantly preaching to me the gospel of 'saving' and 'abstinence.' Very well! Like a sensible, thrifty owner of property I will husband my sole wealth, my labour-power, and abstain from wasting it foolishly. . . . I therefore demand a working day of normal length."[40] The worker here meets the capitalist in his logic: commodities must be bought at their full value. Why do capitalists pay less for the commodity known as labor power?

After the conclusion of the workers' rally, Marx is able to introduce, for the first time in *Capital*, the motif of class struggle. And the struggle is over time: "The establishment of a norm for the working day presents itself as a struggle over the limits of that day, a struggle between collective capital, i.e. the class of capitalists, and collective labour, i.e. the working class."[41] According to Marx, class warfare, this fearful and charged term, revolves around the creation of a just working day. It is a struggle for time, for a just and life-giving time. And more: it is a struggle over the material conditions that allow for a future, one that is under constant threat of consumption by the voracious appetite for profit. The exploitation that workers experience in the hidden abode of production is future-consuming. Their struggle is therefore the struggle for the future. It is the struggle to reclaim a time that is not—yet.

Capital proceeds with a list of reports that attest to the ways in which time has been expropriated from the working class. Marx reproduces reports from factory inspectors, representatives of the home secretary of the British Parliament in charge of overseeing and enforcing labor laws on the factory floor. The Factory Act of 1850 stipulated the working day as ten hours in length on weekdays and eight hours on Saturdays. Yet, as the factory inspectors illustrate, the limitation to the working day does not appease the "voracious appetite of the capitalist for surplus labour."[42] *Capital* catalogs the minutiae of these reports, every minute assigned for workers' breaks and meals, as well as the constant "temptation" of factory owners to multiply "small thefts in the course of the day" by shortchanging workers with regard to those break times, keeping them at work late, or forcing them back to work early. Marx's attention is captured by these expressions: "The 'small thefts' of capital from the workers' meal-times and recreation times are also described by the factory inspectors as 'petty pilferings of minutes,' 'snatching a few minutes' or, in the technical language of the workers, 'nibbling and cribbling at meal-times.'"[43]

From one of these reports Marx learns the expression "Moments are the elements of profit."[44] For workers, however, these profitable moments are deadly. Marx goes on to enumerate instances of premature death among the working class: potters, match producers, wallpaper manufacturers, bakers, agricultural workers, a milliner, and a blacksmith.[45] Marx suggests that by extending the working day to its moral and physical limits, the capitalist process of producing surplus value "produces the premature exhaustion and death of . . . labour-power itself."[46] Furthermore, the production of profit is tied to the "shortening [of] the life of labour-power" to the degree that capitalist production "extends the worker's production-time within a given period by shortening his life."[47]

As Marx saw it, capitalism renders each and every drop of time as value-producing. But the value of these moments is not equally divided among different social groups. He argues that the exploitation of the labor time of workers is the secret of the precious moments of the capitalist's profit. The class differential between capitalists and workers constitutes a temporal gap, a difference between a time projected as profit and time experienced as the consumption of living labor. Under the capitalist temporal regime, the worker "personifies" labor time.[48] That is to say, the worker is constituted as a person in the moment of the expropriation of their labor time.

Capital's account of time is therefore double: on the one hand, time in capitalism is materially constituted by social relations in the process of production. On the other hand, time is socially constitutive of class disparity: the worker is the personification of labor time; the capitalist is the embodiment of a powerful command over the labor time of others. The secret that Marx set out to investigate—the formation of surplus value—boils down to the power wielded by a certain class to command the time of others, that is, to render the time of others profitable. What appears on the side of capital as surplus value appears on the other side of the relation as lost time, lost living time.

Augustine's question rings again: "How does this future, which does not yet exist, diminish or become consumed?" After taking us to the "hidden abode of production," Marx has unveiled the possibility of an answer: the future of multitudes is consumed by the excesses of the few. Under capitalism the pause engendered by the inexistence of the future, the not—yet, is the moment of exploitation.

Chronic Crises

Let us once again follow Marx's invitation to excavate the "hidden abode of production" and observe the temporality of the working day in the age of finance. Sociologists and economists have perceived that the financialization of capitalism unleashed significant shifts in the hours of the working day. While the assumed notion is that workers in the United States work longer hours, some have suggested that the most pressing issue for labor-time dynamics in the United States is *which* hours people work. Economist Daniel Hamermesh points out that evening and night shifts declined in the United States between 1970 and 1990, while significant changes occurred in the "fractions of work at the fringes of the traditional regular working day."[49] These fringes represent small and unevenly dispersed portions of the working day, like shifts that run in the earlier hours of the day and then resume late in the afternoon. Today roughly two-fifths of the American workforce works on those fringes—should we say *edges*?—of the working day.

At these fringes the class divide grows: wealthier individuals tend to work longer hours while working on a more fixed schedule. Poor workers, while working less, are challenged by a growing instability at the fringes of the working day. Literature on the topic grants many names to the new dynamics shaping the labor force. Scholars refer to it as "externalization of employment," "flexible" or "nonstandard work arrangements," or "market-mediated work arrangements."[50] More recently, work flexibilization has reached its zenith with the rise of the *gig economy*, a term that authors Alex de Ruyter and Martyn Brown believe reflects the long-standing tradition of precarious labor conditions under capitalism.[51] Without a doubt, these temporal fringes of nonstandard working hours significantly disempower workers in relation to their employers.[52]

Sociologists Jerry Jacobs and Kathleen Gerson argue that current labor dynamics in the United States shape a multifaceted and interlocked "time divide."[53] The temporal divide names how working hours are unequally distributed among working-class people and how workers experience pressure from insufficient work or erratic and unhealthy work hours. The time divide is truly an intersection of social divides in American society. Jacobs and Gerson refer to the *occupational* divide between workers who have to work too much in order to make ends meet and workers who do not have sufficient work. They also list the *gender* divide "that leaves women confronting the most acute dilemmas and paying the highest price for their efforts to reconcile family needs with work demands."[54] "These time divides," the authors state, "are interconnected, socially constructed, and deeply anchored in processes of work and family change in the twenty-first century."[55] Various power differentials coalesce in a time divide with dire consequences for family dynamics, career choices, personal aspirations for the relation between work and leisure, and gender dynamics.

72

Harriet Presser, also a sociologist, reflects on the social implications of working on the fringes of the working day, arguing that it has engendered new dynamics in how domestic time is organized.[56] *Home-time* is a term that speaks to new family arrangements shaped under nonstandard working hours, whose effects are particularly felt among the working poor. Most of the jobs that function on a nonstandard work schedule are low-paying positions, and single mothers are their major target. Presser's study using data from the National Survey of Families and Households confirms that people who work these nonstandard hours are forced to balance the reality of a low-paying job "with being 'out of sync' temporally with other family members, including their children."[57] For Presser, the absence of synchrony between work and family is the systemic result of a "24/7 economy" in which each fringe of the working day matters for profit making.

It may well be said that the economic inequality that marks our epoch materializes an unequal distribution of life expectancy. In the United States, research conducted by the economists of the Brookings Institution attests to the growing disparity in life span between the rich and the poor, accompanied by rising levels of wealth inequality. The richest 10 percent who were born in 1920 lived, on average, 7.7 years longer than the poorest 10 percent. Three decades later, for those born in 1950, the difference in life expectancy had increased to 13.5 years.[58] Between 2001 and 2014, the gap between the life spans of the rich and the poor widened significantly. In this period "[the] top 1 percent in income among American men live 15 years longer than the poorest 1 percent; for women, the gap is 10 years."[59] Similar differences in rates of life expectancy are witnessed in studies that address differences along the lines of gender, level of education, race, and ethnicity—with the unsurprising conclusion that marginalized communities live for fewer years and that their life expectancy is diminished when compared to the highest brackets of the income ladder.[60]

That the rich live longer lives than the poor is one of those social tautologies that we tend to treat as a natural fact. But a look over recent data from the medical disciplines suggests that even the most "natural" facts have their social counterpart. Take the case of cancer. A study conducted by the Dana-Farber Cancer Institute and Boston Children's Cancer and Blood Disorders Center points out that children from impoverished areas are "substantially more likely to suffer early relapse" after being treated for acute lymphoblastic leukemia—the most common type of pediatric cancer—despite having received the same treatment as other children. The research is paradigmatic because there were no differences in treatment or access to health care that would account for the results. Poor children in this case are more susceptible to relapse for no other reason than being poor. Pediatric oncologist Kira Bona, the lead researcher on the study, reflects on the findings: "In trying to improve cure rates, we, as a field, have focused almost exclusively on biology. If we want to move forward, we also have to look at social determinants. . . . Any 'moon shot' to cure cancer must include interventions that target socio-economic disparities in outcomes."[61] As Bona's research indicates, socioeconomic dynamics make their way into the very cancerous cells of a child's body.

Fundamentally, the driving force of capitalism gains the shape of a consuming power over people's expectations for the future. Economists Anne Case and Angus Deaton have famously studied the widespread phenomenon of "death of despair." Focusing on middle-aged white Americans, they discovered a reversal in the decades-long trend toward a decline in midlife deaths, a fact that distinguishes the United States from other developed countries. The increase in mortality is largely explained by deaths from alcohol and drug use, suicide, and chronic liver diseases and cirrhosis.[62] Case and Deaton hint at the implicit link between these deaths and financialization: "The United States has moved primarily to defined-contribution pension plans with associated stock market risk, whereas, in Europe, defined-benefit pensions are still the norm."[63] In the United States, these pension funds were deeply impacted by the financial meltdown of 2007–2008, which may help explain why the spike in mortality studied by Case and Deaton occurred between 1999 and 2013. "Future financial insecurity may weigh more heavily on US workers," Case and Deaton conclude, "if they perceive stock market risk harder to manage than earnings risk, or if they have contributed inadequately to defined-contribution plans."[64] With their future plans evaporating along with their pension funds, workers are confronted with the consumption of their expectations for the future. Death by despair might be the debris of the futures traded in financial markets.

We may overhear in these descriptions echoes of Marx's own studies on the labor conditions of nineteenth-century Britain: "[Capital] attains its objective by shortening the life of labour-power. . . . It extends the worker's production-time . . . by shortening his life."[65] When we observe dynamics in the working day in the contemporary scene, we continue to wrestle with the consumption of the future. Under financialized capitalism, access to the future is negotiated by financial markets. For workers to get there, they need nothing less than an appropriation of the means of *prediction*.

74

The Means of Prediction

In the fluctuations of the working day, that which is not—yet is consumed. Ivan Ascher has suggested that financialization appropriates, indeed privatizes, the means of *prediction* and *protection*. Ascher argues that ours is not simply a "'civil society' (*bürgerliche Gesellschaft*)" mediated by the exchange of commodities, like the one confronted by Marx in the nineteenth century. Rather, we live in a "portfolio society" in which capital mediated by financial markets assumes a prominent role in determining the future of all members of society.[66] In the portfolio society, the power of the capitalist class lies in its ability to forecast the future and subject people to this projection. Here we notice how the privatizing of the means of prediction and protection consumes the life expectations of workers and indebted persons.

Ascher takes his readers to the hidden abode of prediction. There, similarly to what Marx encountered in the hidden abode of production, we encounter "Moneybags," a character Marx had developed in *Capital* as the embodiment of the unending capitalist drive for profit. In the Marxian account, Moneybags was ultimately concerned with purchasing labor power. In our times Moneybags shifts his attention to the task of lending money. "The result is nothing short of extraordinary," Ascher quips.[67] For Marx, as we have seen, the surprise Moneybags had when going to the marketplace was that labor power was a commodity whose use value was precisely that of creating more value, surplus value. Moneybags, the financier, once again discovers a "miraculous" commodity: the credibility of a borrower.[68] In financialized capitalism, "it appears that Moneybags . . . is now similarly able to claim other people's credibility or probability—that is, their ability to be believed—while himself becoming miraculously more credible as a result."[69]

By the end of the twentieth century, Moneybags had mastered his capacity to assess and predict the profitability of borrowers' promises of future repayment. Ascher describes the development of credit scoring techniques as both a way to calculate the "likelihood of individuals defaulting on their debt" and also a way for lenders to "imagine that they could calculate the probability of several borrowers defaulting at the same time."[70] From the perspective of borrowers, the expansion of credit is as deceiving as the "freedom" of workers who have no other option than to sell their labor power to a capitalist. "[Just] as workers in Marx's account were paid only what they needed to reproduce themselves as workers . . . , a similar arithmetic and a similar ethic have come to surround the allocation of credit."[71] The conceit nevertheless starts to show its sinister backdrop: the "credit" we receive is good for our "repro-duction" as borrowers. Our creditworthiness lasts long enough to make us return to Moneybags for another loan.

Ascher's insight is to indicate the structural similarity between the ex-ploitation that occurs in the hidden abode of production, studied by Marx, and the exploitation that occurs in the hidden abode of prediction under financialized capitalism. The argument, however, is more than a claim about the relevance of the Marxian analysis for our contemporary context. Ascher helps us deepen our understanding of the consumption of the future in our contemporary context. The financialization of capitalism has indeed exac-erbated the future-consuming impetus that I have so far described as en-demic to capitalism. After all, what borrowers and indebted subjects offer to their creditors is their own future, their own future possibilities. In return, creditors monetize these promises of future repayment and become even more creditworthy in the public eye, whereas debtors are vilified as agents incapable of making good on their promises. Echoing a scenario we have encountered in previous chapters, borrowers are "compelled by necessity to make promises and thereby make their probability available to others for gambling purposes."[72]

In the portfolio society, Ascher insists, capitalists "make use of the capa-bilities and probabilities of others in such a fashion that they become more capable and probable in turn."[73] He points out that financialized capitalism cannot disavow labor but that its power to discipline workers expands to the management of their probabilities.[74] Finance shapes class relations accord-ing to the rules of credit offering and promises of repayment. As I antici-pated in my study of Martijn Konings's work in chapter 2, financialization is tied to the growing precarization of labor under neoliberalism whereby workers' opportunities to exchange their labor for a wage are systematically reduced.[75] By deepening the precarity of labor conditions, financialization shapes its own demand: it places individuals and communities in further need of credit.

Ascher suggests that financialization tilts class relations toward the ten-sion between the financial investor and the "subprime" borrower.[76] The predicament of students trapped in the student loan industry illustrates this. Before joining the labor force, students are introduced to class power through their interactions with student loan agencies, which in turn shape their social locations as borrowers indebted to financial corporations. At the time of their professional formation, students are subjectified as "speculative units," gauging their aspirations under the shadow of the promise to repay their debts.[77] Higher education, in the context of financialization, is the pipeline into the logic of debt: one must acquire it in order to become a professional; one must be a professional in order to repay one's debts. Young professionals enter the labor force already indebted. Their futures, professional and otherwise, are from the beginning marked by their indebtedness to a financial corporation that now finds two sites where exploitation can take place: the hidden abode of production and the hidden abode of prediction.

For Ascher, Marx's insistence on workers' capturing of the means of production ought to be coupled with the equally urgent task of capturing the means of prediction and protection. They, too, need to be held in common in a society of "freely associated laborers," a fleeting vision Marx launches in *Capital*.[78] In the portfolio society, Ascher submits, financial commodities are social hedges that socialize future predictions and the protection needed for social existence into the future. Under the capitalist mode of prediction, these hedges obey the logic of the futures capitalists envision and summon for their own sake. A more humane and just society will not only need to "decide together on what is to be produced" but also need to determine "what possibilities are to be pursued, what dangers are to be avoided, what risks are worth taking."[79] This is a society where the means of prediction and protection are socialized, expropriated from the class of financiers who currently assume the role of predicting and protecting the social with their own interests in mind.

I have so far insisted that financialized capitalism has produced its own mode of future-talk and subjected us to it, all the while consuming the future possibilities of workers and indebted subjects. Financialization has engendered a temporal appropriation of our collective expectations and possibilities. The task of occupying the means of prediction is thus an act of defiance of this massive process of appropriation of the means of production and prediction. In a word, what is at stake is the takeover of the means to produce, reproduce, and socialize future possibilities.

The appropriation of the means of prediction is a struggle this book endeavors to embrace more directly in its theological section. I shall stress that theological imaginaries function precisely in this vein: as interventions in the realm of future-talk, a realm that financialization has managed to occupy. In the next section, I continue to theorize the exploitative dimension of finance and its hegemonic power over our understanding of time and the collective directions our world has taken under the senses conjured by financialized capitalism.

Scattered Times

In this chapter I have so far shown that Marx's theory of value excavates the "social hieroglyphic" of society to unearth the hidden texts, bodies, and economies that capitalist discourse effaces.[80] Ascher has expanded this analysis to account for our predicament under the portfolio society ruled by the financial corporation. Literary critic Gayatri Chakravorty Spivak offers a deconstructive reading of Marx's theory of value that continues to bridge from Marx's contribution to our understanding of financialized capitalism. Spivak argues that Marx detects the underside of financialization.[81] The study of value has been a theoretical obsession of Spivak's, whose intellectual prowess and eclecticism make her one of the most intriguing interpreters of Marx in our times.[82] With a deconstructive gesture, Spivak suggests that "Value" is the "lever" that can open up a different reading of Marx and of dominant theories of value, even the ones that survive within the Marxian corpus. Value is the "lever to turn to the text, to de-con-struct it for use . . . , the moment of transgression [and] bafflement" that allows us to approach Marx again, to approach him differently.[83] As we follow Spivak into the hidden abodes of Marx's text, we encounter again the exploitative temporality of the working day—now modulated by the futures of financial markets.

In "Scattered Speculations on the Question of Value," Spivak reads Marx's labor theory of value with the kind of critical attention and intimacy proper to "affirmative deconstruction."[84] For Spivak, Marx's analysis of value uncovers the "economic *text*," an opaque term she deploys with some veiled references to Derrida's work.[85] A possible working definition that should suffice for our analysis here is the following: "[Textuality] as a structural description indicates the work of differentiation . . . that opens up identity-as-adequation."[86] A text, in this reading, is that which triggers the work of differentiation. Différance, Spivak says elsewhere, is the "common-sense fact that to begin with anything is to differentiate it from everything that it is not and therefore there never can be a clean beginning."[87] This is the gateway for the "textuality" of the category of value.[88]

Value, as Spivak reads it in the Marxian corpus, functions in this textualized manner: its origins are irretrievable, it operates through differentiations, and its full meaning is forever deferred. Spivak catches a moment of instability in Marx's account of value, particularly as his theory evolved from his notes in the *Grundrisse*, written in the 1850s, and his more refined theorizations in the three volumes of *Capital*. In his itinerary Marx faced a dual aporia: first, that value cannot be said to be a "thing" or to enjoy a stable substance; and, second, that value has no traceable origin. In Spivak's reading of the Marxian theory of value, facing the instability of the labor theory of value offers an entryway into the temporality of financial capitalism.

First lesson: value is not a "thing." Spivak initiates her reading of Marx's theory of value with "intellectual-historical gossip."[89] Around 1857 Marx set out to investigate the "seemingly unified concept-phenomenon" of money, only to uncover in the process that it is *value*—not money—that forever sets capitalist economies in motion. Spivak maintains that value in Marx "escape[s] the onto-phenomenological question."[90] One cannot say or measure what value *is* but only trace its trajectories. Value is not a positive being but a "slight and contentless" thing that abstractly mediates concrete and particular things.[91]

As Marx began his studies on the category of money in the *Grundrisse*, he did not encounter a "thing" but rather a chain:

$$\text{Value} \;\rightarrow\; \text{Money} \;\rightarrow\; \text{Capital}$$

Marx then put to use his Hegelian inheritance to name the relations between these categories (the arrows in the schema).[92] First, the value of a commodity is *represented* in money, and, second, money is *transformed* into capital.[93] In a "continuist" reading of Marx, the category of labor is added at the beginning of the chain to "seal it off" by granting it a secure origin. Labor, in the following chart, is the stable origin of the chain of value:

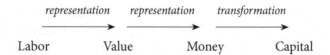

Spivak's crucial move is to perceive a brief slippage in Marx's text and offer a different interpretation of this schema. In Marx, value is not just a representation of labor, nor is money simply a representation of value. Value, for Spivak, is also a *differential*.[94] That is to say: the act of measuring the value of something relies on the negotiation of differences, not merely on the representation of an equality. For Spivak, each end of the chain and the connecting arrows between the elements "harbor discontinuities," rendering the beginnings and endings of the chain as always provisional and shifting.[95]

This comment exposes Spivak's reliance on Derrida's deconstructive gestures introduced in *Of Grammatology*. In her signature introduction to her translation of the book, Spivak is faced with a similar chain—the chain of signification. "In Derrida's reworking, the structure preface-text becomes open at both ends. The text [here we might interrupt to add: "value"] has no stable identity, no stable origin, no stable end. Each act of reading the 'text' is a preface to the next."[96] One may supplement the last sentence to suggest that in Spivak's reading of Marx, in each act of e-value-ation the chain of value slips into yet another chain. Reading Marx's theory of value through the deconstructive textual lens allows Spivak to question the continuity between representation and value to instead perceive how the pursuit of value always already encounters an excess of meaning—a surplus of value, as it were—that may derail any account of value.

And therein lies the second lesson of Spivak's speculations on value: the origins of the chain of value are irretrievable; only their traces remain. Writing, Derrida had noted, effaces its own origins. It "conceals and erases itself in its own production."[97] As Marx sought to weave his narrative of the origins of capital, his theorization must likewise conceal its point of departure. In fact, Marx had confessed in his preface to *Capital* that "beginnings are always difficult in all sciences."[98] For Spivak, Marx noticed—and, eventually, tried to suppress—that the difficulty with beginnings is tied to the fact that value represents *itself*.

Spivak takes us back to *Capital*, where Marx reflects on the double character of the commodity as having both use value and exchange value. I recall what I said before: use value refers to the particular (qualitative) utility of a commodity, whereas exchange value points to the (quantitative) capacity that commodities have of being exchanged for other products. Marx makes value surge from the interplay between these two categories, as indicated in the following passage, which Spivak highlights: "In the exchange-relation of commodities their exchange-value appeared to us as totally independent of their use-value. But if we abstract their use-value from the product of labor, we obtain their value. . . . The common element that represents itself (*sich darstellt*) in the exchange-relation of the exchange-value of the commodity, is thus value."[99] Value, in this passage, is the common element that "represents itself" in an exchange relation between commodities that possess use value. Spivak stresses that in this statement the relation of representation carries no fixed or fixable object, contrary to the continuist assertion that value points directly to labor. "Marx is writing . . . of a differential representing itself or being represented by an agency" that is ultimately indeterminate.[100]

For Spivak, what slips into this crucial passage in *Capital* is that value appears as a "differential and a representation."[101] Value is a *differential* because it is what remains after use value is subtracted from the commodity. It is a *representation* because "it cannot appear on its own, but only appears through its representation as exchange-value."[102] The absence of a referent in this passage confers on the Marxian theory of value a "subtle openendedness at the origin of the economic text."[103] The origins of the chain of value are themselves discontinuous, indeterminate.

Spivak's reading of Marx points to an irreducible problem in the concept of use value, something she claims readers of Marx tend to gloss over. She shows that the "continuist" reading of Marx takes use value for granted, assuming it simply exists a priori. But use value is at once inside and outside the "system of value-determination." It is outside because it is "outside the circuit of exchange" and cannot be properly measured. It is inside because the exchange value of a commodity still relies on its use value.[104] Spivak asks, "How many of Marx's readers remember that use-value appears only *after* the appearance of the exchange-relation?"[105] As hinted in the passage from *Capital* cited above, the buyer must perceive that any given commodity contains use value, but *this* value is realized only at the moment of exchange.[106] Marx's text is attentive to this nuance as it indicates that use value cannot be assessed outside the exchange relation. In the example I offered earlier, I can realize the use value of a soda (to address my thirst) only once the exchange has been consummated. But when that does happen, (use) value is lost. Spivak names the aporetic situation of use value: "Use makes 'value' vanish, yet without the moment of the consumption of the commodity as use-value the value would not be 'real'-lized."[107] That is: value appears when use value is subtracted.

As abstract as this may be, Spivak's Marxism is continuously teasing out the "materialist predication" of abstract "ideas."[108] She reminds readers that Marx makes the intriguing claim that capital consumes the use value of labor power. As stated, the use value of labor power is the ability to produce something in excess of its cost, namely, to produce surplus value even as it is itself consumed. What does capital appropriate when it extracts profit from labor power? Spivak analogizes: whereas capital appropriates the "mind" of capitalists to turn them into "monstrous selves" (Marx refers to them as vampires who consume the blood of others for their own survival), "[the] class of human beings whose *body* capital must appropriate is the working class."[109] In this contrast we see on display Spivak's account of the indeterminacy in the chain of value: even as capitalism shapes the mind of capital-subjects, it cannot help but slip into the hidden abode of the bodily existence of the labor force.

Spivak's speculations on value have their twists and turns but continuously return to the matter of time. And they do so with this constant stress on the materiality of time to which the Marxian theory of value gestures. "Time remains constitutive of value," she asserts. "Capital is a determination of value. Its body is made up of the workers' bodies in time."[110] In fact, from her observations on the indeterminations in the chain of value she extrapolates a narrative that pulls Marx's theory of value from its industrialist milieu right into the core of financialized capitalism.[111] It must be stressed that temporality is the fundamental link in this narrative. Spivak ponders whether or not Marx's labor theory of value becomes "obsolete" under circumstances where the circulation of capital has apparently been "sublated into the speed of Mind."[112] Has the financialization of capitalism released capitalist economy from its material burden and launched it into midair?

Spivak categorically denies this possibility. She addresses this issue by analogizing the simultaneous rise of the "word-processor" and the "wiring of Wall Street." She begins with the word processor. Consider the word processor and the temporal expediency it offers: "It is an extremely convenient and efficient tool for the production of writing. It certainly allows us to produce a much larger quantity of writing in a much shorter time and makes fiddling with [the text] much easier."[113] Still, the reduction of the writer's labor time is not altogether disconnected from other forms of labor. Spivak contends, "Even as circulation time attains the apparent instantaneity of thought . . . [the] attainment of apparent coincidence must be broken up by capital: its means of doing so is to keep the labor reserves in the comprador countries outside of this instantaneity."[114]

The time-saving opportunities that the word processor affords to the critic in the Western academy come at the expense of time-consuming obligations in other "hidden abodes." Spivak's attention to the theory of value in its materialist iteration trains and imbricates her "mind" in the international division of labor where workers—especially women—across the globe are kept in a state of "primitive labor legislation and environmental regulation."[115] Even as she instantly translates her most brilliant "thoughts" onto the screen of the word processor, other "texts" are produced.

It is no different with the acceleration of financial transactions through the wiring of Wall Street. Spivak's essay witnesses to some of the first signs of capitalist financialization as evidenced by the velocity of new forms of financial trading adopted by Wall Street banks. She reads a 1983 *New York Times* report describing the "revolutionary" impact of technology in financial markets. Thanks to the use of computers, this revolution would solve the "major dilemma" of financial markets: "the management of time."[116] The report Spivak reads illustrates how technology was transforming the temporality of financial corporations: "'What we are seeing now is time compression,' says Mark W. Harriman . . . , a veteran of 30 years on Wall Street." Peter Solomon, then chairman of Lehman Brothers, is quoted as saying, "Computers have shown us how to manage risk." The *Times* draws its conclusion: "Computers allow firms to ask the 'what-if' questions."[117]

Back in 1983, Spivak was not impressed by Wall Street's claims about its power to manage time and risk. She asks, What if we were to read the wiring of Wall Street alongside the lines of Marx's theory of value? Her analogy gains force here: technological developments in financial trading no doubt accelerate the circulation of money to the speed of consciousness, much as the word processor accelerates writing to the speed of thought. But can it produce value? Not quite: these technical innovations still fail to do the work of differentiation. "The computer, even as it pushes the frontiers of [temporality], proves unable to achieve *bricolage*, to produce a program that will use an item for a purpose for which it was not designed."[118] The operation of finance fails to produce the work of difference, that is, to trigger an indetermination that can free a different chain of values. The creative juxtaposition of difference—the work of the bricoleur—is a task that can be performed only by labor power.

Likewise, the acceleration of circulation in an electronically wired financial market cannot erase *fremde Arbeit*—the alienated, estranged, disjointed work of others. "This is why," Spivak concludes, "any critique of the labor theory of value, pointing at the unfeasibility of the theory under postindustrialism . . . ignores the dark presence of the Third World."[119] Even in financial times, the theory of value "does not allow the irreducible rift of the International division of labor to blur."[120] With this claim, Spivak's "textual" reading of the theory of value is exposed in full color.

The textuality of value, we recall, irreducibly introduces a differential as the chain of value unfolds. So, when the *Times* describes proud bankers announcing the power of computers to manage time and risk, Spivak destabilizes the narrative by pointing to that which the text puts under erasure. Marx's "inconvenient and outdated" theory of value discloses the mounting crisis that the "management" of risk tries to hide.[121] In the case of the quote from the chairman of Lehman Brothers ("computers have shown us how to manage risk"), it must be said that hindsight is bliss.[122] As the executive speaks so highly about managing risk, one cannot help but leap to the financial meltdown of 2008, a whirlwind that coalesced in the bankruptcy of Lehman

Brothers. It appears that something derailed those executives' capacity to evaluate the what-if questions.

By way of conclusion, Spivak exposes the contrast capitalist discourse elides: the financier who exudes pride in his ability to manage time and risk seemingly warps time itself to earn nearly $2 million for fifteen minutes' worth of work. On a different side of the chain of value, however, a Sri Lankan woman needs to work "2,287 minutes to buy a t-shirt."[123] Spivak cautions us: financialized capitalism portrays these two stories as disconnected, but the trick of the Marxian theory of value brings them together. What on the surface seems to be running unencumbered to produce profit at the speed of light eclipses the pace of a life of toil and oppression.

The Marxian theory of value speaks to the narratives written underneath the dominant stories of economic discourse. The "assessment" of future risks sought by financial techniques casts a large shadow over present economic exploitation. For our times, Marx's theory of value, properly modulated through the protocols of deconstruction, detects the debris of poverty engendered by globalized finance. Hidden underneath the spreadsheets accounting for profit is the labor of exploited workers. The moment that appears as profitable on one side echoes like a vanishing moment on the other.

How does the future, which does not yet exist, come to be such a valuable commodity? The drops of time are precious, the old Augustinian text reminds us, but their value seems to be beyond measure. The future is not—yet, he maintains. For an economic system so concerned about risk assessment and trend predictions, financialized capitalism is constantly treading the ambiguity of pursuing profit out of unknown futures. Financialization thinks itself capable of measuring the drops of time that drip from the future and turning them into profitable moments. It envisions the possibility of a technical, profit-driven capacity to address the what-if questions.

The story is dazzling, almost like the power of sight over future events.

Until it is not. The capitalist production of predictions does not escape the ruptures in the chain of evaluation. As Spivak argues in her deconstructive adaptation of Marx, the story buried underneath the capitalist hope of risk assessment is the story of crisis. The story line of financial profit continues to be punctuated by exploitation. Under the regime of financialized capitalism, exploitation takes shape under the guise of a consumption of future expectations and aspirations. From wage theft to the subject-shaping force of a student loan, from gender oppression under the new work dynamics to the higher probability of cancer relapse in impoverished children: we live and breathe in an economy that turns every single drop of time into profit. And so it is with the future, the time that is not—yet. Capitalist financialization has tried to cross the temporal threshold and occupy that which is to come.

Moments, in fact, are the elements of profit. Might there be a different moment from the ones expropriated by finance for the sake of profit? More than offering an answer, the next chapters try to present this question as a theological matter. Theology, as critical reflection on hope, has a stake to claim in a context where the future has become the territory for financial speculation. I lay bare here that a certain hope remains in me, precisely because hope can only be a matter of the future as that which is not—yet. The inexistence of the future, in this sense, presents financialization with an enduring challenge: something other than financial profit might come. The hedges one makes in financial games are haunted by the edges of that which does not exist—yet.

the time that is money

4

In the previous chapters, I maintained that the financialization of capitalism builds its hopes on a future that can be anticipated for the sake of profit. We have investigated the implications of that mode of futurity. The questions I pose now seek to probe the futures constructed by financialization from the critical perspective offered by liberation theologies. I suggest that the obsession with the future that I identified in financial discourse must be addressed theologically. In the following chapters, I muster the energies of theology as critical reflection on hope and summon an eschatology of liberation that may construe the future otherwise than the futures of financialization. The theological argument that I develop here insists that future-talk may summon different worlds into existence. Attentive to the underside of capitalism, liberation theologians have identified the possibility of different patterns for the social production of future-talk.

My goal in the next chapters is to retrieve and expand the radical legacy of liberation theologians who identified the Christian eschatological imagination as a site of resistance and as a theological locus for imagining different worlds and summoning them into being. Liberationists expose the idolatrous nature of capitalist future-talk, a process that entails uncovering the sacrifices that are made in the name of the future. As critical reflection on hope, the theological work that I perform in this chapter endeavors to reveal the unjust social relations that underlie the production of future-talk under capitalism.

In his "Advice to a Young Tradesman," Benjamin Franklin famously wrote, "Remember that time is money."[1] But what time is this that can become money? Not every time, Franklin observes. Those who spend their time "abroad" or in "idleness" miss out on the opportunity to increase their fortunes. Such time cannot become money.[2] Trivial as Franklin's advice has become, it reveals that for time to be money—for this sentence to make sense—one needs a particular way of constructing time. In the case of Franklin, the time that becomes money is future bound: "Remember that CREDIT is money."[3] The good tradesman is the one who pays by the time he promised to pay. We have seen how this promise makes its mark in the present in the form of debt. As the credit theory of money suggests, money is credit. In Franklin's economy, to be creditworthy requires alignment to the future-talk of capital. To say that time is money is more than advice to be ready to make money in every single minute. It is a request that accepts no breaks in time. No pause, no time to say "not—yet."

In the eyes of Max Weber, Franklin's advice beckons the spirit of modern capitalism. In the opening pages of the second essay of *The Protestant Ethic and the Spirit of Capitalism*, Weber ponders Franklin's pious pursuit of moneymaking even as his devotion to the Christian faith dwindled. Weber observes in Franklin's financial advice a call to duty, a true ethic that associates a person's worth with how much credit that person accumulates. "'Business savvy,'" Weber states, "is here not *alone* taught; rather, an *ethos* is expressed."[4] This ethical orientation in organizing life around the pursuit of money stems from a true sense of calling—a vocation to perform the duties of a business while avoiding the temptations of enjoying the fruits of one's labor too much.[5] This dynamic Weber famously called the *spirit* of capitalism.

For Weber, this spirit is the air we breathe. "[The] capitalist economic order of today is a vast cosmos into which a person is born. It simply exists, to each person, as a factually unalterable casing (*unabänderliches Gehäuse*) in which he or she must live."[6] In modern capitalism, subjects are born into the immovable house of capital, which Weber would also refer to as the *stahlhartes Gehäuse*—the iron cage, in Talcott Parsons's translation.[7] The spirit that breathes into these ironclad cases is normative. Deviant subjects—

the "factory owner who operates in the long term against these norms" or the "worker who cannot or will not adapt to the norms of the marketplace"—will be eliminated. Weber submits, "[Through] a process of economic *selection*, the capitalism that today dominates economic life socializes and creates the economic functionaries that it needs, both owners of businesses and workers."[8] For Weber, there is no escape from the spirit of capitalism.

Weber's analysis is insightful, but it is possible that he missed other spirits in Franklin's letter. For the American founder, the spirit of capitalism is somehow a spirit of time, a zeitgeist, that shapes an entrepreneurial subject. It is the spirit of punctuality, of mastering time, of being on time in the future. Franklin offers the following advice: "He that is known to pay punctually and exactly to the Time he promises, may at any Time . . . raise all the Money his Friends can spare."[9] Alongside the duty of money making, we find in the statement a call for the calculation of the money that can be made in the future. Franklin's vocation as a moneymaker propels his worldview toward the future, toward the becoming of a creditworthy subject. Might we then ask, What is this spirit invoked by the zeitgeist of capitalism?

In his rather cryptic commentary on *The Protestant Ethic*, Walter Benjamin questions the secularizing impetus that Weber identifies in capitalism. Benjamin instead suggests that capitalism responds to the same "worries, anguish, and disquiet formerly answered by so-called religion."[10] He frames capitalism as "essentially a religious phenomenon" and rejects Weber's hypothesis that capitalism is a "religiously conditioned construction."[11] The hallmark of the religiosity of capitalism is its emphasis on *guilt* (*Schuld*). In capitalist religion, we are always guilty, which in German is the same as saying that we are always in *debt* (*Schuld*). My observations in chapter 2 have made clear that this equation of guilt and debt plays a central role in financialized capitalism. Benjamin thus insightfully identifies the essence of capitalist religiosity as perversely future bound: hope longs for the "attainment of a world of despair."[12]

We notice Benjamin's choice of words: in capitalism what is hoped for is a world of despair, a world where no future can possibly come. The religion of capital poses images of the future only to offer a present that eliminates the possibility of the coming of something beyond its stranglehold. In Benjamin's messianic understanding of history, the stakes could not be higher because the future remains the condition of possibility for the coming of the messianic age: "Every second of time [is] the strait gate through which the Messiah might enter."[13] The promises of the spirit of capitalism therefore sacrifice what is to come, even in the name of the future. The religion of capitalism is bound to obliterate the future.

Benjamin's notes, sketched in 1921, remained unknown until the release of his unpublished writings in 1985. Critical theorist Michael Löwy was the first to compile a study of "Capitalism as Religion"; he described the essay as the beginning of a series of reflections that would culminate with Benjamin's *The Arcades Project*, where the topic of capitalism as religion is addressed through the lens of the critique of commodity fetishism and of the "mythical structure" of capital.[14] Löwy identifies Benjamin's fragment as a "creative misappropriation" of Weber's work. Whereas Weber dosed his attitude toward capitalism with "a mixture of 'value-free' science, pessimism and resignation," Benjamin approached the arguments of *The Protestant Ethic* in order to develop "a virulent anticapitalism, of socialist-romantic inspiration."[15] Löwy recalls that the expression "capitalism as religion" was first introduced by Ernst Bloch, yet another figure in the romantic anticapitalist tradition.[16]

The creative misappropriation of Weber's work approaches the capitalist spirit differently. Instead of perceiving it as a secularized form of the Protestant ethic, Benjamin sought to examine the theological disposition of capitalism. As Löwy suggests, what remains implied but not clearly stated in Benjamin's notes is that capitalism is *bad religion*. It is religion that launches us all into the deadening cycle of debt and guilt. Capitalism functions as a religion that entraps people and history in a spiral that consumes the possibility of a different future. One might say: the religion of capital sacrifices everything in the name of a future that never comes—a sentence that finds deep resonances in the work of liberation theologians.[17] Löwy in fact notices the parallels between Benjamin's fragment and the "radical criticism of capitalism as an idolatrous religion" advanced by liberation theology.[18] He comments, "Market theology, from [Thomas Robert] Malthus to the latest World-Bank document, is a ferociously sacrificial theology: it requires from the poor that they offer their lives at the altar of economic idols."[19] As we shall see, Benjamin's insight in "Capitalism as Religion" is deepened by liberation theologians who remained attentive to the numinous quality of capital.

The intuition about the disguised theological disposition of capitalism is echoed in the work of the economist and liberation theologian Franz Hinkelammert, whose lifelong project has been to develop a theological critique of capitalism. Drawing from liberation theology's signature suggestions about idolatry, Hinkelammert indicates that capitalist social structures are idolatrous to the extent that economic development occurs at the expense of the oppression—indeed the *sacrifice*—of the poor.[20] An idol, liberationists insisted, is a figure posing as divine who is much pleased with suffering. Its exaltation results in human and planetary exhaustion and death. The idol lives, but its life is stolen from the worshiper: "The thing it represents when [it] comes face to face with [us] has no heart in its breast. What seems to throb in there is [our] own heartbeat."[21] For Hinkelammert, Karl Marx's critique of capitalism attends to its religious allure and ought to inform the theological critique of the idolatrous imagination that lives under the guise of economic rationality.

I point out in this chapter that Hinkelammert's fundamental contribution to liberation theology is the identification of the correlation between capitalist discourse and future-talk. The sacrificial economy-theology of capitalism is shot through with a portrayal of the future that legitimates economic inequalities in the present. Hinkelammert identifies in capitalism a variation of the Christian eschatological vocabulary in which oppressive images of the future function to preserve the powers that be. But he likewise harnesses some of the spirits within the Christian eschatological imagination to plot a liberating mode of future-talk. Hinkelammert aligns liberation theology and the eschatological imagination within a critical utopian force field. Hegemonic forces, he notices, constantly deploy images of the future to justify injustice in the present. Liberating forces, in contrast, can project the future differently as a way of disrupting sacrificial economic forces and summoning something different into existence. This dialectical tension between unjust projections and the disruption that future-talk affords is paramount to Hinkelammert's theological critique of capitalism. I will demonstrate that the spirit of his critique is crucial for resisting the mode of future-talk produced by financialized capitalism.

This chapter introduces Hinkelammert's thought to suggest that capitalist economic discourse conjures an unjust mode of imagining the future. We have encountered these unjust futures in the previous chapters as we navigated the future-talk engendered by financialization. As my attention now moves to a theological response to financialized capitalism, I build on Hinkelammert's suggestion that the sacrificial logic that undergirds capitalism is enmeshed in its future-talk. Capitalist temporality projects future images—say, of a free-market society where a rising tide is expected to lift all boats—that validate present injustices as necessary "social costs" of the socioeconomic development toward the projected future.[22] Hinkelammert refers to it as a "sacrificial hope."[23] He posits that liberation theology must provide a critical account of this mode of future-talk.

My presentation in this chapter emphasizes Hinkelammert's connection to the emergence of neoliberalism under the dictatorial regime of Augusto Pinochet in Chile while also expanding Hinkelammert's critical work into the context of financialized capitalism. I follow his formulation of a "critique of utopian reason" that can evaluate social imaginaries about the future, critique their oppressive effects on the lives of the poor and marginalized, and ultimately engage in providing an account of a liberating hope that activates resistance to capitalism.[24]

Clouds over La Moneda

Let us unveil a scene that cannot easily escape our memories. It is a Tuesday morning, and its date has become the name of an epoch. September 11. As the morning dawned calm in the busy city, the occasional sounds of sirens blowing here and there suddenly gave way to more sinister news: planes had been attacking the city. Their pilots were apparently trained in foreign nations. The city, now hidden underneath a cloud of smoke, could scent the coming of a new age. Like burnt offerings, the sacrifice of lives would serve the dawn of a new era.

One must be confused by this memory, for the memory in fact has multiple senses. Here it points us to a September 11 normally covered over by the tragedy that befell New York City in 2001. The date I uncover, however, takes us to Santiago, Chile. There, in 1973, the presidential palace was attacked by a coalition of reactionary forces in the Chilean army with ties to the School of the Americas, a training center for the Cold War in the United States.[25] The air strike was directed toward the socialist president Salvador Allende, who remained locked in La Moneda, the presidential palace. After his election in 1970, Allende unfolded plans for agrarian reform, the nationalization of major sectors of the Chilean economy, and progressive social programs in education and labor empowerment. Allende gained support from a large coalition of grassroots movements and, naturally, the contempt of Chilean right-wing forces. In times of Cold War, his government was quickly regarded as a threat to Western capitalist powers. As these forces coalesced around La Moneda, a surrounded Allende addressed the nation for the last time and ended his life.[26]

But the ultimate sacrifice was yet to come. General Augusto Pinochet assumed control over Chile with a fierce hand, closing down political parties, persecuting his critics, and instituting widespread terror. This side of the story is widely known. But the first September 11 also unveiled for the world the first experiment in neoliberal governance. Under Pinochet's rule, Chile's economy was handed over to the "Chicago boys," a group of Chilean economists trained under Milton Friedman in the Chicago school of economics. With Pinochet's unwavering support, the apologists of economic liberalism took control of Chile's economy and started implementing policies of privatization, deregulation, and cuts in social spending.[27] Sociologist Raúl Sohr states, "Professor Friedman followed the progress of the model closely. In March 1975, he flew to Chile and was received almost like a head of state. He promised Pinochet an 'economic miracle' if they followed his advice."[28] Friedman recommended that the Chilean economy needed a "shock," and Pinochet wasted no time in heeding the advice: in 1975 he cut public spending by 27 percent, a trend that continued until it reached half its level during Allende's presidency. Wages would fall 8 percent between 1970 and 1989, and government investments in education, health care, and housing would shrink by 20 percent. Labor's share in the Chilean income similarly fell from 52.3 to 30.7 percent.[29]

In the ensuing years, the example set by Pinochet's Chile would become a global trend. "Not for the first time," David Harvey writes, "a brutal experiment carried out in the periphery became a model for the formulation of policies in the centre."[30] Margaret Thatcher's Britain and Ronald Reagan's United States would be more illustrious examples of the neoliberal model applied to nations at the center of the global economy. The Chilean origins of neoliberalism are nevertheless omitted from the grand narrative of its rise to global dominance. The more typical story is that neoliberalism emerged as a critique of the economic theory developed by John Maynard Keynes, whose "welfare state" is described as creating the conditions for the development of a "Leviathan" government, in addition to interfering with individual liberties and stifling the human spirit of entrepreneurship. In their rebuke to Keynes, neoliberal economists like Milton Friedman and Friedrich von Hayek emphasize the efficiency of market mechanisms to independently drive economic progress. Friedman states, "Government measures have hampered not helped [economic] development. We have been able to afford and surmount these measures only because of the extraordinary fecundity of the market. The invisible hand has been more potent for progress than the visible hand for retrogression."[31] With their emphasis on deregulation, privatization, and entrepreneurship, neoliberal policies quickly gained momentum in the ideological battleground of the Cold War. For Harvey, part of the "genius" of neoliberalism is its capacity to "provide a benevolent mask full of wonderful sounding words like freedom, liberty, choice, and rights," in order to elide the violence that propelled neoliberalism to the global stage.[32] Yet the first September 11 unveils the obscured genesis of neoliberalism: underneath its language of free markets and its pious appeals to liberty, neoliberal forces came to prominence in the guise of Pinochet's torture chambers.

As Latin American activists and scholars claim, one must pay attention to both events known as September 11. Yes, there are indissoluble differences between La Moneda and the Twin Towers, and the connection between the two events is arguably coincidental. But the coincidence nevertheless *speaks*, comments liberation theologian Franz Hinkelammert, a witness to the first September 11.[33] In Chile, he states, we see how the globalizing strategy of neoliberalism grows from state terrorism. More broadly, Hinkelammert perceives the neoliberal appeal to liberty as a vile irony. Their motto could very well be "The welfare state enslaves; the police state frees."[34] Hinkelammert thinks this inversion is part of the global design wrought by neoliberalism, one that typically affirms that which denies life. Throughout impoverished nations, neoliberalism endorsed the political power of governments only insofar as they submitted to police and military apparatuses that preserved the sovereignty of the market.

Hinkelammert watched closely the unfolding of neoliberalism in its first iteration under Pinochet's rule. He had moved to Santiago from his native Germany in 1963 after completing his doctoral work in political economy at the Free University in Berlin. His research there investigated the industrialization process in the Soviet Union and critiqued its appropriation of Marx's ideal of communism.[35] During his years in Berlin, Hinkelammert was exposed to the new developments in critical theory articulated by the Frankfurt school, from which he gained a pronounced interest in Marx, even if that meant going against the grain of Marxist orthodoxy. His interest in political economy put him at odds with both the industrial developmentalism of the Soviet model and the neoclassical model that most of his colleagues in Berlin appealed to in their fight against communism. At the epicenter of the Cold War, Hinkelammert's political position did not obey the protocols of the ideological conflict.

And neither did his theological imagination. Even though his intellectual formation was dedicated to critical theory and political economy, Hinkelammert also attended introductory classes in theology and Catholic social teaching, perhaps to honor his family's Catholic roots. It is said Hinkelammert's ties to Catholicism have a very Protestant origin: his ancestors were linked to an Anabaptist upheaval in the city of Münster between 1532 and 1535. Fearing retaliation, the peasants in the city called on Martin Luther for support, but the Lutheran princes united with Catholic forces to send in the army and crush the movement. Feeling betrayed by the Lutheran princes, the survivors of the massacre joined the Roman Catholic Church. Hinkelammert jokes that he is Catholic thanks to Luther.[36]

In large part owing to this ancestry, along with his interest in Soviet communism, Hinkelammert caught the attention of the Konrad Adenauer Institute in Santiago, a Catholic research institute in the social sciences. Hinkelammert recalls the irony of his appointment: "I had studied the Social Doctrine of the Church at the center of the Cold War so they imagined that I was the best candidate to fight Marxism in Chile."[37] Soon enough, Hinkelammert would frustrate these expectations.

In Chile, Hinkelammert found fertile ground to develop his thoughts on social and political theories. He was active in the conversations that would lead to the formation of dependency theory, and he joined Unidad Popular (Popular Unity), the political movement that led Allende to the presidency.[38] Between 1966 and 1968, Hinkelammert was first introduced to liberation theology in the context of his participation in ILADES, the Instituto Latinoamericano de Doctrina y Estudios Sociales (Latin American Institute for Doctrine and Social Studies), a Jesuit center. Through ILADES, for instance, Hinkelammert first met Gustavo Gutiérrez, who sought Hinkelammert's support for his initial writings on political economy.[39] Hinkelammert wrote with fondness about this period, "In these ten years [between 1963 and 1973] there was such creativity and a wonderful environment. . . . It was like this on every front, in literature, in thought: liberation theology, dependency theory, theater."[40] He recalls the widespread assumption that change was imminent, that society would swiftly move in a different direction: "It was called socialism, but it was not a copy of capital-S, institutionalized Socialism." It was rather an indigenous version, "socialism with *empanadas* and red wine."[41]

Hinkelammert's excitement was nevertheless matched by growing concern. Right-wing movements, he comments, cannot stand "uncontrolled creativity."[42] On that September 11, Pinochet's coup asserted complete control over what had been a creative social process in Chile. Hinkelammert recalls the shock of the aftermath: "We had no consciousness of what the coup would mean."[43] News of bodies appearing in rivers and missing friends being reported dead gave Hinkelammert a clearer perspective on the scale of the calamity Chile was facing. "Red wine was converted . . . into blood

94

and the *empanadas* into human flesh."[44] In Hinkelammert's words, the coup performed a true transubstantiation of these elements: "What Pinochet did was to turn the revolution of *empanadas* and red wine into a deadly eucharist."[45] The vicarious suffering of the persecuted, the tortured, and the executed would be the sacrifice necessary for a new economic dispensation over Chile.

Already in those early days, Hinkelammert perceived that Pinochet's coup was a watershed moment, and not only for Chilean history. For him, a true ideological shift was underway: "Traditionally in military coups in Latin America, the leader wants to be a military dictator, but there is no clear project for social transformation. In Chile, however, we went very quickly to a neoliberal project that was tied to a globalized strategy that sought to re-create society entirely."[46] Instead of the more usual passage toward "state capitalism," Pinochet's coup ushered in the ideology of a "total market." The Chicago boys did not simply analyze the Chilean economic scenario, Donald MacKenzie notes, but rather "sought to reconstruct it along the free-market, monetarist lines whose advantages they had been taught to appreciate."[47] Hinkelammert observes, "Everything that was not aligned with the market was dissolved. . . . [They] intervened in all unions and killed all [their] leaders . . . , the neighborhood associations, students, peasants, everyone. It was a targeted massacre."[48] In Sohr's words, there was a direct parallel between political persecution and the new economic agenda: "The regime of political repression allowed the economic agents to operate with complete laissez faire."[49] Pinochet's Chile exposes that neoliberalism's critique of government interventionism comes to a halt when state intervention is necessary to clear the way for economic expansion.

In the weeks after the coup, Hinkelammert's ties to Allende and to popular movements made his staying in Santiago unsafe. He sought refuge at the German embassy in Santiago, where he furiously gathered notes to report and reflect on what was happening on the ground.[50] The impression created by those days at the German embassy never left Hinkelammert's writing. While his work is fundamentally interdisciplinary and eclectic, the experience in Chile marked a definitive turn to theology in his thought. He is haunted by arguments that depict violence and state-sponsored terrorism as necessary means to obtain a certain type of society. Theologically, what is at stake for Hinkelammert is an implicit and widespread sacrificial theology that renders the death of some as the necessary path toward divine favor. As he excavated the reports from the Chilean context, Hinkelammert was appalled to encounter such a theological sensibility in the rising neoliberal agenda.

Hinkelammert's experience in Chile turned him into a theologian. It may well be said that Hinkelammert is a second-act theologian, a thinker who uncovered the presence of a certain mysterious force operating under the guise of the spirit of capitalism. Instead of addressing that spirit as a secularized embodiment of an ancient religious ethic, Hinkelammert framed neoliberal discourse as a great liturgy of idol worship. The need to reflect theologically on the nature of capitalist discourse arose as Hinkelammert discovered that socioeconomic analyses were insufficient to address the sacrificial discourse underlying the economic policies adopted under Pinochet. The mode of justifying and validating state-sponsored and market-creating violence demanded a thorough investigation of the theological underpinnings of capitalist discourse. The task was to uncover the idol disguised as the "free market."

In 1981 the neoliberal economist Hayek visited Chile to witness the "economic miracle" that had supposedly befallen the Chilean people under Pinochet. Hayek was impressed by what he saw and declared that Pinochet's dictatorial regime would soon lead to a safe transition toward a liberal society. Famous for his antigovernment views, Hayek compromised his neoliberal ideals to insist that "absolute power" should at times be used "to avoid and limit any absolute power in the future."[51] In the name of this future, Hayek embraced the military power of Pinochet's government. He stated ominously that in some circumstances "it may be necessary to sacrifice individual lives to preserve a larger number of lives."[52] In the context of Pinochet's Chile, this sacrificial language is hardly a metaphoric concession. It casts everything that happened after this September 11—the violence, the deaths, torture, and exiles—as necessary sacrifices that would lead Chilean society toward some supposedly brighter future goal. Hayek allowed his vision of a liberal society to sustain him even as the present contradicted his expectations for the future. Everything can be sacrificed in the name of the future.

Hinkelammert observed how the cuts in social spending and wages were tied to a rise in income among Chile's economic elites. "After the military coup in Chile," he wrote, "the public health system was systematically dismantled and salaries in real terms were reduced to half of what they had been, but the incomes of the upper 5 percent of the population doubled." Hinkelammert does not mince words: this money is the "blood of the poor."[53] For Hinkelammert, Hayek's slippage into sacrificial language embodies a model of reasoning according to which the death of some—particularly the death

96

of an innocent figure—is necessary to attain divine favor or, in Chile's case, an economic "miracle." Hinkelammert noticed Hayek's nod to the language of sacrifice as the symptom of the specific spirit of capitalism. For him, it was time to cast this spirit out.

Pinochet's coup and the ensuing market-driven ideology that he inaugurated in Chile must be thought of as a symptom of a deeply theological sensibility. Theologian Joerg Rieger, attentive to the insights generated by Hinkelammert's writings, forcefully argues that the promotion of "moral values" is insufficient to address the most ingrained ideas and unconscious pull of capitalist economics. One must go deeper to evaluate how capitalism indeed shapes our very perceptions of that which is ultimate.[54] It is a mistake, Hinkelammert warns, to approach capitalism as a dispirited attachment to money or avarice for material goods. We need to attend to the "infinity of capital" and the "mysticism of greed" that propels capitalism forever forward.[55]

In a word, what is necessary is a *theological* critique of capitalism. This intellectual project began with Hinkelammert's *The Ideological Weapons of Death*, a book that marked his return to Latin America in 1976.[56] With this text, I argue, Hinkelammert inaugurated a tradition within liberation theology that attends particularly to Marxist political economy and the theological dimensions of capitalism.[57] Attention to economic matters is always on the agenda of liberation theologians, but what distinguishes Hinkelammert's work is an unapologetic attention to political economy and Marx's work as a necessary step into observing and reading the "signs of the times." Moreover, Hinkelammert's training in the insights of the Frankfurt school allowed him to perceive the broad social and cultural implications of capitalist production, including in the shaping of theological dispositions and imaginaries. Hinkelammert especially investigated Marx's theory of commodity fetishism, a theme largely shunned by orthodox Marxism, and drew significant parallels between the Marxian concept and the theological category of idolatry.

For Hinkelammert, the theory of the fetish offered a way to unveil the real, fleshly sacrifices that take place and are effaced by capitalist discourse. He suggests that Christianity and Marxism share a similar hope for an emancipated society and that they are particularly united in their emphases on material life and on the concreteness of the production of that which is necessary for life to flourish.[58] The Marxian theory of fetishism focuses on the material forms of social organization that enable the production of the goods and services necessary for the maintenance of human life. Under capitalism, however, something veils the concrete social relations of production of these goods and services.

Hinkelammert points out that capitalist discourse has its own way of enchanting the world and that Marx's theory of commodity fetishism offers an analytical framework to account for the detrimental effects of this enchantment. "The theory of fetishism analyzes a form of coordination of the division of labor that tends to make invisible the effect of the division of labor over human life and death."[59] The forces that orient a society's production go unnoticed, and the social relations they produce seem "natural": "They appear to be the 'rules of the game,' taken for granted by everyone, whereas in reality they are the rules of a life-and-death struggle between human beings."[60] According to Hinkelammert, Marx found in the theory of fetishism a way to theorize this invisible reality by investigating its visible, tangible *effects*. Marx's arguments about the fetishism that "attaches itself to the products of labour" inaugurates a mode of analysis that inveighs against forces that present themselves elusively in the form of a thing by means of connecting the material good—the commodity—to the social relations amassed to produce it.[61] For Hinkelammert, these material forces, though initially invisible, have quite perceptible consequences. He reflects, "The analysis of fetishism inquires into the way that commodity relationships are seen and the way they are lived. . . . These are social relationships that bring about the coordination of the division of labor. Nevertheless they are experienced and seen as a social relationship between things and objects. . . . They arrogate to themselves the decision over life and death, and leave human beings subject to their whims."[62] As Hinkelammert sees it, Marx encountered in the concept of the fetish a tool to theorize the ways capitalist discourse eclipses the effects of an unjust social division of labor.

This model of analysis is theologically significant for Hinkelammert. He argues that Marx's attention to this invisible realm forced him to reconsider his critique of religious discourse. In his youth Marx had adopted the Feuerbachian thesis that religious images are a projection of the human imagination, a critique that starts with the content of religion and then draws a parallel with concrete reality. For the later Marx, however, the path is reversed: "Now he starts with real life in order to explain how the images of a religious world make their appearance."[63]

This approach offered Marx the chance to see religion not simply as a projection but also as a *reflection* of material reality. This allows for a critique of religious images that reflect unjust social relations, a religion that sacralizes "the power of some persons over others." This is a "religion that canonizes the right of some to decide over the life or death of others, and projects that kind of power onto the image of God."[64] For Hinkelammert, Marx's mature insights changed the course of the nineteenth-century critique of religion. From then on, the critique of religion is fundamentally concerned about beliefs and imaginaries whose constitution negates human life. It is a critique of images of God that deny and oppress humanity.[65] Hinkelammert concludes, "Marx is trying to defend human beings against the religious fetishization of their own works."[66] For Hinkelammert, the logic of Marx's thought makes him portray fetishization as an Antichrist figure that comes to subdue humanity.

Future-talk is paramount in Hinkelammert's theological critique of capitalism. He points out that Marx's theory of commodity fetishism leads to an account of the ways the future is socially imagined and the effects that such future-talk has on social relations. Hinkelammert observes, for instance, that Marx's concept of the "realm of freedom" operates in a certain eschatological register. At face value, the concept refers to a social arrangement in which commodity fetishism is abolished. For Marx, this would be a society without coerced labor and where human production of goods and services would be fully socialized and serve the interests of all. One notices, however, that Marx's projections about the realm of freedom stem from his perception of the injustices of capitalist societies. Commodity relations reveal an "absence that cries out," and struggles for social change assume their starting place in this absence.[67] This cry that Hinkelammert identifies in commodity relations is a cry for justice. The future imagined in terms of the realm of freedom is a "demand of that which commodity production—especially in its capitalist form—has suppressed."[68] In its place Hinkelammert sees in Marx a future projected as fulfillment as "concrete human beings," an accomplishment denied under capitalism.[69]

Hinkelammert concludes *The Ideological Weapons of Death* by weaving Marx's materialism with a theology of the body. "In Christian terms, the relationship between life and death is perceived in reference to the relationship between resurrection and crucifixion."[70] The materiality of productive forces that Marx highlighted finds its analogue in the Christian emphasis on the materiality of the resurrected body. "Resurrection here means coming back to be touched, coming back to eat and drink."[71] In this setting Hinkelammert reclaims the language of "anticipation" to suggest that the "liberation of the body is the anticipation of the new earth in the Spirit." He proceeds, "Life animates mortal bodies even while they remain mortal. . . . Even though the body remains mortal and will indeed die, this present life is already transformed into genuine life, beyond death."[72] For Hinkelammert, this eschatological orientation toward the resurrection of the body informs a new economic paradigm. "Food and clothing, bread and shelter: an economy exists to serve these ends, but hoarding does not. You are oriented toward life if you are seeking food and shelter; you are oriented toward death if you take your sense of direction from love for money."[73] The liberating potential of the Christian message operates within this eschatological canopy that functions in constant tension with the material reality of life.

This hope poses a constant threat to a world order that presents itself as inevitable and immutable. In his account of the rise of neoliberalism in Chile, Hinkelammert observes that the military junta and its sympathizers constantly attacked utopian thinking.[74] For him, it is inevitable that interpretations of Christian theology that dissipate the future orientation of the gospel function to preserve present political authorities and class power.[75] Hinkelammert, however, warns that anti-utopianism is not properly a rejection of utopian reasoning but rather a rejection of *particular* hopes, namely, those that challenge the status quo. In fact, anti-utopianism creates its own way of imagining the future: "[It] promises a future where the utopian is wiped out."[76] For those in power, policing future-talk is as critical as policing subversive activity.

The economic policies forced on the Chilean people during Pinochet's rule functioned in this way. Hinkelammert argues that the anti-interventionist policies espoused by neoliberal economists camouflaged the interests of the ruling class and that the necessary "sacrifices" that Hayek had in mind bespeak a hidden theological agenda. Hinkelammert's reading of Marxian theory allowed him to unveil the oppressive reality hiding in the neoliberal experiment in Chile and its projections for the future. Much as the capitalist commodity effaces unjust social relations of production, projections of a future that merely preserves the present social order eclipse unjust social relations. The social production of future-talk, as it were, serves the interests of the powerful when the imagination of a time to come suppresses current human needs and desires.

Capital Futures

100

The key insight of Hinkelammert's reading of Marx lies in his ability to address the theological dimensions of capitalist discourse. Specifically, Hinkelammert observes that capitalism construes images of the future that inform a particular attitude in the present. The capitalist entrepreneur is forever seeking to enhance their profit margins. This is an infinite pursuit that stumbles on the finitude of resources, market movements, technological development, and so on. As Hinkelammert sees it, capitalism "formulates goals that can never be reached," but this is never an impediment for capitalist development.[77] In fact, a certain form of spirituality is formed around this impossible pursuit: "Because the goal is an infinite value, religious reflection enables it to be sacralized and thus made into an object of devotion. Seeking money becomes a work of devotion *ad majorem Dei gloriam*, and therefore makes the human subject fit for this endless race toward the infinity that money itself points to."[78] The hope for an unending accumulation of capital and the image of the "invisible hand" are projections of a future world order that reproduces present social relations and, ultimately, preserves them. The neoliberal vision of a free market functioning without any friction with any other force apart from the market is itself an imaginary construct. Though the vision is impossible, it still makes sense. Capitalist discourse shapes imaginaries for the future in line with its unjust social relations.

Hinkelammert elaborates these insights in his most influential book, *Crítica de la razón utópica* (The Critique of Utopian Reason). Along the lines of a Kantian transcendental critique, Hinkelammert offers a critique of utopian reason that both dismantles the destructive force of hegemonic ideologies and tests the liberating potential of utopian reasoning. The book opens with the recognition that the social sciences of the nineteenth and twentieth centuries strongly resisted utopian thinking. Hinkelammert refers to this as the "utopian naivete" peculiar to the epoch: "Wherever we look, we find social theories that seek the empirical basis of the greatest human dreams to then discover a manner of realizing them."[79] Hinkelammert worries that the disavowal of utopian reasoning masks conservative forms of thought or, more precisely, antisocialist thought. The goal is "to destroy [socialist] utopias so that no other utopia may exist." This "utopian extremism in disguise" portrays anti-utopia as the true utopia.[80] Anti-utopian thinking for Hinkelammert is a trademark of conservative thought. In the reactionary vein, future-talk represents a menace to a present state of affairs that must be conserved at all costs.

For Hinkelammert, Karl Popper's thought exemplifies this position. Popper launches his epistemological theory presupposing that human action is circumscribed by the limitations of human knowledge.[81] This translates into Popper's assertion that any attempt at social "planning"—a catchword in antisocialist thought—is doomed to failure because human knowledge simply cannot anticipate human behavior in the future.[82] Knowledge of the future, Popper reiterated, is impossible. His epistemological rejection of future-talk is nevertheless interrupted when his economic theory enters the picture. Hinkelammert notices that Popper's articulation of the principle of market efficiency affirms that competition leads to market equilibrium while also acknowledging that competition is never present in its ideal form. Popper's expectation, however, is that perfect competition—an idealized, future-oriented projection—is normative for present economic relations.

Hinkelammert catches Popper's slippage: "The impossible character [of these projections] does not preclude them from being models or scientific theories. Reality can only approach them, but [Popper] still encounters in them a rational point of reference."[83] The sentiment is no different from the attitude adopted by neoliberal economists like Friedrich von Hayek: from the assumption that no knowledge of the future is possible comes the direct command to act in conformity with the protocols of the market. Popper was fond of saying that all who wish to "build heaven on earth" will ultimately bring about hell on earth.[84] Hinkelammert, in contrast, suggests that Popper's avowed realism hides a conservative agenda that portrays every struggle for justice as a hellish endeavor. This maneuver portrays "all values of human coexistence [*convivencia*], all humanism, all ethical universalism, as a monstrous threat . . . [and] a devilish temptation."[85] As Hinkelammert sees it, Popper arrived at a veiled utopian rationality based on a hope for technological progress and infinite technical development. In the expectation of infinite progress, the impossible that Popper sought to abolish from his social theory came to inform his work. More: it came to enforce his conservative politics and his trust in capitalist markets.

Allow me to reiterate: for Hinkelammert, Popper's rejection of utopian reasoning cannot be framed as a rejection of utopia but rather as a migration from a hope constructed through social interactions to a hope constituted by technical progress.[86] Hinkelammert generalizes this argument to suggest that contemporary societies oriented toward free-market capitalism similarly transfer all their hopes to market forces while rejecting as "utopian" all movements that contradict this dominant hope. Still, utopian thinking lingers in free-market ideology: "[Neoliberal thought] is a thought oriented towards the market, and the market is its central empirical concept."[87] This market is construed as fragile and in constant need of protection, particularly from government and public agents. The threat to the market is projected as "increasingly grave" until it reaches its zenith in the projection of a total market collapse. The portrayal of market fragility, on the other hand, ushers in the desire for a more "perfect" market, one where competition reaches its ideal form.[88]

The ideal of perfect competition is not empirical, Hinkelammert insists. And yet it functions as the basis of neoliberal thought. "When the neoliberal pronounces his utopias he poses as a realist."[89] In Hayek's writings, for example, the imagination of perfect competition offered a "necessary model to interpret the market economy" while also informing a societal concern to preserve the market.[90] Hayek started from an analysis of empirical markets to then construct an idealized vision of a market where competitive forces reach equilibrium. He concluded that while perfect competition is impossible, empirical markets will approach this idealized model.[91]

It is a leap of hope from a present of instability to a future of equilibrium. The projection of an ideal market relies on the hope that the pursuit of economic equilibrium will produce socially beneficial results. Joerg Rieger argues that the market in this view operates as an "engine of happiness and balance, guaranteed by a *deus ex machina* . . . : a god that functions automatically and can be trusted to arrive on the scene whenever help is needed."[92] Rieger suggests that what unites religion and economics under capitalism is the assurance that a "transcendent fix" is coming from above to save the economy and, hopefully, us too. It is the "market that will mysteriously bring happiness and prosperity—no matter how badly it may perform this function in the present." Similarly, it is the "divine entity that will eventually bring happiness and salvation—no matter how bad things might be at the moment."[93] Hinkelammert frames this future orientation of capitalist discourse as ideologically charged. Fundamentally, for him, the injustice of this mode of future-talk is that in trying to approximate this ideal, human lives are lost.

Hinkelammert returns to Hayek's interview during his visit to Chile in 1981: "A free society requires certain moral standards that ultimately boil down to the maintenance of lives: *not the maintenance of all lives because it would be necessary to sacrifice individual lives to preserve a larger number of lives.*"[94] Hinkelammert finds in this statement the embodiment of a sacrificial logic operating in the form of future-talk. Approaching the ideal of a *"total market becomes a great sacrifice of human lives."*[95] Hayek concedes that the "only moral rules are those that conduce to a 'calculus of lives': [and these are] property and contract."[96] These two axes of capitalist social relations guarantee "future progress." Hinkelammert sees Hayek's avowal of the calculation of human life on the basis of market principles as the segue to a veiled sacrificial theology: "The sacrifice of lives in the present for the sake of a completely phantasmagoric future is rampant in the ideology of the total market. Everything can be sacrificed in the name of this future that never comes. This is the cursed dialectics that destroys the present for mere imaginations. . . . Everything is promised, as long as one accepts today the contrary of what is promised. . . . Neoliberal thought accepts no present, but sacrifices each present moment for its respective tomorrow. Real-life conditions are lost in the name of a future delusion."[97] Market ideology harbors this idolatrous mode of future-talk: everything is promised, everything has a place in the future, as long as one is ready to sacrifice. The projected future will never come, but not because the future must be forever deferred. The future will not come because its delay is the time necessary for the preservation of the status quo.

In neoliberalism, future-talk is bound to this sacrificial logic. As I suggested earlier, a driving motif in Hinkelammert's work has been tracking how violence and oppression get framed as necessary acts of sacrificial love.[98] Hinkelammert traces this thirst for sacrifice back to some of the founding myths in the Western philosophical canon. In *Sacrificios humanos y sociedad occidental* (Human Sacrifices and Western Society), he probes the myth of Iphigenia as core to understanding the sacrificial logic implicit in Western culture. This particular myth thematizes human death as a necessary means to military conquest. In Aeschylus's tragedy, the first iteration of the myth in Greek tragedy, Iphigenia is depicted as a madwoman who protests against her killers. Later on, in Euripides's rendering of the story, Iphigenia appears as the perfect victim, someone who gladly accepts her fate as a necessary sacrifice so that the Greeks can obtain victory in battle against Troy.[99] The same rendering of the myth extends all the way to Johann Wolfgang von Goethe, as Hinkelammert shows. The myth of Iphigenia, through its life in the Western canon, portrays human sacrifice as effective and legitimate. Its appeal evinces a rationality that obscures violence by coding it as necessary sacrifice. Sacrificial logic offers a rationale for that which is unreasonable, unjustifiable, and unjust.

Hinkelammert holds that this mode of reasoning is indispensable for capitalist discourse. Under capitalism, the market dubs violations of human and ecological integrity as the "social costs" of economic progress.[100] In Adam Smith's theory of progress, for instance, Hinkelammert detects the remnants of a doctrine of divine providence according to which all of society will prosper as long as every individual pursues their own self-interest. Yet as people strive to save themselves alone, they mutually impede the possibility of salvation for each other.[101] This is as necessary as it is inevitable: the success of some is implied in the sacrifice of others. In Smith's vision of progress, to obtain salvation one must either bow down to the sacrificial logic or become the scapegoat that keeps the sacrificial system alive.

In the eschatology of liberation one can distill from Hinkelammert's work, future-talk must be resisted mightily when it nods to sacrificial language. No sacrifice. No more victims. That is not an argument but the *criterion* of any possible liberating mode of future-talk. Hinkelammert argues forcefully: theology must unveil every form of sacrificial theology by revealing its victims. That there exist no victims is what makes theology a theology of liberation.[102] For nothing that projects itself onto the future as worthy of sacrifice can be liberating.

Utopian Captivity

It is worth stressing the prescience of Hinkelammert's reflections on the future-conjuring impetus of capitalist discourse. This foresight is all the more intriguing given that his analysis of capitalism focuses primarily on industrial forms of production. As I indicated in previous chapters, recent debates in political economy associate the rise of neoliberalism with a shift in the balance of power from the industrial to the financial sector. This change of focus evinces even more the importance of future-talk in economic discourse insofar as finance is based on the economic analysis and prediction of future market movements.

In the context of financialized capitalism, Hinkelammert's theological production gains a new dimension and renewed importance. As he observed in 1973, Pinochet's coup in Chile was a watershed moment for the global economy as it triggered an experiment in neoliberal policies that would introduce a profound shift in economic discourse. Hinkelammert's insight was to perceive in this transition a transformation in the social production of future-talk. The rise of neoliberalism was accompanied by a new way of imagining the future, one that sought to monopolize the formation of human expectations and abolish all dissonant hopes. The ideology that "there is no alternative" not only projects the future as the inevitable outcome of present power relations but also functions to maintain these structures in place.

Hinkelammert terms our predicament under neoliberal capitalism as the "captivity of utopia." In the expectations conjured by capitalist discourse, he sees the "inversions of utopias of liberation" and the construal of an "infinite future promised as the outcome of an infinite submission to the powers of the system."[103] The dream of a just society has been "sequestered" by market forces and is used as a weapon against the world's peoples.

THE TIME THAT IS MONEY

Future-talk under the neoliberal regime assumes an uncritical position, promising "the construction of a new world while celebrating present conditions."[104] This is the society to which there is no alternative—a society, in Hinkelammert's terms, where utopian thinking is set up to "create a world whose conservation is worthwhile."[105] Hinkelammert offers us a critical impetus to probe the realities that hide behind the human imagination of what is to come.

Alongside Marx, Hinkelammert observes that religious projection functions ambivalently: if, on the one hand, religion can sacralize the "power of some persons over others," it also functions as a "protest against this situation."[106] And so it is with future-talk. The imagination of a time to come stands in direct relation to the ways in which human communities experience the present. In the spirit of liberation theology, Hinkelammert points out that the dreams and expectations of those who suffer in the present—the poor, the excluded, and the outcasts of society—imagine the future differently. "I speak of hope from the perspective of the excluded, a hope that springs from the problems of life," says Hinkelammert.[107] The time that capitalist production suppresses for multitudes fuels these dreams and conjures alternative visions for the future.[108]

Liberation theology, which Hinkelammert defines as a *theology of life*, is the "affirmation of human hope in all its forms, of utopia as the Christian *anima naturaliter*."[109] In Hinkelammert's work Christian hope is enmeshed in reality even as it launches itself into imaginary utopian narratives. "There is not only a utopian image of the new world but also an anticipation of the new earth present in human activity."[110] The stuff that comprises these visions of utopia is the material assembled in the present in all its tragedy and oppression. The Christian vision for the future for Hinkelammert is grounded in the bodily, material realities of life: "The theology of liberation is a theology of the liberated body by the satisfaction of needs and the enjoyment of pleasures. . . . When human beings experience liberation in their real, material life, they can establish contact with God."[111]

Returning to Marx's theory of fetishism, Hinkelammert encounters in it a method to distinguish between a "fetishized transcendence" and a "humanized" one. He acknowledges, "The main contrast and contradiction here is that between values and the reproduction of real material life. In the fetishist view, values are raised up as elements standing over real life. They live because they make human beings die."[112] The future as imagined in capitalist discourse projects and validates an image that camouflages unjust social relations in the present. Real life is stifled by the future. In contrast, the Marxian model of transcendence exists "within real material life." Marx's appeal to transcendence does not simply project itself onto the future but fundamentally "anticipates" worldly transformation. This is a "transcendence that emerges from the transformation of this world into another kind of world [es la transcendentalidad de este mundo transformado en otro]."[113] According to Hinkelammert, one can imagine the future otherwise. It is a future horizon made possible as we struggle to create possibilities out of historical engagement. The meaning of liberative action is not accomplished in its fulfillment but is lived out in the struggle itself.[114]

Future-talk in this register speaks from the whirlwind of transformative activity. In light of the calamity created by economic oppression, this eschatology of liberation forgoes any promise of future victory. Hinkelammert remains utterly pessimistic with regard to the prospects of a civilized progression toward social justice. The calculus of potential outcomes for a world so steeped in tragedy and oppression simply cannot offer a bright vision for the future. But Hinkelammert will not succumb to despair. On the other edge of his appeal to future-talk we notice an eschatological imagination that pushes the boundaries—the edges—of what is historically possible. Under the rules of the status quo, it is fair to say that there is no alternative to neoliberalism. This is so "because there are powers capable of and intent on destroying [any emerging alternative]."[115] But the liberating role of the eschatological imagination is precisely to sidestep the realism of the status quo and offer a different set of expectations.

Hinkelammert turns his theological work toward the impossible that the Christian eschatological imagination entertains. The hope that springs from his writings is a "transcendental concept" that orients history. It gives sense to history, as it were. I insist that this is not a way of granting "meaning" or resolutions to historical tragedy but rather a way of producing meaning and directions—*sentido, sens*—out of a calamitous situation. It is fundamentally a matter of creating paths where alternatives have been shut down by hegemonic forces. With Hinkelammert we are after an "eschatological limit" that connects the perception of what "is" to the realization of what is not—yet. For him, the construction of social reality and worldly transformation requires an imaginative leap into the possibilities of what reality *can* become. The imagination of the impossible is part of the constitution of reality, he says.[116] What is normally referred to as utopia is an elastic and imaginative dimension of human rationality—a way of stretching reason to envision present limitations and future possibilities.[117] Capitalism appropriates this faculty of human reasoning to elide its injustices, but Hinkelammert wants to bend his imagination toward justice by engaging a place that has no room in our world. Liberating activity unveils for us a reality that is otherwise impossible within the confines of the present.

Eschatology casts a long and *critical* shadow over Hinkelammert's corpus. It is the name under which he critiques capitalist discourse and its sacrificial logic. His work derails the projections of capitalist discourse by exposing the violence and injustice on which its projections for the future are built. We recall that Franklin advised the good tradesman to always fulfill his promises. Such promises, however, trap people in an iron cage of guilt and debt. Capitalist temporality admits no pauses, for every single minute brings the possibility of profit making. Likewise, it accepts no difference in the social production of future-talk. The credit relation that Franklin thinks of as foundational to a successful business renders the future as the repetition of present social relations between creditors and debtors. Hinkelammert unearths the deceitful nature of these promises, suggesting that in the promises offered by capitalism we encounter the invisible hand of class power. His theological critique of capitalism is an exercise in discerning the spirits that come when one speaks of the future. And to the spirit of capitalism he invites us to say no.

But Hinkelammert is equally attentive to the future-talk that capitalist discourse cannot police. The Christian eschatological imagination for him can function as the lever that turns the hidden scripts of capitalist temporality on their head. Not every time is money. Not every future promise binds us to the burden of debt. In the language of his recent work on spirituality and liberation, what is indispensable for liberation is also useless under the evaluation system of capital. What is indispensable is "coexistence [*convivencia*], peace, and care for nature."[118] Indispensable and useless. Useless because these are gifts that do not subscribe to the logic of profit making, according to which time is money. Indispensable because these are the subversive gifts that do not get used up.

Hinkelammert's theology takes us to the outer limits of history to probe that which cannot possibly exist—yet. This in-between time, the pause on which I have been focusing my attention in this book, is the location of an eschatology of liberation. The future is beyond us as a "present absence" that pleads for a different world from the crevices of this world.[119] We cannot let our theological imagination forgo these present absences and these brief moments when we gather our breath to say "not—yet." The eschatology of liberation finds its breathing room in this pause. The spirit of the pause indeed haunts the spirit of capitalism with its sacrificial inability to take a break. Savoring the pause, staying within its liminal temporality, might offer us the imaginative and political strength to resist the stifling presence of capitalist hegemony.

sighs of the times

5

Religion is the sigh of the oppressed creature, the sentiment of a heartless world, and the soul of soulless conditions.
—KARL MARX, "A Contribution to the Critique of Hegel's Philosophy of Right: Introduction"

What would we be without the help of things that don't exist?
—PAUL VALÉRY, quoted in Rubem Alves, *Transparencies of Eternity*

I release a deep sigh as we move into this chapter. Religion is the sigh of the oppressed creature, writes Karl Marx. "Can there be a more beautiful definition?" asks a liberation theologian in response.[1] In these sighs of oppressed creatures, liberation theology has encountered its breathing room within Marxism. And together these traditions of the oppressed have conspired—indeed breathed together—so that at every single sigh of the oppressed creature, a different future is announced. Both Marx and his liberationist readers found in the sighs of the oppressed not only the cry of a wounded world but also the sign of a different time, "a certain experience of the emancipatory promise."[2] I suggest in this chapter that liberation theologians embraced the call to read the "signs of the times" by attending to the sighs of the oppressed creature. The liberationist critique of capitalism is attuned to the different senses that future-talk makes when it emerges from painful realities. In Rubem Alves's theological work, the stifling presence of oppression is met with the creative and subversive force of sighs that stem from the depths of bodies in pain. As we register these sighs, they signal different times, breathing into us new senses. For liberation theology, they conjure different futures.

Marx, too, sought to read the signs of the times. *Capital*'s first preface speaks of a growing anxiety that haunted the ruling classes: a transformation in social relations was imminent. "These are the signs of the times," Marx says, himself forever haunted by theological memories.[3] These signs "do not signify that tomorrow a miracle will occur," but they do signal that something is coming: "[They] show that, within the ruling classes themselves, the foreboding is emerging that the present is no solid crystal, but an organism capable of change, and constantly engaged in a process of change."[4] For Marx, the sense of change, the possibility of an alternative, the very coming of the future—these forebodings hit the ruling classes with the scare of a twist in their timelines.

For liberationists, the transforming movements of this social organism give flesh and history to Christian hope. In liberation theology the sighs of the oppressed creature encode the signs of the times. Liberationists sought to excavate images and hopes for the future in these sighs of oppression—in fact, from the very guts of the oppressed, as we shall see—in order to produce new modes of future-talk. In this liberating eschatology, theology goes to its own edges to encounter the margins of the social body. Precisely here we merge and repurpose Gustavo Gutiérrez's two definitions of theological labor that I announced in the introduction to the book. The critical reflection on praxis, which defined the early epoch of liberation theology, is modulated as a hermeneutics of hope—Gutiérrez's later definition—to conspire a theology performed as critical reflection on hope.[5] The approach, as I plan to unveil it in this chapter, maintains the critical impetus that Gutiérrez and the first generation of liberation theologians breathed into Christian theology. But it also embraces an imaginative and poietic expansiveness in order to explore different modes of theological writing that construe future-talk as a critique of the status quo.

Not coincidentally, the crafting of Gutiérrez's later definition of theology came in the context of his induction to the Peruvian Academy of Literature. He positions theology as a word about a mystery before which we cannot *not* say a word. Gutiérrez gestures favorably toward novelist José María Arguedas's tantalizing suggestion: "We know so much less than the great hope we feel."[6] Gutiérrez opts to remain with hope's "disquieting assurance" against the "tranquility of an innocuous knowing."[7] I suggest that the contrast between disquieting assurance and innocuous knowing can be refigured as the contrast between, on the one hand, a stubbornness to remain in the struggle for the future and, on the other, the hegemonic sense of futurity engendered by financial discourse. The innocuous knowledge that Gutiérrez resists is tantamount to the calculating, profit-seeking mode of futurity endorsed and socialized by financialized capitalism. Likewise, Gutiérrez's casting of theological work as a creative act of interpreting the hopes we live by is for me an invitation into a modality of future-talk ignited in the confrontation with calamity. The *critical* reflection on hope that I embrace is critical in its inability to conform to the present and in its passion for absences that must be summoned for this present to be truly just.

In this chapter I deepen my attention to the possibilities of an eschatology of liberation by construing hope as an affective, creative, and imaginative force that can support the takeover of the means of production of future-talk. This theme, introduced earlier in chapter 3, is presented here as an important step taken by liberation theology, prefigured in and unveiled by the work of liberation theologian and poet Rubem Alves. His attention to the theological category of hope, I argue, does not distract but rather teaches him to pay attention to the pain and suffering in the world. Building on Alves's work, the critical reflection on hope that I stage harbors a passion for that which does not exist—yet. It is a summons that prepares the way for what may come.

This chapter engages the work of Alves, an author whose scholarship cannot be framed in any particular disciplinary regime. Walking freely among fields as diverse as philosophy, poetry, psychoanalysis, education, and children's literature, Alves remained enamored by the political and poetic force of things that do not exist. In some of his texts and at certain periods of his life, Alves thought it necessary to disavow God-talk altogether and separate himself from fellow liberationists. More often than not, he failed. Words about ultimate mysteries, the sacrament of communion, the imagination of bodies resurrecting—all of these motifs were as close to Alves's thought as his own body. In fact, he states, he embodies these words and their enchanted *sentidos* (senses).[8] Throughout his life he continued to code his theological sensibilities in myriad genres of writing, disciplinary fields, and epistemological registers. His writings offer an embodied mode of future-talk, typical of liberationist discourse, alongside a poetic impulse that expands the outer limits of Christian theology. As I shall argue, this, too, was a liberationist maneuver.

Though often neglected in some accounts of the history of liberation theologies, Alves figures at its inception, already suggesting that the work of

112

liberation goes through the reconfiguration of our concepts of the future. Alves also signaled different trajectories for liberation theologies, and I intend to trace some of these steps. In the literature surrounding Alves's work, it is common to contrast his concern for beauty and theopoetics, found more often in his later writings, with his earlier commitment to liberation. One form this argument takes is to indicate that Alves did not employ Marxist analysis, contrary to his liberationist companions. At some point, he concurs with this narrative, pointing out that his assessment of reality relies on psychoanalytic theories and poetry, not on historical materialism.[9] Yet a more nuanced perspective might be warranted. As I intend to show in this chapter, Alves could be said to be tapping into a spirit of Marx's thought throughout his writing, especially when he considers the roots of the religious imagination in the dreams and struggles of those who have been oppressed. The sighs of a pained body turn into signs pointing to different worlds. For Alves, Marx's work provides more than an analytical framework for the critique of oppressive social relations. He once wrote, "It seems to me that the simplest explanation for the historical force of Marxism is not in its analytical rigor but in its power to catalyze and express the desires of those who suffer under alienating conditions and therefore dream of their abolition."[10] While Alves cautions against embracing a strict socioeconomic analysis, he remains loyal to Marx's power of catalyzing the desires of the oppressed.

For Alves, liberation requires and *is* a dream one can have only when one is attentive to the sighs of the oppressed creature. This gesture is one that I embrace. The category of hope remains with me in my critical account of financialization as I perceive the lingering cries for a future as they continue to emerge even in this future-consuming economy. I propose that Alves appropriated the vocabulary of Christian eschatology as a visceral reality that echoes the sighs of the oppressed creatures and defies the roots of human suffering. Alves paid close attention to the groans and moans of oppressed bodies to craft a poetics of the edge, an eschatology that liberates precisely by imagining a world upside down and summoning it from the depths of its yet-inexistent state.

The sighs of the oppressed, the anguish of indebted subjects, the strife of precarious workers—these are not the signs of an incoming miracle, as Marx warned. But they are the foreboding that the present harbors discontinuities, that alternatives to capitalist futurity exist and are emerging. Training our imagination to perceive these sighs of oppression taken for signs of the times is the work of liberation theology.

Gut Theology

Theologian Harvey Cox introduced Rubem Alves's seminal book, *A Theology of Human Hope*, by arguing—and warning—that the work was breaking new ground: "Beware, all ideologists, theologians, and theorists of the affluent, so-called 'developed' world! The 'Third World' of enforced poverty, hunger, powerlessness, and growing rage has found a ringing theological voice."[11] Despite Cox's excitement, the editorial police found it necessary to translate this "Third World" voice of Alves's into language palatable to the dominant tongue of theology. Under the motif of a "theology of human hope" hides a more telling title: "Towards a Theology of Liberation," the title of Alves's doctoral dissertation.[12] Alves's editor read his manuscript with the lenses of Jürgen Moltmann's *Theology of Hope* and missed his most poignant comment: that hope is constituted by human liberation. Alves would later write, "Not only did I want to have hope, I wanted to perceive the signs of its possible realization in the lives of individuals and peoples. . . . Hope had to be expressed as politics."[13] At this moment of inception, Alves entwined the political pursuit of liberation with the eschatological imagination of the coming of a new world.

The demand for concrete signs of hope is itself a sign of the times Alves lived through as he labored toward a theology of liberation. In the early 1960s, he joined Union Theological Seminary in New York City for his master's degree and found there a welcoming place to vent some of the concerns he brought with him from his native Brazil. His thesis, "A Theological Interpretation of the Meaning of the Revolution in Brazil," gives voice to a conversation that had been underway among Brazilian Protestant theologians since the 1950s.[14] These were revolutionary times, and Alves sought to produce revolutionary theology. But on a rare day of rest after the completion of his program, Alves took a stroll in the city. On the subway a man unfolded the newspaper, and the headline read: "Revolution in Brazil." This was not the revolution Alves had in mind. The date was April 1, 1964, the infamous day of the Brazilian military coup. "My thoughts were maddening, in the solitude of the room, spinning around itself, tied, impotent. . . . Fear and rage became diarrhea, my eyes glazed through the night. Nausea. Claustrophobia."[15] That night, Alves's guts spoke.

A month later, Alves returned to Brazil only to discover that some of his colleagues in the Presbyterian Church had denounced him to the military authorities. He reminisces of the night when he had to run to his library and get rid of some of his books: "I remember that one of them was *Communism and the Theologians* by Charles West—a profoundly innocent thing. But the cover was red and contained the hammer and the sickle."[16] In the following months, Alves surrendered his ministerial credentials to the church: "I have always understood the Gospel is a call to freedom," he wrote to his ecclesial leaders. "I no longer find this freedom in the [Presbyterian Church]. It is time, therefore, to find the communion of the Spirit outside of it."[17] In March 1965 Alves fled the country and landed at Princeton Theological Seminary for his doctoral studies. Though safe, he remained restless, seeking words to name his visceral fears and hopes. The signs of *these* times speak loudly in Alves's theology.

Alves insists on the intrahistorical dimension of hope and of theological language as a whole. This is not to say that hope speaks only to the present "now" but rather that our imagination of the future must be grounded in history and in constant relation to our material realities. Alves thinks of this in terms of a historical transcendence and the human proclivity to exist "between times."[18] That is: in times of exploitation and suffering, new futures can be projected as alternative temporalities that function to question our present reality. Historical transcendence, as Alves portrays it, is directed toward the future, but it is neither external to nor "above history."[19] This hope is both born out of history and committed to history. Its "ethical exigency, its categorical imperative for the transformation of the world . . . [comes from] its participation in the sufferings of the human community."[20] Future-talk *makes* history, precisely because it rejects what "is" in order to construct something new.[21]

Alves encountered support for his project in Marx's identification of religious sentiment with human suffering. Religion, we recall, is the sigh of the oppressed creature. Alves refers to the rise of a "proletarian consciousness" that gathers people across the world around a common exploitation—from the peoples of the Third World to Black Americans and students. This oppressive reality takes shape in history as the proletarian consciousness finds itself "being dominated by a power which does not allow it to create its own history."[22] The world's proletariat is denied both power and hope: the freedom to envision a future and act on this vision.[23] And yet something different emerges: "Although the future still remains closed, [human] consciousness is open to the future. [Man] inserts himself into his historical present as a contradiction to it, as a negation which presses toward a new tomorrow."[24]

For Alves, hope is the outcome of a historical consciousness that recognizes the injustices that plague our times: "The present is negated because

man ... apprehends what creates pain, suffering, injustice, and defuturization in history. Because the present is historically painful and therefore dehu-
manizing, it must be negated. ... [H]ope is not derived from an ahistorical
idea of the perfect society; it is rather simply the positive shape which the
negation of the negative and inhuman of the present takes."[25] Alves's nod
to Marxist language signals his perception of the entanglement of the sighs
of the oppressed creature and the signs of the times. In Marx's *Capital*,
the "negation of the negation" is portrayed as a process in which those
whose means of production have been usurped by capital rise as a "mass
of people" to bring about revolution.[26] It is a true twist in the oppressive plot
of capitalist hegemony: the forces capitalism suppresses gather together to
reverse the course of oppressive social relations. In Alves's work the negative forces of "defuturization" are negated to open up new horizons for the
future. In the social unsaying of suffering, the negation of the negation, we
may hope that something liberating is to come.

Alves contrasts liberating hope with three philosophical and theological projects: existentialism, Karl Barth's transcendental theology, and Moltmann's theology of hope. First, Alves commends the existentialist concern
for human freedom and human transformative potential in history, while
also indicating that the subjectivist bent in existentialism hinders the
possibility of conceiving of transcendence as causing real change in the
"structures of time and creating thereby a new time."[27] Alves fears that
existentialism creates a split between time and eternity and thus reduces
hope "to a dimension of subjectivity, without any import for the transformation of the world."[28] He identifies a similar polarization between time and
eternity in Barth's theology, particularly in his insistence on the separation
between God and the world. So, despite Barth's "radically critical ... 'theology
of crisis,'" his "docetic" portrayal of transcendence renders human action in
history futile.[29]

Many of these concerns about the historical dimension of hope are addressed by Moltmann's theology of hope and its significant attention to
the political undertones of Christian theology. Alves finds Moltmann's
work "remarkably close" to his own project. The dialogue that he stages
in *A Theology of Human Hope* would in fact anticipate and prefigure the
fertile, sometimes tense, conversation between Latin American liberation
theologians and Moltmann.[30] This conversation begins with the recognition that biblical narratives speak of a God whose presence in history interrupts existing reality to unveil a promise for the future. God's name, in
Moltmann's wording, "is a wayfaring name, a name of promise that discloses

a new future, a name whose truth is experienced in history inasmuch as his promise discloses its future possibilities."[31] Moltmann's formulation ought to be contrasted to the oppressive force of promissory notes that I exposed in chapter 2. Whereas the debt economy binds debtors to the promise of repayment and to the repetitive cycle of submission to creditors, Moltmann's theological understanding of the promise speaks of a promise that creates crevices in reality and unveils liberating possibilities for the future.

Alves is quick to indicate the political potential of Moltmann's eschatology in resisting any historical system that affirms itself as the "end of history."[32] By placing God as the God of the future, Moltmann leaves room for political action in history to have theological significance.[33] Still, Moltmann's use of the term *promise* suggests an extrahistorical reality. "It is from the promise," he writes, "that there arises that element of unrest which allows of no coming to terms with the present that is unfulfilled."[34] Alves counters this to propose that the "element of unrest" that triggers human hope comes not from an external promise but rather from the suffering experienced in the present. In Moltmann the "promised future gives birth to the crisis of the present," whereas Alves contends that the crisis of the present conjures hope for the future.[35] The inadequacy of the present is bodily felt, not superimposed from an external promise. Alves firmly argues that the human consciousness of the future is born out of the *inadequatio* of the inhumanity of the reality of suffering. Confronting the inadequacy of the present initiates the work of surpassing the negations of the present moment.[36]

The priority of suffering as the triggering moment of hope distinguishes Alves's visions of the future from Moltmann's. In Alves's work human suffering and the identification of the roots of suffering make creativity possible, desirable, and historically necessary. Alves thinks of this creative act in temporal terms: "Through an act whereby subjectivity invades the world of space and time, man is able to create a break in history, to produce a qualitative change in time, which is, indeed, the event of the birth of the new."[37] For Alves, the shape that hope assumes is a sublimation of the pain we embody.

Alves's theological reflections about time form a looping spiral in which present and future are coconstituted and forever turning together, informing one another, challenging each other. On the one hand, future-talk *reflects* present reality and current relations of power that engender human suffering. On the other hand, human suffering *projects* a future reality that contradicts the present and resists conservative claims for an "eternal now." With this Alves avoids a vision of hope that denies history for the sake of the future while also rejecting romantic visions of humans' capacity to create the future on their own. He submits, "[Never] hope without history; never history without hope." His future-talk "remains realistic without despair and hopeful without being romantic."[38] With a single stroke, Alves here rejects both the futurism of a hope undeterred by the present and the anti-utopian realism that presumes to concern itself only with the present.[39]

Alves is therefore aware of the ambivalence harbored by imaginaries of the future. He states that not *all* projections of future time, much less of Christian eschatology, are liberating. Much like Franz Hinkelammert's call for a critique of utopian reason, Alves understands that future-talk can become yet another tool to manipulate history and suppress alternative visions for the future. The images and hopes constructed from the centers of power are projections of the status quo that aim at its preservation. "What about the hopes of kings and lords?" he asks. For the rich and the powerful, he observes, wealth and power are not sufficient; they also need to validate their power and privilege with a religion of their own—a religion that projects their wealth and power as divine gifts.[40] Alves puts it in poetic form:

> The idols announce their program
> To preserve the past in the future.
> To impede the advent of the future.[41]

Similar to Hinkelammert's claims about anti-utopian rhetoric, Alves suggests that the control of our future imaginaries is a central axis of systems of oppression. The "futurology" of these systems projects onto the future the current dominant conditions of power while also eliminating all "dysfunctional elements" that deviate from its timeline. This implies "a conquest of [the] imagination" that makes people love a future imposed on them by others.[42] In the first part of this book, I have suggested that financialization has been this dominating presence that stifles our very capacity to imagine a future outside the parameters established by the futurology of financialized capitalism.

Alves specifies the role performed by hegemonic economic discourses in the conquest of our longings for the future. Our destination as well as our love for the future is dictated by a "system of production that fills all its horizons with ready-made products, and the only initiative left is to choose and to buy."[43] But the transience of these products and of the multiplicity of our choices simply effaces the *permanence of the economic system.* Alves concludes, "Time will be determined by the rhythm of the 'healthy economy.' . . . The logic of the economy plans its endless expansion, and while it does, imagination is [funneled] into proper channels so that men will behave in a functional way."[44] Already in 1972 Alves anticipated what would become a central tenet of the dominant economic model of our times: "[Behind] its most exciting promises futurology tells something, almost in a whisper, that makes us shudder: *there is no way out*. The future is inevitable. It is useless to look for alternatives."[45] Not too long after this, Margaret Thatcher would make this the slogan for neoliberalism.

In the hands of hegemonic forces, particularly economic forces, time is normalized so as to render the future as inevitable. What shall be is but a continuation of what is. Alves, however, takes the proclamation of the lack of alternatives to the status quo as something else than the arrogance of a system that thinks of itself as self-sufficient. For him, the suppression of voices that struggle and dream of alternative futures unveils the fragility of hegemonic systems. The stifling of dissenting voices is for Alves an indictment of the status quo: "When a system affirms something to be impossible, it is simply disclosing its own limits."[46]

Alves therefore speaks of the need to identify and combat "pseudo-hopes" that stem from an unjust and incorrect reading of the signs of the times.[47] Hope for preservation of the status quo is met with the injustice of the present. The primacy that suffering gains in Alves's eschatology aligns the edges of his future-talk to the margins of the social body. His association between hope and human suffering anticipates what would be canonized as the landmark idea of liberation theologies—the preferential option for the poor. He says, "[The] slaves, the wretched of the earth, the outcasts and marginal . . . , these are [the ones] who can have the vision and passion for and are able to understand the language of hope, freedom, and liberation."[48] Alves uses the term *messianic humanism* to name this way of constructing the future where the reality of present suffering is not received as fully present but rather as a "time-toward-the-new-tomorrow."[49] The language of hope, he insists, "[names] the 'things that are absent.'"[50] I shall return to a more detailed account of this statement, but for now it must be stressed that in Alves's eschatology of liberation, the grammar of hope at once acknowledges a void in the fabric of reality while also creating room for something to come.

The recognition of suffering as the condition of possibility of a liberating hope is Alves's most meaningful contribution to the shaping of liberation theology. I have argued before that in Marx the assertion of a commodity's value requires an excavation into the realm of production and the social relations therein. For Alves, when we excavate the Christian eschatological imagination in its liberating potential, we, too, encounter a weak, oppressed body that desires and protests for a future. The imagination of the future is already a witness to the pain of the world. But it witnesses something else too. The Christian eschatological imagination, as envisioned by Alves, overhears the sighs of the oppressed creature under the voice that speaks of a time when all tears shall be wiped away. Imagination is, as Alves proposes, a mirror to reality, a mirror that directs our attention to the injustices of our world while also projecting different futures.

The Flesh of Hope

The liberationist impetus of *A Theology of Human Hope* is to make hope a fleshly matter for Christian theology. And, in the process, to identify the incarnations of liberating hopes that construct the future differently. The spiraling paths engendered by future projections and reflections construct a variety of directions, as I have been suggesting. In Alves's theology of liberation, the imagination of the future gains the sensory contours and sinews of the suffering body. His theology is forever haunted by the affirmation of faith: "I believe in the resurrection of the body."[51] He argues that this is the only possible theme for theology: the hope that flesh and word will forever meet and that the body will come alive. "Theology is . . . an endless poem about the mystery of the incarnation."[52] The theological imagination thus speaks deeply—indeed *viscerally*—to the depths of the human body.

To track the different senses that future-talk makes and to conjure liberating hopes, Alves leads us into the guts of the suffering body. He identifies liberating hope as a function of the incarnations of suffering in the world. The hope that liberates springs from the suffering of those who suffer in their own flesh the forces of "defuturization." Alves defends that the "slaves" of history are "those who can have the vision and passion for and are able to understand the language of hope, freedom, and liberation."[53] While hegemonic forces seek to "preserve their 'now,'" Alves positions suffering as the "the starting point for the dialectics of liberation that negates the old and stretches itself, in hope, toward the new."[54]

Alves's focus on the body, particularly the suffering body, directs his future-talk to the materiality of bodies in pain—and their dreams. Oppressive power relations pierce these bodies with the burden of the "now," yet the suffering body sighs a breath of pain that signals toward a different future. It whispers of a "world without lords and slaves" and color these imaginary spaces with projections of liberation "symbolically filled with ultimate desires."[55] The projections of the oppressed body are neither descriptive nor

120

predictive statements about the future, but rather they perform the "ethical and religious task" of prophecy.[56] The religion that affirms life against the forces of oppression cannot dream the dreams of the oppressors, but it finds ways of producing future-talk nevertheless. It does so out of the crevices of human frailty.

Future-talk in its liberative sense is the sigh of a weak body. Alves employs bodily metaphors as he explains the entanglement between our desires and our hopes: "To name our desires is to acknowledge our condition of exiles, of being out of place, u/topics, bound to a present that suppresses the body."[57] And yet Alves perceives the oppressed subject as the carrier of "an erotic/heretical project for the liberation of life."[58] Such a project starts with a "small body, limited by our skins, [and then grows] into the spaces of society, nature, until we reach the corners of the universe, large body, until we are constituted as Body of Christ."[59] Alves's thinking starts in displacement, in the pain wrought by exile. The sighs of displaced bodies signal more than pain, however. They long for a regathering of bodies conjoining with a universal body, a messianic body. The hope of liberation is engendered by the passage of a desire enclosed within the body to the cosmic edges of reality.

Alves acknowledges that writing *A Theology of Human Hope* was a testimony to his own fragility, his own experience of exile. The image of a people wandering in the desert in search of a new land, he says, was a poetic metaphor that amplified his experience of anguish and displacement. It was a "[hope] in movement, fighting for a future, an affect [*(a)feto*] that pushes forward through the anguish of a tight path, as if giving birth—to *liberation*."[60] The hope Alves embodied in his own experience of exile casts a deep shadow over his corpus.

Alves cites a sermon of the seventeenth-century Portuguese Jesuit priest António Vieira that speaks to the prophetic and fleshly dimension of the sighs of the oppressed body: "The Ancient, when they wanted to foretell the future, sacrificed animals and consulted their guts. . . . This superstition was false, but the allegory was very true. There is no surer light of prophecy than the one which is found in the guts of men. Of whose men? Of all? No. Of those who have been sacrificed. If you want to prophesize futures, consult the guts of those who were sacrificed: consult the guts of those who were sacrificed. . . . And whatever they say, this must be taken as prophecy."[61] The kind of future-talk that speaks from within the guts of oppressed bodies— this is prophecy. The entrails of the suffering body signal a future coming, it codifies the longing for the Messiah, Alves says.[62] A body that is equally broken and that partakes in worldly pain. This is Alves's form of probing into

121

the entrails of human misery and making it the stuff of hope. Future-talk speaks with world-creating "groans, whispers, prophecies."[63] "We groan, the earth groans, a symphony of groans having the Holy Spirit as the conductor: labor pain, hope for the redemption of the body."[64] Theology speaks with symbols that become flesh and bread, making sense of suffering while nourishing bodies in pain.

The "religious and ethical task" of a Christian eschatology of liberation is to be attuned to these socially embodied sighs of oppression and to hear in them the signs of the times.[65] They are the foreboding that some other time is coming, that society is no solid crystal but an organism—a body, truly—that is constantly changing.[66] "What is hope?" Alves asks. "It is the *hunch* that the overwhelming brutality of facts that oppress and repress is not the last word. It is the *suspicion* that . . . the frontiers of the possible are not determined by the limits of the actual."[67] The signs of the times do not signify that "tomorrow a miracle will occur," as Marx suggested, but that something "is preparing the creative event which will open the way of freedom and resurrection."[68] For Alves, the flesh of hope is socially embodied. The sighs of oppression gather in the life of the community of hope to form a new tune whispering of a different time.

In the critical and liberative contours of Alves's future-talk, hope is the confession of the strongest desires of the weakest bodies.[69] When the hopes of weak bodies coalesce with other bodies and their hopes and desires, "heavenly dreams invade the earth," and the future gains the shape of protest against the present.[70] And something comes with these breaths: "[The] community of hope is a partial realization of the dream of utopian visionaries. For it is the future actually taking place in the present. The community is a 'sample' of the 'not yet,' the *aperitif* of a banquet still to come."[71] The creative event that points to a different imaginary of the future erupts in history and assumes a social form in the midst of oppressed communities. Alves revisits Paul's letter to the Romans: "Those who live in the pain-delivering sectors of our society . . . , even before they can articulate in speech the evil of this world, are already doing it by means of their inarticulate groans (Rom. 8:26). And this is the raw material the Spirit takes unto Himself."[72] Materialized in the bowels of planetary life and its painful groans, the Spirit conspires against insipid presents to season them with a foretaste of a banquet to come.

Alves's theology takes pleasure in these aperitifs that, from the present, wet our mouths for that which may come. He particularly delights in Father Vieira's taste for future-talk: by taking us to the entrails of the slain, Vieira imagines the prophet savoring the pain of the victims while excreting the logic that turns bodies into sacrifices. Alves in turn projects a eucharistic feast that resurrects the bodies of the victims. "The dialectics of the prophetic word is the dialectic of eating: one eats and one is eaten. One is possessed by the Wind which dwells in the food."[73] The prophet thus feeds on the interrupted dreams of the victims and, by incorporating them, brings them back to life. This is hope in its fleshly form, hope as the incarnation of a multiplicity of dangerous memories and bodies. That hope resurrects the dead, breathes life into the body, and prepares us for feasts to come.

123

For Alves, every theology attentive to the prophetic word spoken from the guts of human life speaks to the meaning—*sentido*—of life and death. Even as Alves engages theological symbols in unorthodox ways and privileges playful and imaginative forms of God-talk, he insists that theology is a matter of life and death. The words we craft to name our desire for liberation and life abundant are to be eaten.[74] Theological imagination gains its political character as the space where new modes of sociability and social relations are prefigured, anticipated, and experienced. The enfleshed mode of future-talk we encounter in Alves puts the body in motion, transfiguring it to "[make] love, dance, smile, and sleep."[75] Fiddling with the theological category of hope allows Alves to unravel a subversive mode of future-talk. For him, imaginative world creation is as necessary for liberation as political engagement.

Father Vieira's sermon further allegorizes the reason for consulting the guts of sacrificed bodies as opposed to their heads. In his anatomical imagination, the head is the seat of understanding, but the entrails are where love resides. For Vieira, gut-prophesying energies instill an affective form of future-talk. The future is summoned not by those who "better understand but rather [by] those who love most."[76] We remember Arguedas's maxim that captivated Gutiérrez's imagination: "We know so much less than the great hope we feel." Alves is also raptured by the passion that engenders future-talk against all attempts to plant theology on firm ground and capture an uncapturable future. Future-talk speaks affectively precisely because it addresses the mystery of our love for that which is not—yet.

Naming Absences

Rubem Alves was fond of citing Paul Valéry: "What would we be without the help of things that don't exist?"[77] What in fact would our times be without a time that is not—yet? In the all-consuming temporality of financialized capitalism, mustering the forces of that which does not exist might offer us a hope that derails a system that proclaims itself to be all there is. Is this not what hope does, after all? That is to say: is not hope a statement that what "is" is not all there is to be? That something may come, hope—fully? Future-talk in this register suspends the perception of what "here" and "now" is in order to invoke absent realities. In Alves's theology this is performed by means of a poetic summoning of absences. Hope for him is a way of naming things that are absent.[78] It is language that calls on the coming of something that is not—yet.

I suggest we consider the interplay between presence and absence in Alves's work under the influence of Jacques Derrida's mysterious overture into the apocalyptic imagination. Derrida claimed that the apocalyptic pronouncement about the imminence of the "end" fundamentally requires a certain "derangement" of reason and of language.[79] For Derrida, the voice that speaks with an "apocalyptic tone" exists through perversion and mixture. In fact, the voice that speaks of the future is not one. It takes place when two voices speak together, or rather when one voice "whispers secrets to you in uncovering your ear for you, jumbling, covering, or parasitizing [the dominant voice]."[80] Nothing is therefore "less conservative than the apocalyptic genre," Derrida submits.[81] Precisely because nothing about an apocalyptic utterance can be properly conserved and definitively censored. "By its very tone, the mixing of voices, genres, and codes, and the breakdown [le détraquement] of destinations, apocalyptic discourse can ... dismantle the dominant contract or concordat" and offer some "detours" that can mislead the "vigilance" of censorship.[82] The apocalyptic tone unleashes excessive images and metaphors that escape censorship and policing forces. As Derrida concludes, when one adopts this tone, a "poetico-metaphorical overabundance" is unleashed.[83]

The abundance of striking images, incisive graphic metaphors, and poetic exuberance binds Alves's theology to the apocalyptic tone of which Derrida speaks. As I unveil this entanglement, we should note how the performance of the apocalyptic pronouncement gives salience to the critical liberationist task of reading the "signs of the times." For Alves, reading these signs requires different modes of theological signification. His theology construes future-talk as the naming of realities that cannot properly be named but that can and must be summoned. Hope becomes the stuff of *poiesis*, of creative activity. In Alves's work this gesture deepens the project of liberation by releasing its aesthetic possibilities.

In texts and interviews, it is common for Alves and his interpreters to speak of his passage from theology and politics into the realm of play and

124

poetics at some point during the early 1980s.[84] In a documentary filmed close to the time of his death in 2014, Alves himself divides his life into three periods. "In the first phase, we only spoke of things as big as the universe: God. Then God died, and we stepped back a little and searched for political heroes. We left theology for politics. Then politics failed us, and we went to our backyards to play with spinning tops."[85] These passages can be traced to Alves's writings, undoubtably. His mature writings demonstrate a disciplinary eclecticism and a religious incredulity that distanced him from theological circles. He confessed to being an unbeliever.[86]

But Brazilian philosopher and poet José Lima Júnior cautions against neat divisions in relation to a writer who indeed defies disciplinary boundaries. For him, the triad religion-politics-play is present throughout Alves's corpus with differing degrees of emphasis or intensity.[87] Lima Júnior teases out, for example, how Alves's appreciation of play is core to his understanding of religion articulated during an earlier phase of his career.[88] A poetic sensibility is certainly visible in Alves's second book, *Tomorrow's Child*, written in the early 1970s.[89] Raimundo César Barreto Júnior rightly suggests that ethics and aesthetics, justice and beauty, politics and imagination are poles that Alves did not conceptualize as opposites.[90]

These might be better heard as voices that he intended to mix, jumble, and parasitize in order to dismantle any type of dominant contract. In Alves's theological *poiesis*, the work of justice encompasses the defamiliarization of theological language itself. He displays exuberant images and poetic language to destabilize ossified assumptions in the Christian vocabulary and spark new modes of theological imagination. While one can easily trace rejections, passages, and sublimations in Alves's corpus, his theological imagination remained active, playful, and transgressive.[91] Reminiscing about his ties to the birth of liberation theology, he indicated his own *Aufhebung*. "The Rubem Alves of the theology of liberation, the one who spoke about action, changed. I became different. I believe God has strange ways of doing things. One of them is turning them upside down."[92] Alves's texts indeed turn theology upside down, derailing the voice that privileges what he commonly referred to as "Cartesian rationality." But the uncanny nature of Alves's theology remains liberating precisely because of his attention to the flipping of narratives, to the world turned upside down.

In Alves's theopoetics, hope is to be encountered in the cracks of the text, in its ruptures and ellipses. By the "mixing of voices, genres, and codes," as Derrida will have wanted, Alves's writing derails the linearity of the present-future nexus in order to make future-talk an exercise that unleashes a multiplicity of senses.[93] *A Theology of Human Hope* does exactly that. A fruit of political exile, the book already shows vestiges of a metaphoric exuberance that offers detours from the stranglehold of the present. Alves met a stifling censorship with the Christian vocabulary of hope precisely as a tactic to derail dominant theological concordats.

In the book Alves approaches the vocabulary of Christian eschatology as an imaginary way of naming absent times. He writes, "Imagination is a form of critique . . . [that] is able to 'name the things that are absent,' and . . . [break] the spell of the things that are present."[94] Naming our absences is an act of defiance of dominant temporalities according to which what is present is all there is. In this sense, giving name to someone or something absent can be framed as an act of mournful resistance: it incorporates the memory of the departed—the slain, those who have been sacrificed, as we saw—while enfleshing a hope for a new story. It is the dual gesture of naming absences while invoking something to come. It is the resolute denial and resistance of the present order of things and its devouring force. And it is also the stubborn remaining within the pause that persists in saying that the future is not—yet in active defiance against the forces that continue to consume what is to come.

Theology here is unveiled as critical reflection on hope. Alongside other liberationists, Alves learned that the language of hope speaks more than what it says.[95] In his writings liberation theology is constructed in this interplay between the spoken word of hope and the unspoken sighs of the oppressed creature. For Alves, hope speaks in many tongues: as the acknowledgment that something hurts and as the naming of our absences. Moreover, hope offers a protest against oppressive forces and a summons for the coming of a new epoch. At first, as Alves heard it, this voice is nothing but a "shout of pain, anger, and refusal." But listen to this announcement: "[This shout of pain] expands; it becomes a 'symphony of negation'" that will "project itself in the direction of the future, giving birth to hope."[96] As we saw earlier, the language of hope is the "positive shape which the negation of the negative and inhuman of the present takes."[97] Marx's "negation of the negation" acquires in Alves a poetic, imaginative edge: "I say that the goal of all political struggles, the goal of all our struggle for justice is for the world to be more beautiful."[98] Alves foregrounds beauty as the necessary companion to justice and refuses to subscribe to any political project that topples aesthetic concerns as subjective, romantic, or needless for liberation. He calls it the "politics of beauty."[99]

The absence of which Alves speaks beckons imaginative activity as a mechanism to construe the object of our desires and summon it into being. Alves therefore affirms that the future cannot "be." It is not. Yet. In "the world of absences . . . we can only dispose of word and imagination as instruments to construct that which is *not yet*."[100] We tend to conceive of the passage of time as the necessary and unchanging flow of being from past to present, from present to future. But Alves's eschatological imagination offers a different ontology of time, perhaps even what might be perceived as a hauntology of time.[101] In the language of hope, what is not yet matters the most. "*From the future, from the not yet, something comes*," Alves proposes.[102] That which is to come haunts presence. Hope tears apart the linearity of time, the timeline that assumes a straight line from here to there. Alves concurs with Ernst Bloch: "What is, cannot be true."[103] Future-talk exposes the present and all there *is* to the haunting reality of the yet inexistent.

By exhuming a poetico-metaphorical overabundance, Alves's text unleashes theological work to critically craft our desires for inexistent realities in the shape of future-talk. As Lima Júnior writes, Alves's poetic work must be perceived as his ongoing struggle to mine different forms of naming the ineffable.[104] His unwieldy writing, his many ellipses, and his textual ruptures bespeak his attention to this nameless mystery that he could not avoid beckoning, even when he disavowed God-talk. In fact, Alves prepared a way for God in the crevices of his early theological reasoning precisely by proposing that God is what we call on when we name our absences. Future-talk in Alves performs this task of naming that which is not present—including God.

In our shared mother tongue, Alves and I have a word that names absences while conjuring their coming, even their resurrection. In Portuguese, *saudade* gives name to absences that comprise who we are. This untranslatable word is normally rendered in English as "nostalgia" or "longing." It often signals things, people, and experiences one misses, like missing a loved one who has passed away or missing a time gone in the past. On the one hand, yes, *saudade* names the missing of things past. But it also activates a movement, a desire—for the future. A longing, which led one of Alves's translators to render *saudade* as "longing remembrance."[105] *Saudade*, in this sense, names the memory that longs for reuniting with something absent. Alves's own reflection on *saudade* indicates a similar passion: *saudade* is the affect one inhabits when one loves that which is absent. He takes this to be the foundation of his poetic and theological thinking.[106]

But how can one *love* that which is not—yet? What might the love for an absence mean? Truly, such a love cannot come into being. It cannot "be." Likewise, I suggest that the love for the future is the love of something that *is* not—yet. And yet loving the future may be the affect one needs in order to love in the times without a pause. Loving the future directs us to that which does not exist but somehow must. It is a love that summons. For that affect to occur, *saudade* will actualize and materialize this absence in the interim time-space of a not—yet. In Alves's theology God occupies the space opened up by this actualized absence. He locates God in that in-between temporality activated when one summons an absence into be-coming. "God dwells in [*saudade*], there where love and absence take their places."[107]

Saudade as the longing for an inexistent yet necessary reality is how Alves describes liberating hope. We overhear Alves's passion for that which is not—yet in the following verses that break into his prose:

> Can this be?
> Perhaps . . .
> We, who try the first fruits
> We, who experience the aperitif of the future
> We, who were caressed by Someone, from the future.[108]

For Alves, the touch of the future reaches us from the infinity of a time that is not—yet. Its nourishment offers no assurances of a divine presence but reveals the "open wound of an Absence."[109] We touch this open wound, and it touches us back with a caress that comes from the future. How can we exist without that which is not—yet?

The poetico-metaphorical overabundance of Alves's writing speaks to his commitment to the naming of absences as the proper name for Christian hope. Naming absences is an unveiling, a true act of revelation. For Alves, what is hidden is both the ineffable mystery *and* that which has been suppressed. The appropriation of the apocalyptic "unveiling" of a mystery is the necessary political and poietic act of going to the oppressed body and overhearing in it the signs of the times. In Alves's writings, both those that are explicitly theological and those that veil his passion for the divine through the language of absence, liberation remains implied even when unwritten. It is stated even when it is not voiced. Liberation is coded in a poetic excess that derails periods into ellipses, and hegemonic presences into future comings.

Future-talk is forever a double entendre, a statement that cannot be one precisely because it always already summons more. The future is a time derailed by the excess that escapes the grasp of a single time. It is therefore a time that must be named and invoked with the poetico-metaphorical over-abundance we encounter in Alves's writing. Future-talk produces the sense of the very thing it defers. And this sense matters: in its passing it haunts and produces other things. It generates other senses, other directions, other meanings, other affects. In its liberating spirit, future-talk channels sighs of pain into signs of future becomings. Conjure, now, Alves asks: may the future come.

fugitive futures

6

Fallen, fallen is Babylon
the great!
—REVELATION 18:1

Standing on the edges of the biblical canon, the book of Revelation casts a large shadow over the history of musings about the future. The scene of the fall of the great city of Babylon and the collapse of its economy has oriented the imagination of movements who mobilized around the hope that, yes, even the greatest empires collapse. For these movements, future-talk offers the necessary camouflage and the inspiration for their critique. The strategy is not unfamiliar to John of Patmos, who disguised his critique of the Roman Empire in the rags of "Babylon." From heaven above, John saw the coming of a very bright angel announcing with a loud voice: "Fallen, fallen is Babylon the great!" (Rev. 18:1).[1] The announcement confounds our senses of time: *When* does that come to be? The voice speaks in the present, but Babylon is long gone in the past, and the Roman Empire, supposedly the city informing John's imaginary, is still strong and far from fallen. In the confusing temporality of this apocalyptic statement, might the attack on Babylon summon the fall of other empires and economies?

One can hope. And that, I submit, is not nothing. For hope might be one of the voices we need to summon as we stand before the imperial city of Babylon. The indefinite temporality of the pronouncement of the fall of the imperial city quickens the liberating spirit of future-talk. The factual fall of Babylon is not what the statement seeks to address. That it *must* fall is what is at stake. This mode of speaking of reality by means of a detour into an indefinite temporality is a key tactic for an eschatology of liberation. The future unveiled by the vision of the collapse of Babylon and its economy *makes sense*. It directs our attention to the injustices of the imperial commerce while also providing a direction. As I present it in the following pages, this direction gains the contours of an escape route. Hope, in this sense, differs from escapism and the refusal to confront reality. The escape cannot neglect the stifling present, but it must deviate from it through a step into the edges of future-talk.

The edges of the eschatological imagination nurture the hope of the demise of imperial cities and their economies. Constructive theologian Catherine Keller proposes we remain within the "forcefield" of apocalypse in order to cherish its concern for justice as well as its announcement of the unveiling of a new city, a new heaven, and a new earth.[2] Keller's probing allows us to detect a relational and liberating temporality in the pause one makes when saying that the future is not—yet. In the second section of the chapter, I follow the work of scholars in Black studies who have problematized and construed hope in light of the Middle Passage and the calamity of Black life in order to elaborate my argument about future-talk as an escape tactic. Joseph Winters has named this as a "melancholic" hope, a "hope draped in black."[3] At this juncture in my reflection, I should like to summon the wisdom that comes from a proclivity for the escape. I depict this as a maneuver that can offer an alternative to hegemonic forms of future-talk and sustain resistance to the forces of financialization.

In this chapter the apocalyptic pronouncement about the imminent collapse of the imperial city coalesces with a fugitive disposition. Theorist Fred Moten has embraced an optimistic stance and plotted paths for "fugitivity," an attitude of refusal and resistance to any reality that cages us in the hold of the present.[4] As I envision it in this chapter, future-talk offers an escape tactic that is supple and capacious enough to create paths of liberation. I venture to name the future as the fugitive reality that escapes any present hold.

My work here therefore concludes my reflections on the possibilities opened up by an eschatology of liberation to confront the consuming temporality of financialized capitalism. The future has been unveiled for us in the past two chapters as a critique of the sacrificial futurology of capitalism and as a summoning of things that do not exist yet. In this final unveiling, I portray future-talk as a creative way to circumvent reality and sidestep its harmful forces. I speak of a hope that does not deny suffering and oppression but that indeed straddles the edges and marginal spaces of the present. My path consists of a constructive engagement with apocalypse and a reflection on future-talk as a mournful resistance and world shifting. My remarks ponder the image of a fugitive future. Financialization has produced our collective sense of the future by subjecting us to the force of its futures. In this final seal that I seek to unravel, capitalist futurology is met with a fugitive futurity. To indebted subjects living in the iron cage of financialization, I offer the escape as a tactic of temporal displacement: a way of inhabiting the present bent on running away.

Future Unveilings

Catherine Keller, the first constructive theologian to write comprehensively about the future imagined in apocalyptic literature, has pointed out that Christian theology has shaped Western visions of history and temporality. She writes that the plots of our cultural imaginaries are informed by an apocalypse *script* with iterations that transgress the boundaries of religious belongings.[5] The script informs popular culture, art, and politics— from images of a postapocalyptic scenario in literature and film to military interventions in the Middle East. The all-pervasive force of the apocalyptic imagination shapes a particular *habit* that accustoms us to visions of cataclysmic events, moral dualism, and an "explosive futurism."[6] As a social habit, apocalypse inclines people to perceive things like the burning of rain forests as somehow expectable features of a world approaching its end.[7] As Keller argues, from the edges of the biblical canon, apocalypse determines the "outer edges of our time frame."[8] Our sense of the passage of time and our expectations for the future are shaped by apocalypse.

As a habit, Keller argues, apocalypse is destructive or even self-destructive. But she is clear: each and every critique of apocalypse cannot avoid its habitual protocols. Ingrained as they are in our social, cultural, and political patterns, disavowing apocalyptic habits may lead to repeating and even reinforcing them. Keller therefore induces us to probe into a "third space" opened up by apocalypse's oppositions. Therein we may face the apocalyptic imagination with a constructive ambivalence: "to poke openings *into* the apocalypse pattern" and then "disarm its polarities" while also "savoring its intensity, its drive for justice, its courage in the face of impossible odds and losses."[9] Keller calls this maneuver *counter-apocalypse*. She describes it as an ambivalent, careful, and cautious reading of apocalypse geared toward disarming the destructive effects of the apocalypse habit. For her, a careful reading of apocalyptic texts and effects may disclose some openings into our present crises.[10] For me, this attentiveness to apocalypse proves useful in my articulation of an escape route from the imperial commerce instituted by contemporary finance.

Keller instills her counter-apocalyptic gesture with a strong liberationist impetus, inflected by the demands of a feminist political stance. In fact, liberation theologians, while attentive to the revolutionary intrigue of the apocalypse script, have often failed to recognize the violence and the misogyny encouraged by apocalyptic fervor. When uncritically entangled in the apocalypse script, the politics of time will betray even the most justice-seeking readings of the biblical apocalypse. As Keller rightly points out, apocalyptic revolutionary fervor may reinscribe that which it intends to oppose.[11] Yes, it is tempting to turn the promise announced in hope into guarantees that the future will be what we think it shall be. Politically, revolutionary "determination" can quickly turn into totalitarian "determinism."[12] True to its feminist spirit, counter-apocalypse holds the temporality of apocalypse and the politics of time in constant tension.

In this register hope is "agonized and agonistic, confronting critical difference, mourning unbearable loss, and yet struggling for the new."[13] Keller locates the hope of counter-apocalypse not in habitual predictive patterns that seek to set an end date to history. Instead, Keller gently leads us to the "vibrating edge, the *eschatos*, of a precarious present becoming."[14] As readers will note, I have positioned my reflections on future-talk on similar ground. With Keller, I affirm that something "real if not actual" presents itself under the guise of the future: a "possibility not yet actualized but *presenting*."[15] The "to-come may not come": that is the precarity embraced by future-talk. The future is always a precarious not—yet.

But the unknowability of the future proves itself a reliable deconstructive lever. Its indeterminate state deconstructs every determinism, including the preemptive predictive impetus that is so central to financial markets. The futurology of finance, as we have seen, is set on gathering data, predicting, and anticipating market movements. The underside of the story of financialization is the enclosure of the future of the multitude of indebted subjects who remain bound to the power architectonics of financialized capitalism. But in contrast to these exploitative futures engendered by financialization, there remains the irreducible fact that the future is not—yet. The controlling impetus of capitalist futurology is derailed by the inability of the future to satisfy our projections. Future-talk interrupts every totalizing claim about the present with a pause: not—yet. Likewise, it destabilizes every deterministic claim about the future by reminding us that what is to come is not yet here. The future looms and lures Keller's constructive theological project with its energy to displace the present age and its unjust forces. We cannot "disallow" hope, not without letting go of possibilities "tucked in" every present moment. Yes, I, too, "would rather hold hope's feet to the fire of its most amorous—most *remaining*—desire" than allow the forces of financialization to consume all possibilities of future becomings.[16]

Keller insists that apocalyptic habits be encountered in the spirit of resistance and solidarity that opens up different plots that the apocalyptic script may perform. Counter-apocalypse therefore supplements the liberationist prophetic imagination with a methodological ambivalence that can "sustain resistance to destruction without expecting triumph."[17] Constructive ambivalence incorporates the prophetic dimension of future-talk while also cautioning against an unconditional and apologetic acceptance of apocalyptic literature. Keller's counter-apocalypse conjures new *senses* of time—a new temporal sensibility that soon will translate into a different *spirit* of time.

The cultural patterns and habits induced by apocalypse constitute for Keller the "ontology of the West." The project condenses itself in the call to be "on top of time," that is, to manage time in such a way as to control it.[18] In previous chapters we witnessed some of the economic iterations of this chronic ontology in the need employers have to manage the time of workers and the impulse that financialized capitalism has to predict market movements. I have framed the endless pursuit of financial profit as a contemporary iteration of this search for mastery over time, for the coding and decoding of the signs of the times that can secure one's future, even when all else is left behind. Keller takes us a step further by teasing out the ethico-theological implications of such mastery over time: "To master time one does not merely control one's time and that of others, but one finally transcends it. Thus time-control guarantees personal immunity to apocalypse; come what may—even the End of History—being on-time ensures that the successful time manager will not be left behind."[19]

Mastery over time assumes one can absolutely capture the future, a time that is not—yet. The master of time is the one who assumes ownership of this pause and construes it as ultimately manageable. And who is the financier other than the successful manager of futures? What is financialized capitalism other than this self-perpetuating system for codifying risks and monetizing worries about the future?[20] In the disjointed temporality of apocalypse, one ought to witness to the ties between John's rampant critique of the imperial economy of his age and our own predicament under the empire of finance. In Keller's case, minding John's attack on imperial commerce is the distinguishing factor between her account of apocalypse in the "last millennium" and her most recent one.[21] In *Facing Apocalypse*, she insists that John's "satire" about how merchants mourned the fall of Babylon "delivers a loaded critique of what we now term the 'global economy.'"[22] Financialization, as I have sought to frame it, might be the newest dispensation of an apocalypse habit. The mastery over time that Keller identifies as one of the gravest symptoms of this habit gains shape in financial maneuvers to assess risk, anticipate future market movements, and make a profit out of the management of uncertainty.

With futures under the control of the financial behemoth, I suggest that we summon the spirit of counter-apocalypse, which Keller describes as capable of deconstructing the "relentless timeline of alpha-to-omega" by maintaining these poles alive in the synergy of a "messianic forcefield, not as two poles of a timeline."[23] Rather than portraying the passage of time as a manageable sequence of moments moving in the direction of the future, Keller introduces a relational ontology of time that construes time as a "series of relations configured as differences."[24] The present moment is not a self-sufficient reality but a complex web of "eco-social" relations. In Keller's work the edges of Christian theology show their relational potency: "Eschatology, posing its questions of collective ultimacy, meets us if at all in the minute acts of timing constitutive of life's rhythm, the rhythm of our relations."[25] In this reading the present moment exists in relation to a future coming, much as the self is constituted by its relation to others. Difference manifests in time through the infinite presence and deferral of the future, a time that is irreducibly other.

Future-talk, in this sense, uncovers the temporal motion of difference. That time is not one. The present cannot be perceived nor justly lived without a *sense* of what may come from it. For Keller, a relational ontology of time will usher in a politics of dis/closure. In her work on political theology, she revisits some of the themes broached by her writings on apocalypse to suggest that we may need to relearn to inhabit the no-place called utopia. Keller traces the unfolding of a radical utopian thread that moves from Ernst

Bloch's utopian Marxism to Jürgen Moltmann's *Theology of Hope* and into José Esteban Muñoz's *Cruising Utopia*. The paths taken by radical utopians unveil the no-place as a site of inception where life creeps from the underground. In particular, Keller detects in Muñoz's work the possibility of a "political queering of hope," a gesture that I have also affirmed in my introduction. Keller's work unfolds in the possibility of this queer and edgy temporality while attending to climate change and eco-social catastrophes. Future-talk here is a matter of neither postponement nor predictions. For Keller, the eschatological imagination may begin to "perform" or to "*ingather*" that which is to come.[26]

This gives contours to a messianic ontology of time that ties radical otherness to a future coming. In dialogue with Jacques Derrida, Keller suggests that messianic time is heterogeneously coconstituted by both a now and a then. The irreducible difference of the other is construed in a messianic temporal framework: the other comes prior to the moment that I am, "[upending] the linear determinism of any closed system." When these systems of enclosure seek an end, counter-apocalypse offers a "dis/closure." Meanwhile, Keller continues, the messianic other places the subject in relation to a heterogeneous future coming. In fact, the "I" of the present moment is "coconstituted" by this other who is to come.[27] Keller's theology vibrates in the messianic force field, not in the pursuit of control of the other, but gesturing to the dis/closures that the future may bring. I insist: this future is not untethered from the present moment but rather inhabits the present with a resolute disposition to what may come. Keller's attention to the present moment and its *depth* is the counter-apocalyptic way of "conceiving a sustainable, just, and lovable future by living it *already*."[28]

Once again, we confront the mystery of a love for that which is not—yet. The lovable future of which Keller speaks is actual and material but not captured by any present moment. Apocalypse now *and* then: here and there, now and later. As we follow Keller's steps into the edges of time, we notice how apocalypse unveils more than some there-and-then. It reveals, more deeply, the coconstitution of present and future. Instead of dissolving difference in either absolute presence or lofty futurity, Keller maintains the present and the future in infinite relation: "[The] edges of (my) being at any given moment are the edges of (my) time."[29] Subjectivity and temporality herein are thought of relationally. The limits and possibilities of self and time exist in relation to that which is other. The future, in this formulation, is totally other, infinite in its possibilities, and not ever captive to any one master of time.[30]

Mastering time elides the relational dimension of time. It is a form of making impermeable the edge between now and then, self and others. On the contrary, a relational ontology of time affirms the permeable boundaries between now and then, between self and others. Like the fragile and permeable edges between self and other, the temporal relations between now and then constitute our experiences of time. Here the present moment is not *only* in the here and now but is constituted by a future coming. Keller attends to the ways that becoming constitutes time not as the straight line toward the end but as the curves and interruptions of the messianic to-come. "Becoming neither trumps nor smooths the path of the *to come*—it enfolds and pluralizes it, it diasporizes it, it prepares its ways and follows in them."[31]

Babylon is fallen, apocalypse reveals. But when? Now and then, now and ever, forever and never. Time as revealed by apocalypse is out of joint. Present and unpresent: a true fugitive. The resolution to remain within the influence of the eschatological imagination is my way of persisting in this fugitive state where we may indeed "[savor] its intensity, its drive for justice, its courage in the face of impossible odds and losses."[32] So far I have named this disposition, in language that is not unfamiliar to Keller, with the refrain: the future may not be yet but might make things become. In our time we may enter into this edgy, dirty commons, not expecting resolutions for our economic or ecological predicaments, but with a steadfast resolution to remain.

Melancholic Hopes

Difference exists in the pause one makes when claiming that the future is not—yet. And the pause harbors the realization of past calamity and a precarious hope that the future might be different. Hope for the future cannot offer guarantees of successful outcomes, but it can assemble mournful memories to give flesh to an equally mournful hope. Draped in the tragedy of Black life, Joseph Winters has conjured a melancholic hope that construes the future not as a time of resolutions but as yet another way to bear witness to tragedy and oppression.[33] In my previous chapter, I argued with Rubem Alves that hope might be construed as an act of mournful resistance. With Winters and other theorists in Black studies, I propose that we investigate hope in light of the Middle Passage.

The gesture is a necessary step for the realization of the deep ties between Black oppression and financial extortion. As I pointed out in chapter 2, the mode of subjectivity founded by financialization recodes racist tropes and submits Black communities to a debt economy. Financialized capitalism deepens the legacy of white supremacy through its lending practices and its segregating effects. The "predatory inclusion" of which Keeanga-Yamahtta Taylor speaks shows the entanglement of white supremacy, the legacy of slavery, urban development, and financialization.[34] In this sense, approaching future-talk with attention to the calamity of Black life amplifies the awareness of the ties between financialized capitalism and what Cedric Robinson has termed *racial capitalism*.[35]

For some, as we shall see, white supremacy and the condition of Black existence do not authorize the language of hope, a stance that I consider even as I follow Winters in embracing the possibility of a hope draped in black. The persistence of future-talk may be construed as a residue of the fugitive disposition that marked the resistance to slavery and anti-Black racism. This remainder does not allow itself to be captured by optimism, but it remains steadfast in the pursuit of escape routes. I consider that this escape harbors its own mode of future-talk.

The question of the future is central to Black studies. The poles of the debate often bounce between Afro-pessimism and optimism, but the lines cannot be neatly divided.[36] In Fred Moten's words, pessimism and optimism are asymptotic: they come in the shape of a curve and a line approaching each other continuously, even if through different trajectories. "Which one is the curve and which one is the line? Which is the kernel and which is the shell? Which one is rational, which one is mystical?" Definitive answers are not the point, Moten writes. "Let's just say that their nonmeeting is part of an ongoing manic depressive episode called black radicalism / black social life."[37] For Moten, this episode does not present itself as a disavowal of future-talk but as a wrestling within the gap created by the asymptotic nonencounter of optimism and pessimism, nothingness and celebration, despair and hope.

From the outset we must clarify that Afro-pessimism does not make a claim about pessimism common to philosophical traditions stemming from nineteenth-century European thinkers like Arthur Schopenhauer and Friedrich Nietzsche.[38] Jared Sexton argues that Afro-pessimism is not even a direct claim on the future based on the calamity of the present and its bleak prospects for what is to come. The pessimistic stance, in its Black iteration, is a response to the "*longue durée* of racial slavery" and its defining role in the shaping of modernity.[39] For Sexton, the radicality of Afro-pessimism lies in its rejoinder that slavery is the matrix of oppression that induced the formation of the modern racial paradigm and its accompanying structures of domination. Building on Frantz Fanon's terminology, Sexton describes Black existence as arising out of the "metaphysical holocaust" of the Middle Passage.[40] Anti-Blackness forms an "unconscious cultural structure, a grammar, a *weltanschauung*, a metaphysics that lives on well after, and despite, the destruction of metaphysics."[41] For Afro-pessimists, the Black slave marks the abject location of that which is not.

Blackness is construed as beneath being, as an anti-ontological position. Philosopher Calvin Warren has dubbed this position *ontological terror*. The modern category of the human, he maintains, is fundamentally tied to its negation in the figure of the slave, whose ontological status is always under this horrifying erasure. White supremacy owns being and terrorizes all that threatens its proprietary rights. Blacks are depicted as nonbeings while also threatening the claim over being made by white supremacy. "Black Lives Matter," Warren comments, seemingly assumes an ontological ground for the Black person, only to then expose the terror that such a person might, after all, not be a human *being*.[42] Anti-Black hatred is ambiguously projected onto something construed as nothing: "What is hated about blacks is this nothing, the ontological terror. . . . Every lynching, castration, rape, shooting, and murder of blacks is an engagement with this nothing and the fantasy that nothing can be dominated once and for all."[43]

Warren's Afro-pessimism therefore rejects any "politics of hope" that insists on accommodating Blackness in the structures of racist ontologies. The political deployment of hope "depends on the incessant (re)production and proliferation of problems to justify its existence."[44] In this reading the diagnosis of present misery necessitates the discourse of future solutions, forming a vicious cycle that entraps all of us in continuing suffering. More to the point of Warren's critique, the politics of hope is a facade that obfuscates anti-Black violence. Warren says that to sustain their hopes for the future, political theologians and Black optimists must "avoid the immediacy of black suffering."[45] Warren's own recipe is Black nihilism, which "hopes" for the end of political hope. This is an attempt to reconfigure the politics of hope as a task proper to a Black nihilistic hermeneutic.[46]

Writing as a political theologian, Vincent Lloyd takes the claims of Afro-pessimism seriously while flipping the question of hope to interrogate the possibility and the conditions for whites to hope. Lloyd argues that hope is often a function of the status quo and, more specifically, a tool for the maintenance of white supremacy.[47] He intimates that it takes a great deal of despair to abandon the hope of whiteness. To hope against hope, in fact, is for whites to renounce privilege and dive into a "despairing hope, a hope for hopelessness."[48] With time, Lloyd indicates, this may engender the possibility of hope, if properly accompanied by a communal effort. This community, however, cannot belong to the present. Lloyd calls it an eschatological community, and, as such, it points to a postracial mode of sociability that we cannot foresee in the present. For Lloyd, the "post" of a postracial community is tainted by its impossibility in the present. And yet his gesture toward the impossibility of an eschatological community summons ethical dispositions that may usher in something that may escape the hold of white supremacy. As Lloyd envisions it, the community that stands on the edge of the sublimation of racism still can make a claim on the present.

In the work of religious studies scholar Joseph Winters, this mode of future-talk gains the contours of a melancholic hope.[49] Against the backdrop of political discourses that suggest that the United States has reached its postracial phase with Barack Obama's election in 2008, Winters inflects his future-talk with a more somber tone. Winters shows that the rhetoric of progress functions as a buffer against loss and tragedy.[50] Black literature and, more broadly, Black experience resist narratives of progress by speaking of hope with attention to "melancholy, loss, and a recalcitrant sense of tragedy."[51]

Melancholic hope does not capitulate to despair while rejecting hope as a whitewashing mechanism. Winters builds on responses to Sigmund Freud's theorizations to argue that melancholy is not just a mourning process gone rogue.[52] Rather, melancholia "signifies the remains and leftovers from past experience and loss."[53] For Winters, this remainder is the stuff of melancholic hope: "By imagining and relating to the past as congeries of remainders and fragments, we refuse the tendency of progress to integrate past events, ideas, and possibilities into a coherent, status quo-affirming framework."[54] The future is not a point at the end of a timeline nor a time that depicts past oppression as part of a great narrative arc. Rather, the future is here approached as an ambiguous, opaque reality that mourns over the calamities of history, particularly the tragedy of Black life in the American context. As we melancholically contemplate this past, its remainders inform the formation of something akin to hope.

Winters grounds his future-talk in the cadences and dissonances of Black music. The Black musical tradition formed in slave plantations "inculcate[s] dissonant memories and feelings while articulating desires for liberation." The hope sung in these melancholic tunes offers hope as critique and resistance "intertwined with vulnerability, sensitivity to the agony of others, and memory of past suffering."[55] In the musical amalgamation of mourning and hope, "dislocated black bodies become grievable, worthy of lament, compassion, and remembrance."[56] This musical sensibility imparts a historical awareness: progress must always be confronted by its underside. That is, historical progress "necessarily involves and generates conditions that are typically imagined as incompatible with progress—loss, suffering, disappointment, and death—even as these inescapable realities must be downplayed for progress to be a desirable concept and ideal."[57] For Winters, the melancholia engendered by the sedimentation of past suffering cannot offer assurances for the tragic nature of reality. It does offer, nevertheless, a way into this tragedy.

Black fragmented memories drape Winters's sense of hope. The tone of this mode of future-talk assembles these tragic historical fragments not in pursuit of a neat narrative nor to offer assurance of what the future may bring. Like its past, Black futurity is mournful, melancholic, vulnerable, tragic. Like its past, hope draped in black is fragmented. But, like its past, Black futurity remains. It makes a claim on the present while pulling toward some opening, like a cut in jazz. This cut, both a "wound and an opening," is for Winters the ethical and creative possibility that might enable a more "generous and promising world."[58] It is a despairing hope, longing for something irretrievable from the past and yet something that Black experience cannot avoid summoning.

The tradition of Latin American liberation theology showcased a similar appreciation for a form of future-talk that rises in protest against past and present oppression. Gustavo Gutiérrez's foundational *A Theology of Liberation* depicted the Christian eschatological imagination as embedded in the historical struggle for liberation.[59] My retrieval of both Franz Hinkelammert's and Rubem Alves's theological work demonstrates the liberationist commitment in treating future-talk in the midst of struggle. By extending the tradition to the context of financialization, I modulated this driving eschatological motif to our contemporary economic predicament. Winters's work and the radical tradition of Black thought are crucial because they do not gloss over the effects of white supremacy and its comfortable place in the language of hope.

It is possible that some will perceive that this stance still holds on to too much and that this holding is a symptom of a neglect of Warren's notion of ontological terror. Admittedly, hope shall remain interrupted in the Afropessimistic position. The gesture I make in the direction of hope is not an attempt to avoid the terror of the Middle Passage nor to safeguard hope as a mechanism that glosses over the calamity of Black existence and the depths of white supremacy. By following Winters's account of hope closely, I seek both to acknowledge the magnitude of the oppressive apparatus that continues to terrorize Black people into breathlessness and to name a certain disposition toward hope. This disposition is framed as an escape from a stifling present.

Summoning the energies of this escape is a known tactic in the resistance to financial capital. Already in 1854 the fugitive slave John Brown noticed the proximity between movements in financial markets and the exploitation of slave labor. He observed that cotton was the prime commodity produced in the southern states and that variations in its price in English markets were imprinted on the slave body: "When the price rises in the English market," Brown stated, "the poor slaves immediately feel the effects, for they are harder driven, and the whip is kept more constantly going."[60] Recent scholarship has indeed pointed to the irreducible connection between chattel slavery and the rise of the modern financial system. For sociologist Matthew Desmond, a contributor to the *New York Times* 1619 Project, chattel slavery was entirely financed by the London money market and secured the central position that London bankers would have in an emerging global economy. "Years after abolishing the African slave trade in 1807, Britain, and much of Europe along with it, was bankrolling slavery in the United States."[61] For the runaway Brown, the whip on the slave's back is the underside of the rise of the modern financial system.

Runaways escaping slavery were also escaping the hold of a financial system growing its roots on the backs of slave labor. In financialized capitalism, financial mechanisms similarly entrap people in a cycle of debt while racializing the Black body as forever indebted to society. Financialized capitalism extends its oppressive arms in the constitution of indebted subjects, whose futures are held captive by the owners of the means of prediction.

Fugitive hope situates the escape I envision from the hold of financialized capitalism. This echoes theologian Keri Day's call for a "radical hope" as she develops a womanist critique of neoliberalism.[62] In Black feminism and womanist thought, Day shows how hope is introduced as a *social practice* that takes place in the ordinary movements and experiences of Black women struggling to survive.[63] For Day, future-talk neither projects perfection nor demands closure. It rather enacts alternative forms of subjectivity and community that transcend the "hegemony of the visible."[64] As a social practice, radical hope is constituted through eco-social assemblages that bring together past suffering and engender a social commitment to resist hegemonic forces and their grip on the present. It does so, quite often, by summoning a reality yet unseen.

Radical hope steps away from simple optimism and the easy assurance that things will be all right. On the contrary, hope in this guise is a refusal to accept reality on the terms offered by the status quo. Day submits, "[Hope] is more of an existential stance imbued with new meaning, along with more just structural-social practices, than wishful thinking or calculable guesses that mark optimistic thinking."[65] Enfleshed in the real pain, the concrete struggle, and the subversive joy of Black women, Day's radical hope occupies the hegemonic forces of the visible with hope-producing movements that create a way out of no way.[66]

A social disposition toward hope thus engenders the displacement necessary for resisting financialization. In the spirit of womanist thought, we may picture fugitive futurity as a hush harbor, the spot in space and the temporal interval in which the escape takes place to interrupt the hegemony of the now.[67] It is the clearing one makes in the middle of the forest, which opens up a different time-space. In this scene futurity is not a time ahead of us or something one predicts. Rather, the future is more fundamentally a crevice in temporal hegemonic regimes. It allows us to sidestep timelines and summon something into becoming. Future-talk always puts us in some different place and time.

The insistence on the language of hope speaks to a spirit of struggle that persists and insists that there is a way out of calamity, even if that way needs to be created. Like Winters's melancholic hope, my motion in the direction of hope is fragile, mournful, and tentative. But it is also quite stubborn. The hope I embrace persists; it keeps coming back, haunting me forward. In the motion of this future-bound movement, I plot hope as an escape tactic. It is the improvised stance of someone who must move (away) because the present is not a place one can justly inhabit.

Fugitive Futures

Melancholic hope exposes the impossibility of separating hope and despair, optimism and pessimism. For Fred Moten, these are terms that point to a single image—the calamity of Black life. But hope and despair do figure differently, and they represent different responses to such experience. In Moten's work fugitivity is the name for a certain escape from reality that cannot properly be thought of as escapism or denialism. For an eschatology of liberation, future-talk would be the escape tactic to circumvent reality, to slip through its hold and course different paths. The fugitive runs (away) from the present toward an indeterminate time-space. Such an escape is the maneuver around and beyond the ironclad hold of the present, an escape route that may unveil the encounter with a future that, like the runaway, gets away from the grip of the present. I refer to this as *fugitive futurity*. Future-talk conspires escape routes in the interval we make when saying that the future is not—yet. I approach this interval as the breathing room for the fugitive conspiracy that plots the collapse of the imperial city.

The difference—not the separation—between Afro-pessimism and Moten's position lies in what is perceived as the condition of possibility of Black thought. In the pessimistic register, nothingness. For optimists, celebration. Moten contends that Blackness is not "relative nothingness," as Afro-pessimists like Warren hold. Rather, there "is" something that can be excavated as Blackness, a something that is utterly common and improper, an "anoriginal dispossession" that nevertheless summons a response. Its subterranean existence is what Moten and his colleague in Black study, Stefano Harney, call the undercommons.[68] Along with Harney, Moten adopts the concept of the "prophetic" precisely in its relation to the future—this need and this commitment to "get there." Prophecy, they claim, is a way of being "in two places at the same time, but also to be able to be two times in the same place." The prophet cannot embrace the now, for their senses are always already doubled. The prophet tells the "brutal truth" while also "see[ing] the other way, to see what could be."[69] The sight over the other way and the need of occupying multiple time-spaces put the prophet forever on the run. The prophet is, in a word, engaged in fugitive planning.

Fugitivity exists as the movement of flight of bodies and things from all that is properly housed. Moten suggests that fugitivity is a "desire for and a spirit of escape and transgression of the proper and the proposed. It's a desire for the outside, for a playing or being outside."[70] Black existence comes about in the escape from the house of being, which can host Blackness only in its underground. The undercommons is a space that can be discerned in "the strangely known moment, the gathering content, of a cadence, and the uncanny that one can sense in cooperation, the secret once called solidarity."[71] In the secrecy of the gathering, Blackness can summon something into existence by plotting the escape.

In fugitive planning, the runaway does not set their course toward the destination because such a thing cannot exist apart from the fugitive act itself. The escape is not about achievement, not even the achievement of freedom. "If there is such a thing as freedom whatever it is is much more accurately denoted, precisely because it is emphatically deferred/displaced/deconstructed, by the term/activity of escape."[72] For Moten, Black optimism is the runaway hope of the fugitive. It lacks a telos, but it remains always on the edge of running. Escape here is a tactic to hijack the hold of the present.

For our time, this maneuver is pivotal as an act of displacement that eludes the hold of financialization on our lives. The grip of financialized capitalism on the present is strong, disguised under projections of profitable futures. The hegemonic forces of financialization speak with impunity about projecting, predicting, and anticipating a future time in their incessant pursuit of profit. The urgency of profit making consumes future possibilities along with our hopes and expectations. Financialized capitalism profits from its future predictions, but it entraps us in the iron casing of a present of debt and anxiety. As subjects made in the image of the futures of finance, we are bound to the promise of future repayment, to offering guarantees that our debts shall be repaid, that we shall be in the future as we are expected to be. By colonizing the future, finance captures the means of engendering hope. Our imaginations stifled, we succumb to the promises of future wealth and are subjected to the forces of financialization.

The edges of our senses of time, I have argued, are set by the hedges of financial discourse. And yet is not the future precisely that which escapes the most accurate system of predictions? The future runs away, escaping the most meticulous attempt at predicting and managing it. The time that is not—yet remains the indeterminate time that shall forever frustrate the hopes of financialized capitalism. In this necessary pause, I have been locating the force of a liberating future-talk that summons a different reality. That which financialization seeks to control for the sake of profit continues to escape. It escapes because the future is indeed the ultimate fugitive. What I have named as fugitive futurity speaks to this future-bound escape. It is a symptom of a present time that suffocates us under the dictum that there is no alternative to the status quo. We desire to escape, to create passages—underground if necessary—to a future that we cannot imagine yet but that summons us. And so the plot of an eschatology of liberation is to gather forces in taking over the means of production of future-talk.

The eschatology of liberation that this book summons bases its hope on the fugitive character of the future. Hope, the mode of future-talk that is conjured by the liberationist sense of eschatology, may be after all the energy that interrupts the inexorable force of the futures produced by financial discourse. Hoping against the futures that trade in financial markets might be the best way to occupy the means of prediction engendered and enforced by financial discourse.

Liberation theology confronts capitalist exploitation and the futurity of financialization, insisting that the present is not exhausted by the presence of injustice. In its liberating sense, future-talk is a mode of address that occupies the present with a sensory disposition toward justice.[73] The senses that liberating future-talk makes maneuver around injustice, creating crevices in the fabric of the present that allow us to move in different directions. Liberative hope gathers the sighs of oppressions and parasitizes the hold of financialization on our senses of time. The persistence of hope in a financialized world that colonizes future-talk strikes me as a symptom of the ways that the future escapes the control of financial discourse. But also as the creative, emancipatory force of communities that summon the future as a necessary component of their resistance to financialized capitalism.

The runaway faces the present from its edges. Every moment carries with it the weight of injustice, but such a weight takes the fugitive to the edges of time, where a twist in the plot is possible and imminent. The fugitive is fully aware of the painful and oppressive reality of the hold. But the pressure pushes the runaway into an undercommons where the escape is plotted. Fugitivity meets the awesome force of the present with a cut, a break, and then the escape. Every single gesture is policed to shackle the fugitive in the hold. But the fugitive escapes, precisely. Present captivity weighs on the runaway, but the runaway furiously runs, twists, and curls into the escape.[74]

A fugitive eschaton is the escape route of the maroons, the escape from the circumscribed territory of the present into the territory known as the undercommons. It is uncharted territory, unknown to the fugitive, who must nevertheless clear a path in its direction. The practice of escaping toward nonachievable freedom is what constitutes fugitive futurity. Moten takes us there, to the edges of fugitive planning: "Freedom is a practice—a fugitive act—of its own (un)making, a structure that is the very apotheosis of the terribly redoubled double edge."[75] We run (away) toward the edge by way of "disorganization" of the "end point, of, more emphatically, the end or the idea of the end."[76] It is appropriate to situate Moten's conceptualization of freedom as a fugitive act along the counter-apocalyptic spirit I have tried to tease out from Keller's work. In inhabiting the edges of the alpha-omega continuum, one might indeed disorganize the end point and let go of the quest for ends. The *eschatos*, after all, is not a telos. A fugitive hope will release the pursuit of the end while remaining steadfast along the edges of the plot for liberation.

The gesture toward the future carves out entryways into hidden paths, covered over by a mounting debris of pain and injustice. In the debris the fugitive finds a crevice into the undercommons, the coalition of bodies and energies that commune in the undergrounds of imperial commerce to plot the escape. The city must fall, they say.

Fallen is Babylon the great, we might say in the secret gatherings of fugitive futurity. As Keller plotted, whenever we encounter apocalypse, we run into a now and then. Our present is inflected by the many tongues that speak of a time to-come. The future announced by the book standing along the edges of the canon indeed makes multiple senses. Revelation escapes the definitive outcome, the homogeneity of meaning, the synchrony of the single time—present or otherwise. Apocalypse unveils, among several things, that time is unfolding, that time is out of line.[77] It might be the case that apocalypse invites us to overhear the stifled voices murmuring of a future that is not just to-come but that makes things become. The vocation of fugitive hope is to summon a just unknown. It calls on absences and quickens them into becoming.

John's apocalypse unveils the plot for the collapse of imperial commerce. Babylon and its economy are fallen. When? Apocalypse cannot tell, for the time-space disclosed by this fugitive future digresses into a summons: Babylon must fall. Keller holds that the prophetic force of apocalypse is its capacity to "dreamread" our own context. The prophet who utters a word about the future cannot possibly speak factually. Predictions cannot coexist with the future-talk of the prophecy because the prophet speaks of "unrealized possibilities" that have this "dreamlike quality."[78] The fall of Babylon is one such dream that jumbles our imagination when we confront the empire of finance. Babylon, in its financialized iteration, must fall. Whether it will is beside the point. That it must is the point that we run with.

A fugitive eschatology, modulated by the spirit of counter-apocalypse, discloses escape routes, detours that circumvent the stranglehold of the present. While the inexorable force of financialization hedges on our futures, the hope of fugitives runs to the edges to twist the plot of the economy of the imperial city. In this register future-talk is a maneuver out of a reality that devours the very possibility of a future. Of any future. The escape does not run away from the present, but it runs away so that a present can take place, more justly. Fugitivity happens precisely because the present cannot address the demands of justice, because one needs more time. We need more time.

This book has tracked the futures traded in financial markets and how they engender our collective futures, subjecting us to their promises of future wealth. And yet future-talk continues to offer multiple senses. It exceeds the future-predicting aspirations of financialized capitalism. Hoping against the futures of financial discourse is a symptom of the abject conditions of life under financialization. It signals that hope is not exhausted by the capitalist colonial ventures into the future. There is cause for hope because there is a material need for hope. On the edges of the capitalist control over the means of prediction there remains the cut, the break, the bleak hope of an escape route.

No, we cannot escape the future, for it escapes us first. The future, forever deferred, forever coming and departing, is the everlasting fugitive. Such a time cannot be escaped, but in its name we escape as we fail to accommodate to the iron cage of the present. This fugitive future escapes us, escapes our grasp, escapes our predictions, runs away from our most endearing hope. But in our escape routes, we may ourselves be conjured by hope. For it is the future itself that is unveiled before us in our fugitive routes. The future: the time that is not. Yet. The future, the fugitive, impossibly captive, forever captivating.

CHAPTER SIX

NOTES

INTRODUCTION

1 Augustine, *Confessions*, 243. Catherine Keller is a contemporary voice that has seriously "minded" the fact that the future is not *yet* while not disavowing the importance of engaging in forms of future-talk. See Keller, *Facing Apocalypse*, 195.
2 For the expression "breathing room," see Keller, *Apocalypse Now and Then*, ix.
3 My use of *conjure* in this book is informed by Jacques Derrida in *Specters of Marx*, 40–48.
4 Keller, *Apocalypse Now and Then*, x.
5 Derrida, "Of an Apocalyptic Tone," 68.
6 Keller, *Apocalypse Now and Then*, xi.
7 Wariboko, *Split Economy*, 13–14.
8 Fabozzi and Modigliani, *Capital Markets*, 189.
9 Esposito, *Future of Futures*, 4.
10 Drake and Fabozzi, *Basics of Finance*, 1.
11 Drake and Fabozzi, *Basics of Finance*, 1.
12 See, for example, Schwartz, "Recovery Threw."
13 US Department of Treasury, "Financial Crisis Response."
14 For data on losses experienced by retirement funds, see VanDerhei, "Impact"; Wolman and Colamosca, *Great 401(k) Hoax*; and CBS News, "Retirement Dreams Disappear." For a theological commentary on this dynamic, see Rieger, *No Rising Tide*, 38–39.
15 Lapavitsas, *Profiting without Producing*, xv–xvii, 288–305. For a global perspective on the crisis, see Lysandrou, "Global Inequality."

16 Hardoon, "Economy for the 99%."

17 Coffey et al., "Time to Care."

18 Hardoon, Ayele, and Fuentes-Nieva, "Economy for the 1%"; and Oxfam International, "62 People Own."

19 Harvey, *Brief History of Neoliberalism*, 178–79; and Harvey, *Companion to Marx's "Capital,"* 310–13.

20 Marazzi, *Violence of Financial Capitalism*, 39.

21 Ascher, *Portfolio Society*.

22 McClanahan, *Dead Pledges*, 9–10.

23 Kantor, "Working Anything but 9 to 5."

24 See, for example, Krippner, *Capitalizing on Crisis*.

25 The term is first mentioned by economist Milton Friedman in a 1951 paper where he attacks forms of "collectivism" and tracks the emergence of a new "faith." Neoliberalism, he avers, "would accept the nineteenth century liberal emphasis on the fundamental importance of the individual" and envision market competition as the means to freedom. Friedman speculates, "The state would police the system, establish conditions favorable to competition and prevent monopoly, provide a stable monetary framework, and relieve acute misery and distress. The citizens would be protected against the state by the existence of a free private market; and against one another by the preservation of competition." See M. Friedman, "Neo-liberalism and Its Prospects."

26 The expression "a rising tide will lift all boats" was famously articulated by President John F. Kennedy, and I return to it in chapter 4. For a critique of this image and its detrimental impact on the economy, see Rieger, *No Rising Tide*. For further historical and critical commentary on neoliberalism, see Harvey, *Brief History of Neoliberalism*; and Cahill and Konings, *Neoliberalism*.

27 Duménil and Lévy, *Capital Resurgent*, 110.

28 Giddens, *Runaway World*, 22, 24.

29 Kotsko, *Neoliberalism's Demons*, 122.

30 Graeber, *Debt*, 382.

31 Rieger, *No Rising Tide*, 60–61.

32 Tanner, *Christianity*, 28.

33 Tanner, *Christianity*, 136.

34 See Tanner, *Christianity*, 30–31. For Tanner, this is where one must locate the critical role of Christian theology. While financialized capitalism confines subjects to a present that can only replicate the past, and to futures that can only conserve the status quo, Tanner calls Christian theologians to "think the break itself," that is, to tap into Christianity's own easiness with disruptions, much like the discontinuity all Christians are called to perform in the act of conversion.

35 Goodchild, *Theology of Money*, xiv; see also Goodchild, "Exposing Mammon," 54.

36 Goodchild, *Theology of Money*, 105–6.

37 Goodchild, *Theology of Money*, 56.

38 Goodchild, *Theology of Money*, 54.

39 Gutiérrez, *Las Casas*.

40 Las Casas, *Historia de las Indias*, 469. Translations from all titles not in English are mine.

41 See Piketty, *Capital in the Twenty-First Century*, 377.

42 See Hinkelammert, *Ideological Weapons of Death*; Hinkelammert and Assmann, *A idolatria do mercado*; and Hinkelammert, *Teología del mercado total*. More recently, Eugene McCarraher has insightfully investigated the history of this mode of capitalist enchantment, thus challenging the Weberian hypothesis that capitalism is a secularized and disenchanted worldview. See McCarraher, *Enchantments of Mammon*.

43 See Alves, *Transparencies of Eternity*, 58.

44 Gutiérrez, *Theology of Liberation*, 3–15.

45 As I later describe, Alves's editor suggested the change in title so that the book would speak to the market's positive reaction to Jürgen Moltmann's *Theology of Hope*.

46 Gutiérrez, "Lenguaje teológico," 160.

47 This is especially developed in Rieger's writings on class and religion. See Rieger, "Why Class Matters"; and Rieger and Henkel-Rieger, *Unified We Are a Force*.

48 M. Taylor, *Erring*, 150.

49 M. Taylor, *Erring*, 155.

50 M. Taylor, *Erring*, 156–57.

51 Edelman, *No Future*, 2.

52 Edelman, *No Future*, 11.

53 Edelman, *No Future*, 30.

54 Berlant, *Cruel Optimism*, 1. At face value, Berlant's concept could be portrayed as another instance of the disavowal of future-talk. Their project, however, is focused on the present and the affective dimensions of optimism. One of the central arguments of *Cruel Optimism* is that "the present is perceived, first, affectively" (4). My approach to futurity is amenable to the thought that the future, too, is perceived affectively.

55 Pinn, "Theology after Hope," 27.

56 Pinn, "Theology after Hope," 28.

57 Pinn, "Theology after Hope," 41.

58 De La Torre, *Embracing Hopelessness*, 4–5.

59 De La Torre, *Embracing Hopelessness*, 5.

60 De La Torre, *Embracing Hopelessness*, 52.

61 De La Torre, *Embracing Hopelessness*, 48. Understandably, De La Torre's attacks are often directed at Moltmann, whom he frames as a "Christian determinist" who tried to "convince us that an eschatological hope rooted in salvation history is the only way to interpret reality." For De La Torre, Moltmann's theology offers nothing but unfounded optimism based on Eurocentric readings of history as a linear and progressive process. His theology of hope proves comforting only for "middle-class Euroamerican Christians."

But the "present age has too much oppression to be distracted by visions of kingdoms not yet seen." De La Torre, *Embracing Hopelessness*, 24, 52, 139.

62 De La Torre, *Embracing Hopelessness*, 139.

63 Throughout this book I endorse Keller's warning against the dangers of the denial of future-talk: "Succumbing to a reasonable hopelessness, a critical plausible nihilism, we become one—in effect—with reactionary denialism." Keller, *Political Theology of the Earth*, 123.

64 Keller, *Apocalypse Now and Then*, 276. "So I do not abandon apocalypse. I have argued that our history cannot delete it without committing it." Keller's sentence makes a veiled reference to Karl Marx, who stated that one "cannot transcend [*aufheben*] philosophy without realizing [*verwirklichen*] it." See Marx, "Contribution to the Critique," 250. For Keller's more recent discussion about the possibilities "disclosed" by apocalypse, see Keller, *Facing Apocalypse*.

65 Muñoz, *Cruising Utopia*, 22.

66 Muñoz, *Cruising Utopia*, 1.

67 Muñoz, *Cruising Utopia*, 27.

68 Muñoz, *Cruising Utopia*, 32.

69 Muñoz, *Cruising Utopia*, 12.

70 Betcher, *Spirit*.

71 Betcher, *Spirit*, 33–34.

72 Betcher, *Spirit*, 62.

73 Betcher, *Spirit*, 37.

74 Betcher, *Spirit*, 66.

75 Betcher, *Spirit*, 171; see also 195.

76 Betcher, *Spirit*, 171.

77 Betcher, *Spirit*, 197.

78 Betcher, *Spirit*, 4.

79 Betcher, *Spirit*, 204.

80 Betcher, *Spirit*, 199.

81 Rambo, *Spirit and Trauma*, 6.

82 Rambo, *Spirit and Trauma*, 146–47.

83 Rambo, *Resurrecting Wounds*.

84 Rambo, *Spirit and Trauma*, 156.

85 Rambo, *Spirit and Trauma*, 158.

86 Rambo, *Spirit and Trauma*, 168.

87 Betcher, *Spirit*, 42–43.

88 Muñoz, *Cruising Utopia*, 185.

89 See Puleo, *Struggle Is One*, 190.

ONE. FUTURES DEVOURED

1 Piketty's work has triggered a number of controversies within the field of economics. I certainly lack the competence to enter into this feud, especially as it relates to the specificities of Piketty's economic analysis. I have, nevertheless,

benefited greatly from the response Piketty's book has received from scholars in Marxist studies. They have pointed out, for instance, that Piketty naively assumes the principle of "structural growth" as the necessary component of economic justice without properly questioning the social and ecological implications of such growth. Marxists have also pointed out that Piketty fails to provide a robust analysis of the social implications and dynamics of *capital*, a term he uses rather uncritically, if not shallowly. For more on this debate, see Varoufakis, "Egalitarianism's Latest Foe"; and Harvey, "Afterthoughts on Piketty's Capital."

2   Piketty, *Capital in the Twenty-First Century*, 227–30.

3   Piketty, *Capital in the Twenty-First Century*, 377.

4   Kantor, "Working Anything but 9 to 5."

5   See Froud et al., *Financialization and Strategy*; Borghi, Sarti, and Cintra, "'Financialized' Structure of Automobile Corporations"; and Do Carmo, Sacomano Neto, and Donadone, "Financialization in the Automotive Industry."

6   Foster, "Age of Monopoly-Finance Capital," 9.

7   Marazzi, *Violence of Financial Capitalism*, 28.

8   In chapter 3 I return to Karl Marx to argue that the capitalist mode of production, as portrayed by Marx, systematically consumes the lives and futures of workers. I show that the passage to financialized capitalism does not abandon, but only accentuates, this tendency toward the devouring of future possibilities.

9   Galbraith, *Great Crash, 1929*.

10 Bell, *Cultural Contradictions of Capitalism*.

11 For a detailed discussion of this transition, see Harvey, *Brief History of Neoliberalism*.

12 Krippner, *Capitalizing on Crisis*, 139.

13 Krippner, *Capitalizing on Crisis*, 140–42.

14 Joseph, *Debt to Society*, 93.

15 The argument of the economists of the *Monthly Review* echoes Marx's claims about the declining rate of profit, a tendency he identifies as inherent to capitalism and associates with improvement in the "social productivity of labor." See Marx, *Capital III*, 319. For a further analysis of the relation between Marx's hypothesis of the falling rate of profit and Magdoff and Sweezy's theory of stagnation, see Lapavitsas, *Profiting without Producing*, 16–17. For a more in-depth analysis of the theory of the falling rate of profit and its ties to the surplus absorption problem, see Duménil and Lévy, *Capital Resurgent*, chap. 3.

16 Magdoff and Sweezy, *Stagnation and the Financial Explosion*, 145.

17 Baran and Sweezy, *Monopoly Capital*; and Magdoff and Sweezy, "Merger Movement."

18 Baran and Sweezy, *Monopoly Capital*, 72.

19 For a detailed account of this process, see Harvey, *Enigma of Capital*.

20 Lapavitsas, *Profiting without Producing*, 17.

21 For a detailed chronicle of the historical context for the economic shifts described in this section, see LiPuma and Lee, *Financial Derivatives*, chap. 3.

22 Graeber, *Debt*, 2; and Harvey, *Enigma of Capital*, 28.

23 Foster, "Age of Monopoly-Finance Capital," 11.

24 Magdoff and Sweezy, *Stagnation and the Financial Explosion*, 146.

25 Magdoff, "Problems of U.S. Capitalism," 14. Magdoff gives numbers to flesh out this scenario: "During the ten years prior to 1957, state and local governments added on average a little over $3 billion a year to their total debt load. Since 1957 these government units have been adding close to $6 billion a year. . . . The net debt owned by private individuals and institutions . . . increased on average $32 billion a year during the ten years prior to 1957. Since 1957 the average annual increase has been 50 percent higher—close to $48 billion a year."

26 Magdoff and Sweezy, *Stagnation and the Financial Explosion*, 15.

27 Amadeo, "National Debt by Year." See also Foster, "Age of Monopoly-Finance Capital," 4–5: "In the 1970s, the increase in U.S. GDP was about sixty cents for every new dollar of debt. By the early 2000s, this had declined to about 20 cents for every new dollar of debt."

28 Marte, "U.S. Household Debt Increased by $1 Trillion in 2021."

29 Magdoff and Sweezy, *Stagnation and the Financial Explosion*, 147. A further problem addressed by these authors is the coexistence of a stagnant productive sector with a robust expansion in the financial sector. The problem is accentuated by the assumption, fitting for Marxist analyses, that finance indeed does not add value to the economy. Finance, in short, belongs to the realm of *circulation*, whereas value can be formed only in the sphere of production. Magdoff and Sweezy presciently maintain that this tension between stagnant industry and robust financial growth can exist for long periods of time (as it actually did), but they point out that this tension is not perceived because of the ideological dimension of capitalist economics: "[The] underlying attitudes of the capitalist class . . . are dominated by a set of expectations deeply rooted in the history of the capitalist system. Capitalist ideology takes for granted that the *normal* state of the economy is prosperity based on vigorous growth." Magdoff and Sweezy, *Stagnation and the Financial Explosion*, 104. See also Krippner, *Capitalizing on Crisis*, 12–13.

30 Lapavitsas, *Profiting without Producing*, 2.

31 Lapavitsas, *Profiting without Producing*, 240; see also 39, 70.

32 See Martin, *Financialization of Daily Life*.

33 Adkins, *Time of Money*, 4.

34 Marazzi, *Violence of Financial Capitalism*, 34.

35 Allon, "Speculating on Everyday Life," 368.

36 For more on the work of the group, see their edited volume: Lee and Martin, *Derivatives and the Wealth of Societies*.

NOTES TO CHAPTER ONE

37 Vogl, *Specter of Capital*, 62–63. For Friedman's paper, along with Melamed's reflections on its inception and impact, see Melamed, "Milton Friedman's 1971 Feasibility Paper."

38 M. Friedman, "Need for Futures Markets," 638. This citation is of a reprint of Friedman's 1971 essay, originally prepared for the Chicago Mercantile Exchange.

39 Arnoldi, "Derivatives," 25.

40 Lapavitsas, *Profiting without Producing*, 6.

41 Drake and Fabozzi, *Basics of Finance*, 350.

42 Drake and Fabozzi, *Basics of Finance*, 350–51.

43 For more on the connection between futures and food production, see Westhoff, *Economics of Food*. I thank Norbert Wilson for a serendipitous conversation over a Thanksgiving meal for calling my attention to the agricultural origins of futures markets.

44 See Arnoldi, "Derivatives," 26.

45 Arnoldi, "Derivatives," 27. By 2011 derivative contracts accounted for about $700 trillion in the global economy. For the sake of comparison, in 2000 the world's entire GDP amounted to approximately $147 trillion, whereas the combined value of the derivatives traded in the first quarter of 2003 was $197 trillion. See Lapavitsas, *Profiting without Producing*, 6. See also MacKenzie, *Engine, Not a Camera*, 5; and Arnoldi, "Derivatives," 28. For a fuller argument about this staggering growth in derivatives, see Hunt and Kennedy, *Financial Derivatives*.

46 Arnoldi, "Derivatives," 32–33 (emphasis in the original). For a detailed study of the "epistemology" of financial innovations, see Martin, *Knowledge LTD*.

47 For further explanation of the technical aspects of the Black-Scholes model, see LiPuma and Lee, *Financial Derivatives*, 78–83; and Ayache, *Blank Swan*, 65–70.

48 Lee, introduction, 6.

49 Ayache, "On Black-Scholes," 243.

50 Ayache, *Blank Swan*, 167.

51 See Callon, *Laws of the Markets*; MacKenzie, Muniesa, and Siu, *Do Economists Make Markets?*; MacKenzie, *Material Markets*; and Lee, "From Primitives to Derivatives." For a summary list of this body of literature, see MacKenzie and Hardie, "Assembling an Economic Actor," 58–60.

52 Owing to its capacity to shape social relations, cultural anthropologists have maintained that derivative trading is analogous to the category of the gift as famously studied by Marcel Mauss in *The Gift*. Similar to financial instruments, rituals of gift giving rely on the interval between the gift and its reciprocating act while hedging on the social volatility that the ritual seeks to mitigate. As Benjamin Lee states, derivatives and gifts "share the volatilities and uncertainties of social life and transform them into manageable risks by equating things that are different." Derivatives exist because they are capable of measuring the value of an underlying asset by "analogically equating their

present and future volatilities." Notice that what is valued in derivatives is therefore *not* the value of a commodity but the value of its volatility. Like the temporal gap between the gift and the social obligation of a countergift, derivatives function in the time between changes in value of a given commodity. See Lee, introduction, 2.

53 Appadurai, "Wealth of Dividuals," 23.

54 LiPuma, *Social Life of Financial Derivatives*, 28.

55 For more on this process, see MacKenzie, *Material Markets*, 68–69.

56 Lee, "Deriving the Derivative," 245; see also MacKenzie, *Engine, Not a Camera*.

57 MacKenzie, *Material Markets*, 64–65.

58 Vogl, *Specter of Capital*, 114.

59 Drake and Fabozzi, *Basics of Finance*, 1.

60 See Lee, "From Primitives to Derivatives."

61 Knight, *Risk, Uncertainty and Profit*, esp. chap. 8. As a theoretical economist, Knight engages in an imaginary effort to picture a society where perfect knowledge exists. The introduction of the element of uncertainty in this context, he wagers, gives shape to a true "enterprise organization" that is constantly pursuing knowledge of the future. Uncertainty is what generates a market economy as we know it. See Knight, *Risk, Uncertainty and Profit*, chap. 9.

62 Knight, *Risk, Uncertainty and Profit*, 311.

63 Black, "Noise," 530. Social ethicist Nimi Wariboko has termed this financial paradox a "crack" in the economy itself. For him, "finance is the symbol of the separation" between the "real" economy and financial speculation. This economic chasm is what makes finance possible. The struggle between Main Street and Wall Street is for Wariboko the struggle of the economy itself. See Wariboko, *Economics in Spirit and Truth*, 21–28.

64 Konings, *Capital and Time*, 22–23.

65 Konings, *Capital and Time*, 29.

66 Konings, *Capital and Time*, 67.

67 Konings, *Capital and Time*, 67.

68 Konings, *Capital and Time*, 30.

69 Konings, *Capital and Time*, 103–4.

70 Konings, *Capital and Time*, 104.

71 Appadurai, "Ghost in the Financial Machine," 525; see also Appadurai, *Banking on Words*.

72 See Lee, "From Primitives to Derivatives," 103–5.

73 See Weber, *Protestant Ethic* (2010)

74 Appadurai, "Ghost in the Financial Machine," 532. Appadurai further observes that Knight, the theorist of economic risk and uncertainty, was fascinated by Weber's hypothesis and captivated by ethical questions related to how financial markets deal with the uncertainty of the future. For Knight, uncertainty cannot be suspended by economic calculations, much as the state

of one's election cannot be discerned by mortals. Appadurai, "Ghost in the Financial Machine," 530–34.

75 LiPuma, *Social Life of Financial Derivatives*, 38.

TWO. PROMISSORY NOTES

1 The theme of inscribing theopolitical ideas onto coinage has been treated insightfully in Singh, *Divine Currency*, 106.

2 See K.-Y. Taylor, *Race for Profit*.

3 Byles, *Byles on Bills of Exchange*, 315.

4 Graeber, *Debt*, 17–18. For Graeber, this entails dismissing the tale economic textbooks tell about how barter economies were the norm in "primitive" societies and how commercial societies could exist only after the advent of coinage. Anthropological research is clear that such barter societies never existed as narrated by economists. Graeber quips, "No one has been able to locate a part of the world where the ordinary mode of economic transaction between neighbors takes the form of 'I'll give you twenty chickens for that cow'" (29). When barter does appear in the historical record, it almost exclusively relates to transactions between communities that harbor suspicion toward each other precisely because, between trusting neighbors, tallying who owes what to whom is socially preferable. Graeber insists that the story told by economic textbooks about money is backward: first, he says, there was credit, a mode of keeping a record of promises made and promises paid. Later, much later, money arose as coinage to serve as a medium of exchange.

5 Graeber, *Debt*, 46.

6 Graeber, *Debt*, 47.

7 For Graeber, the ties between the modern banking system and state-sponsored violence are paramount. For this reason, the creation of the Bank of England is exemplary but certainly not an exception. See Graeber, *Debt*, 364–370; see also Dodd, *Social Life of Money*, 95–96. Devin Singh has further explored how sovereign power is "originary" to debt economies. The sovereign, in his analysis, is the original debtor. Singh, "Sovereign Debt," 245.

8 Graeber, *Debt*, 49.

9 In his philosophical and theological account of money, Philip Goodchild takes the creation of the Bank of England as the revelation of money's ontology. The being of money is credit, he offers. "Since metal coins had always been tokens of value, the creation of money as credit does not so much change as reveal the essence of money." Goodchild, *Theology of Money*, 7; see also 9–14.

10 Chitty, *Practical Treatise*, 17.

11 For an account of this legal debate and a summary of contemporary discussions about it in the field of legal history, see Rogers, *Early History*, 177–86; and Dylag, "Negotiability of Promissory Notes."

12 The reference to the laws of Lombard Street overpowering the laws of West-minster Hall appears in a court decision in *Buller v. Crips* (1703) by Chief Justice Holt, cited in Trimble, "Law Merchant," 988. See also Rogers, *Early History*, 177–78.

13 Court decision in *Miller v. Race* (1758), ruled by Lord Mansfield, quoted in Byles, *Byles on Bills of Exchange*, 323.

14 Dodd, *Social Life of Money*, 108.

15 It is common to supplement insights from the credit theory of money with the state theory of money articulated by Georg Friedrich Knapp, who argued that monetary value is generated by the institutional power of a govern-ment agent. State theorists therefore treat money as legal tender backed up by government. As Graeber's genealogy of debt indicates, these two theories about the origins and role of money in society are not easily distinguishable. It is beyond the scope of this section to develop a detailed account of the rela-tion between credit and state theories of money. My approach in this section privileges the insights from credit theorists in order to present the centrality of debt to the modern financial system.

16 Mitchell Innes, *Credit*, 42.

17 Dodd, *Social Life of Money*, 104.

18 For Dodd, debt is what makes money a social category. As he indicates, money is the socialization of the particularized promises people make to each other. Citing Georg Simmel's work, Dodd argues that money takes on the form of a "collectivized debt," one that encompasses the "relationship that each of us has 'with the economic community that accepts the money.'" Dodd, *Social Life of Money*, 93; see Simmel, *Philosophy of Money*, 177. Philip Goodchild is aligned with this perspective as he states, "Money does not provide a source of social cohesion until it brings with it an obligation: the obligation of debt." Goodchild, *Theology of Money*, xv.

19 Court decision in *Miller v. Race* (1758), ruled by Lord Mansfield, quoted in Byles, *Byles on Bills of Exchange*, 323.

20 Singh, "Sovereign Debt," 246. Graeber also calls attention to the ties between debt economies and political regimes of sovereignty. In Graeber's account, empires, nation-states, and governments all function as "guardians of the debt that citizens have to one another," as the policing agents that guarantee that all promises will be kept and debts paid. For Graeber, underneath all monetary and coinage systems, there is the hidden presence of a promise of repayment, an IOU, backed by a mighty imperial agent ready to assure that all debts will be repaid. Graeber, *Debt*, 56.

21 Singh, "Sovereign Debt," 247.

22 Vogl, *Specter of Capital*, 53.

23 Vogl, *Specter of Capital*, 54–55.

24 Vogl, *Specter of Capital*, 56.

25 Adkins, *Time of Money*, 83.

26 As I further explain in the next section, the expression "material memory" comes from Foucault, *Order of Things*, 181.

27 A. Smith, *Wealth of Nations*, 124.

28 A. Smith, *Wealth of Nations*, 147–48.

29 A. Smith, *Wealth of Nations*, 6. Political economist Benjamin Friedman argues that the "central point in *The Wealth of Nations* . . . was that when economic activity is guided by commerce, the public interest is advanced not despite but *because of* individuals' self-interest." For Friedman, Smith's ingenious theory of progress accepts the Christian medieval prescription that all economic activity must serve the common good, with the crucial caveat that self-interest successfully—even when unintentionally—functions for the greater good of society. B. Friedman, *Moral Consequences of Economic Growth*, 40. Christopher Lasch calls this Smith's "moral rehabilitation of desire." Lasch, *True and Only Heaven*, 52–55. For Smith's positive view of human self-interest, see A. Smith, *Theory of Moral Sentiments*, 300–314.

30 In his *Lectures on Jurisprudence*, Smith connected historical progress to progress in government, development in productive forces, and the improvement of the social division of labor. For Smith, history progresses in four stages that reflect four different modes of producing and exchanging the basic necessities of life. These stages are hunting and gathering, farming and other forms of control over livestock, agriculture, and, finally, commerce. Each subsequent stage, he said, evinces a more refined form of producing goods led by a more robust social division of labor, enhanced commerce within and beyond a country's territory, and better forms of government. Each stage, Smith contended, also advanced better forms of "laws and regulations necessary to maintain justice" and property rights. See A. Smith, *Lectures on Jurisprudence*, 14–16, 404–26.

31 A. Smith, *Wealth of Nations*, 182–87.

32 A. Smith, *Wealth of Nations*, 187.

33 A. Smith, *Wealth of Nations*, 124.

34 A. Smith, *Wealth of Nations*, 125, 127–28.

35 A. Smith, *Wealth of Nations*, 128.

36 A. Smith, *Wealth of Nations*, 138.

37 It is worth stressing that in Smith's political economy, as is the case for all classical political economists, this is an absurd supposition insofar as wealth or capital can be generated only through *production*, never in the sphere of *circulation*.

38 A. Smith, *Wealth of Nations*, 133–35.

39 See A. Smith, *Wealth of Nations*, 147–48.

40 See B. Friedman, *Moral Consequences of Economic Growth*, 40.

41 Political economist Martijn Konings points out that the fictitious or even "irrational" aspects of money and other economic categories cannot ignore the "constitutive effects of this fantasy, its ability to generate an affective charge

and serve as a binding force, as an unimagined version of the functional cohesion that it imagines." Konings, *Capital and Time*, 25.

42 It might be useful to establish Foucault's definition of *episteme* as the general conditions of possibility of human science. An episteme thus seeks to uncover the conditions that make knowledge possible, the framework with which one investigates reality in the pursuit of knowing it. See Foucault, *Order of Things*, xxi–xxii.

43 Foucault, *Order of Things*, 181.

44 Foucault, *Order of Things*, 224–25.

45 Foucault, *Order of Things*, 225.

46 Foucault, *Order of Things*, 225.

47 Foucault, *Order of Things*, 226.

48 The conceptual historian Reinhart Koselleck has in fact argued that one can identify a particular mode of temporality emerging in the modern period. Beginning during the Enlightenment, historical time was no longer perceived as a collection of examples from the past that authorizes some predictions about the future. Rather, history is understood as providing knowledge of the secret laws governing historical progress. See Koselleck, *Futures Past*, 21; see also 26–30.

49 Konings, *Capital and Time*, 58.

50 A. Smith, *Wealth of Nations*, 138.

51 Foucault, *Order of Things*, 181.

52 Amato and Fantacci, *End of Finance*, 29.

53 Tanner, *Christianity*, 49.

54 Notably in Deleuze and Guattari, *Anti-Oedipus*. As I show below, Gilles Deleuze and Félix Guattari's combining of Nietzsche's work on the morality of debt with Karl Marx's political economy has been influential in recent debates that discuss the financialization of the global economy. See, for example, Lazzarato, *Making of the Indebted Man*. For a critique of Nietzsche's economic thought and those who find in him a model to critique contemporary capitalism, see Graeber, *Debt*, 75–80. For an argument about Nietzsche's disregard for political economy, see Andrew, *Genealogy of Values*. For the opposite argument, see Kaufmann, *Nietzsche*, 412; and Sedgwick, *Nietzsche's Economy*, x.

55 Nietzsche, *On the Genealogy of Morality*, 35.

56 Nietzsche, *On the Genealogy of Morality*, 35.

57 Nietzsche, *On the Genealogy of Morality*, 36.

58 As Derek Hillard points out, for Nietzsche, "[the] first communal human was an entrepreneur. . . . Wheeling and dealing, setting prices and making measurements: these, Nietzsche asserts, were the original forms of thinking." Hillard, "History as a Dual Process," 44.

59 Nietzsche, *On the Genealogy of Morality*, 38.

60 Nietzsche, *On the Genealogy of Morality*, 40.

61 Nietzsche, *On the Genealogy of Morality*, 40.

62 Nietzsche, *On the Genealogy of Morality*, 45.

63 Graeber suggests that Nietzsche took up the premises of Smith's political economy and exposed what Smith himself tried to avoid, namely, all the violence that undergirds commercial relations between creditors and debtors. Graeber, *Debt*, 336.

64 Nietzsche, *On the Genealogy of Morality*, 39.

65 Nietzsche, *On the Genealogy of Morality*, 60.

66 Nietzsche, *On the Genealogy of Morality*, 61.

67 Wortham, "What We Owe to Retroactivity."

68 Lazzarato, *Making of the Indebted Man*, 45.

69 Lazzarato, *Making of the Indebted Man*, 45–46.

70 Lazzarato, *Making of the Indebted Man*, 45–46.

71 Lazzarato, *Making of the Indebted Man*, 49.

72 Lazzarato, *Governing by Debt*, 87.

73 Amato and Fantacci, *End of Finance*, 29.

74 Allon, "Feminisation of Finance," 19; S. Smith, "Owner-Occupation"; and Langley, *Everyday Life of Global Finance*.

75 McClanahan, *Dead Pledges*, 1.

76 McClanahan, *Dead Pledges*, 59.

77 McClanahan, *Dead Pledges*, 60.

78 McClanahan, *Dead Pledges*, 65.

79 Ascher, *Portfolio Society*, 89.

80 McClanahan offers illuminating examples of this mechanism of assessing a person's creditworthiness. Credit card firms, for instance, gather consumer data to construct "particularized behavioral and psychological profiles characterized by . . . unprecedented 'quantitative granularity.'" Here is how granular it gets: credit agencies perceived that customers who bought "premium bird seeds, rooftop snow rakes, and furniture-leg pads to protect floors from scratches were unlikely to miss payments, whereas those who purchased generic motor oil or 'chrome-skull car accessories' were highly likely to default." McClanahan, *Dead Pledges*, 64; see Duhigg, "What Does Your Credit-Card Company Know."

81 McClanahan, *Dead Pledges*, 66.

82 McClanahan, *Dead Pledges*, 74.

83 Joseph, *Debt to Society*, 8–9.

84 For a discussion about biocapitalism, see Marazzi, *Violence of Financial Capitalism*, 49.

85 Joseph, *Debt to Society*, 25.

86 Allon, "Feminisation of Finance."

87 Allon, "Feminisation of Finance," 14.

88 Allon, "Feminisation of Finance," 20.

89 Allon, "Feminisation of Finance," 24.

90 K.-Y. Taylor, *Race for Profit*.

91 K.-Y. Taylor, *Race for Profit*, 4.

92 K.-Y. Taylor, *Race for Profit*, 4.

93 K.-Y. Taylor, *Race for Profit*, 18–19.

94 K.-Y. Taylor, *Race for Profit*, 19.

95 K.-Y. Taylor, *Race for Profit*, 254.

96 Kotsko, *Neoliberalism's Demons*, 121.

97 Kotsko, *Neoliberalism's Demons*, 84.

98 Kotsko, *Neoliberalism's Demons*, 122.

99 See McClanahan, *Dead Pledges*, 79–80. By stressing the material conditions of debt, McClanahan departs from Lazzarato's account of the debt economy as it does not sufficiently tie material and historical conditions to the formation of the indebted subject. As becomes even more evident in my next chapter, I, too, consider debt from its concrete and material dimensions.

100 McClanahan, *Dead Pledges*, 82–84, 94–95.

101 McClanahan, *Dead Pledges*, 126.

102 McClanahan, *Dead Pledges*, 127.

103 Lazzarato, *Making of the Indebted Man*, 46.

THREE. TIMES THAT MATTER

1 Augustine, *Confessions*, 221.

2 Augustine, *Confessions*, 239.

3 Augustine, *Confessions*, 242–43.

4 Marx, *Capital I*, 376–77.

5 Derrida, *Given Time*, 28.

6 Derrida, *Given Time*, 28.

7 Marx, *Capital I*, 279.

8 Ascher, *Portfolio Society*.

9 Marx, *Capital I*, 90.

10 Marx, *Capital I*, 129. George Henderson suggests that these concepts perform in the drama that Marx seeks to describe in *Capital*. He sees Marx as a "scenic thinker" and argues that each concept of value has its own "appearance" in *Capital*, much like the appearances of characters on the stage. See Henderson, *Value in Marx*.

11 Harvey, *Companion to Marx's "Capital,"* 19–21.

12 Marx, *Capital I*, 199.

13 Marx, *Capital I*, 129.

14 Marx, *Capital I*, 142.

15 Marx, *Capital I*, 129–30.

16 Marx, *Capital I*, 167.

17 Marx, *Capital I*, 168.

18 Marx, *Capital I*, 279.

19 Marx, *Capital I*, 270.

20 Marx, *Capital I*, 342.

21 Marx, *Capital I*, 128. Spivak explains labor power as the "human capacity to produce, not objects, nor anything tangible, but that simple contentless

thing which is *not* pure form, yet perceptible only formally." Spivak, *Outside in the Teaching Machine*, 61. She further suggests that the category of labor power allows Marx to materially "predicate" the subject. Spivak claims that labor power points to the "irreducible possibility that the subject be more than adequate—super-adequate—to itself." See Spivak, "Scattered Speculations," 73.

22 Marx, *Capital I*, 279–80.

23 Marx, *Capital I*, 340.

24 Marx, *Capital I*, 341.

25 Marx, *Capital I*, 341.

26 For a commentary on the constant changes in genre, tone, and style in Marx's *Capital*, see Harvey, *Companion to Marx's "Capital*," 38.

27 In this chapter I refer to the figure of the capitalist with masculine pronouns. When discussing Spivak's work in the final section of the chapter, I point out the connections between the rule of financial capital and patriarchy.

28 Marx, *Capital I*, 342.

29 Marx, *Capital I*, 342.

30 Marx, *Capital I*, 342.

31 Marx, *Capital I*, 342; see also 344.

32 Quoted in Marx, *Capital I*, 342n4.

33 Marx, *Capital I*, 342.

34 Linguet, *Théorie des Lois Civiles*, 466, quoted in Marx, *Capital I*, 342n5.

35 Marx, *Capital I*, 342.

36 Marx, *Capital I*, 342.

37 Marx, *Capital I*, 342–43.

38 Marx, *Capital I*, 343.

39 Marx, *Capital I*, 343.

40 Marx, *Capital I*, 343.

41 Marx, *Capital I*, 344. The same emphasis on the regulation of the length of the working day reappears in the third volume of *Capital*, where Marx claims that the rise of the "realm of freedom" in the form of a society of "associated producers" is predicated on the reduction of the working day. See Marx, *Capital III*, 959.

42 Marx, *Capital I*, 349.

43 Marx, *Capital I*, 352.

44 Marx, *Capital I*, 352.

45 Marx, *Capital I*, 354–64.

46 Marx, *Capital I*, 376.

47 Marx, *Capital I*, 376–77.

48 Marx, *Capital I*, 352–53.

49 Hamermesh, "Timing of Work over Time," 51, 64.

50 For a full catalog of these titles, see Kalleberg, Reynolds, and Marsden, "Externalizing Employment," 525–26.

51 Ruyter and Brown, *Gig Economy*. See also Prassl, *Humans as a Service*.

52 See Clinton, "Flexible Labor"; and Kalleberg, "Evolving Employment Relations."
53 Jacobs and Gerson, *Time Divide*.
54 Jacobs and Gerson, *Time Divide*, 8.
55 Jacobs and Gerson, *Time Divide*, 8.
56 Presser, *Working in a 24/7 Economy*, 2.
57 Presser, "Employment in a 24/7 Economy," 64.
58 Bosworth, Burtless, and Zhang, *Later Retirement*.
59 Irwin and Bui, "Rich Live Longer Everywhere."
60 Montez and Zajacova, "Why Is Life Expectancy Declining"; David and Collins, "Layers of Inequality"; Firebaugh et al., "Why Lifespans Are More Variable"; and Ansell, *Death Gap*.
61 Dana-Farber Cancer Institute and Boston Children's Cancer and Blood Disorders Center, "Childhood Leukemia Patients."
62 Case and Deaton, "Rising Morbidity and Mortality."
63 Case and Deaton, "Rising Morbidity and Mortality," 15081.
64 Case and Deaton, "Rising Morbidity and Mortality," 15081.
65 Marx, *Capital I*, 376–77.
66 Ascher, *Portfolio Society*, 24.
67 Ascher, *Portfolio Society*, 67.
68 Ascher, *Portfolio Society*, 67.
69 Ascher, *Portfolio Society*, 67.
70 Ascher, *Portfolio Society*, 77.
71 Ascher, *Portfolio Society*, 77.
72 Ascher, *Portfolio Society*, 78.
73 Ascher, *Portfolio Society*, 81.
74 Ascher, *Portfolio Society*, 99.
75 Konings, *Capital and Time*, 111.
76 Ascher, *Portfolio Society*, 26–27.
77 Konings, *Capital and Time*, 111. Konings further suggests that interactions with student loan agencies form students as "entrepreneurs" of the self, a term coined by Michel Foucault. See Foucault, *Birth of Biopolitics*.
78 Marx, *Capital I*, 171.
79 Ascher, *Portfolio Society*, 59.
80 Marx, *Capital I*, 167.
81 One can observe a similar pattern of argument in Spivak's reading of the "Asiatic mode of production," a discussion in Marx that reveals his different mode of reading history. Spivak contrasts that with Immanuel Kant's and Georg Wilhelm Friedrich Hegel's ideas about historical progress. See Spivak, *Critique of Postcolonial Reason*, 67–111.
82 For a brief catalog of Spivak's account of the Marxian theory of value, see Spivak, *Outside in the Teaching Machine*, chap. 5. See also Spivak, "Ghostwriting"; Spivak, *Critique of Postcolonial Reason*, 63–68 ; and Spivak, *Aesthetic Education*, chap. 9.
83 Spivak, *Critique of Postcolonial Reason*, 99.

84 Spivak, *Critique of Postcolonial Reason*, 425.

85 Spivak, "Scattered Speculations," 74.

86 Later in the essay, Spivak cites Paul de Man's definition, which goes in a similar direction: "We call text any entity that can be considered from . . . a double perspective: as a generative, open-ended, non-referential grammatic system and as a figural system closed off by a transcendental system that subverts the grammatical code to which the text owes its existence." De Man, *Allegories of Reading*, 270, quoted in Spivak, "Scattered Speculations," 90n20. For further elucidation of Spivak's use of the category of text as structural differentiation, see Spivak, "Translator's Preface."

87 Spivak, *Aesthetic Education*, 185.

88 Spivak, "Speculations on Reading Marx," 40.

89 Spivak, "Scattered Speculations," 74.

90 Spivak, "Scattered Speculations," 74.

91 Spivak argues that Marx's use of the term *value* is a *catachresis*, a term with no literal or "adequate" referent but still a term that one cannot *not* use. See Spivak, "Interview." One can find the development of a similar thesis in George Henderson's reflections on Marx's theory of value. See Henderson, *Value in Marx*.

92 For Spivak, one must qualify Marx's use of Hegel's dialectics. The *Grundrisse* exposes "Marx's effort to open up the seemingly unified phenomenon of Money through the radical methodology of the dialectic-opening up." Dialectics, as Spivak is employing it here, betrays the habit of introducing a contradiction only to quickly resolve it by means of a "synthesis." Spivak submits that the chain of value in Marx offers no clear moment of contradiction but only indeterminations. See Spivak, "Scattered Speculations," 78.

93 Spivak, "Scattered Speculations," 77.

94 Spivak, "Scattered Speculations," 74; and Spivak, "Speculations on Reading Marx," 40.

95 Spivak, "Scattered Speculations," 76.

96 Spivak, "Translator's Preface," xii.

97 Derrida, *Of Grammatology*, 7.

98 Marx, *Capital I*, 89.

99 Marx, *Capital I*, 128. I maintain the changes that Spivak makes to the translation. See Spivak, "Scattered Speculations," 77.

100 Spivak, "Scattered Speculations," 77.

101 Spivak, "Speculations on Reading Marx," 40.

102 Best, "Postcolonialism and the Deconstructive Scenario," 488.

103 Spivak, "Scattered Speculations," 77.

104 See Spivak, "Scattered Speculations," 80. As critic Beverley Best states, Spivak notices that Marx needed a starting point for his narrative about capital. Value is that starting point, even though Marx must acknowledge that this category exists only once the circuit of capital is in motion. Marx must therefore "[posit] the concept of use-value as a 'theoretical fiction', as the

fictional origin of the story from which we can arrive at a concept of value." Best, "Postcolonialism and the Deconstructive Scenario," 489–90.

105 Spivak, *Outside in the Teaching Machine*, 106.

106 See Best, "Postcolonialism and the Deconstructive Scenario," 489–90.

107 Spivak, *Outside in the Teaching Machine*, 106; see also Spivak, "Speculations on Reading Marx."

108 The following claim by Best seems quite appropriate: "For both Marx and Spivak, the detour through philosophical interpretation can be a very useful step in the *practice* of anticapitalist or antineocolonialist struggle. This is where the always potentially dangerous intellectual work of producing explanations can have political and transformative import." Best, "Postcolonialism and the Deconstructive Scenario," 493.

109 Marx, *Capital I*, 342; and Spivak, "Speculations on Reading Marx," 52.

110 Spivak, "Speculations on Reading Marx," 52.

111 In her "Scattered Speculations on the Question of Value," Spivak calls this "micro-electronic" capitalism—a term that I approach as an early iteration of Spivak's later and more developed concept of "financialization of the globe." See Spivak, *Critique of Postcolonial Reason*, 3; see also 358.

112 Spivak, "Scattered Speculations," 82. Though this is impossible to affirm with certainty, Spivak is most likely targeting her critique at the work of Jean-Joseph Goux, who argued that the critique of capitalism needed to abandon the materiality of labor and focus instead on it as a "discursive" issue. Annie McClanahan summarizes Goux's position: "Because the value of commodities is no longer driven by productive labour but rather by the 'intensity of desire', the labour theory of value is . . . inadequate to the forms of value that characterize late capitalism." In her own critique of Goux, McClanahan affirms Spivak's position. See McClanahan, "Investing in the Future," 85.

113 Spivak, *Aesthetic Education*, 195.

114 Spivak, "Scattered Speculations," 84.

115 Spivak, "Scattered Speculations," 84.

116 D. Smith, "Wiring of Wall Street."

117 D. Smith, "Wiring of Wall Street."

118 Spivak, "Scattered Speculations," 87.

119 Spivak, "Scattered Speculations," 84.

120 Spivak, "Scattered Speculations," 88.

121 Spivak, "Scattered Speculations," 88.

122 Quoted in D. Smith, "Wiring of Wall Street."

123 Spivak, "Scattered Speculations," 87.

FOUR. THE TIME THAT IS MONEY

1 Franklin, "Advice to a Young Tradesman."

2 Franklin says, "He that can earn Ten Shillings a Day by his Labour, and goes abroad, or sits idle one half of that Day, tho' he spends but Sixpence during

his Diversion or Idleness, ought not to reckon That the only Expence; he has really spent or rather thrown away Five Shillings besides." Franklin, "Advice to a Young Tradesman."

3 Franklin, "Advice to a Young Tradesman."
4 Weber, *Protestant Ethic* (2010), 79.
5 Weber, *Protestant Ethic* (2010), 81.
6 Weber, *Protestant Ethic* (2010), 81.
7 Weber, *Protestant Ethic* (2001), 164–65.
8 Weber, *Protestant Ethic* (2010), 81.
9 Franklin, "Advice to a Young Tradesman."
10 Benjamin, "Capitalism as Religion," 259. For a fuller argument for the rejection of the secularist thesis from the perspective of liberation theology, see Sung, *Desire, Market, Religion*, 55–63.
11 Benjamin, "Capitalism as Religion," 259.
12 Benjamin, "Capitalism as Religion," 260.
13 Benjamin, *Illuminations*, 264.
14 Löwy, "Capitalism as Religion," 71.
15 Löwy, "Capitalism as Religion," 71.
16 See Bloch, *Thomas Münzer*. Perhaps not coincidentally, Bloch's attack on the religious aura of capitalism comes in his utopian Marxist endorsement of the radical tradition within the Reformation, particularly the peasant uprising in the shadow of Thomas Müntzer.
17 Hinkelammert, *Crítica de la razón utópica*, 177.
18 Löwy, "Capitalism as Religion," 72n28.
19 Löwy, "Capitalism as Religion," 72n28.
20 For the centrality of idolatry in the inception of liberation theology, see Segundo, *Our Idea of God*, 12; Gutiérrez, *Power of the Poor*, 92; and Gutiérrez, *God of Life*. For recent meditations on the theme, see Rieger, *No Rising Tide*, 86–88; and Espín, *Idol and Grace*. For discussion that explicitly relates the theme of idolatry to oppressive socioeconomic systems, see Richard et al., *A luta dos deuses*; Hinkelammert and Assmann, *A idolatria do mercado*; and Sung, *Idolatria do dinheiro*.
21 Marx, *Capital I*, 343.
22 As stated previously, President John F. Kennedy often used the expression that a rising tide will lift all boats. See note 26 on page 150. On the validation of social costs of development, see Hinkelammert and Assmann, *A idolatria do mercado*, 329.
23 Hinkelammert, *Lo indispensable es inútil*, 127.
24 Hinkelammert, *Crítica de la razón utópica*.
25 For more about the connection between Salvador Allende's death, the White House, and the involvement of the Central Intelligence Agency in the Chilean military coup, see Verdugo, *Salvador Allende*; and Kornbluh, *Pinochet File*.
26 Since Allende was inside the palace during the bombings, his sympathizers have claimed that he was in fact assassinated. Others have claimed that he

killed himself after broadcasting his last communiqué to the nation. After conducting a full judicial process and forensic investigation, a commission recently officially classified his death as a suicide. The nature of this suicide and the context in which it occurred is still debated. See Bustamante, "Chile ante la 'verdad histórica'"; and Benítez, *Las muertes de Salvador Allende*.

27 On the role of the Chicago school of economics in Chile, see Valdés, *Pinochet's Economists*; and Klein, *Shock Doctrine*. For a more apologetic reading from the perspective of neoliberal scholars, see Caldwell and Montes, "Friedrich Hayek."

28 Sohr, "Prologue," xxi.

29 Sohr, "Prologue," xxii. Sohr provides further data to substantiate this claim: "By all measures, the average worker was worse off in 1989 than he had been in 1970. . . . [T]he top ten percent of the population, who in 1980 accounted for 36.5 percent of national income, saw their share increase to 46.8 percent by 1989. By contrast, the bottom 50 percent of wage earners saw their share fall from 20.4 to 16.8 percent over the same period. The level of income inequality was among the worst in the region."

30 Harvey, *Brief History of Neoliberalism*, 9.

31 M. Friedman, *Capitalism and Freedom*, 200.

32 Harvey, *Brief History of Neoliberalism*, 119.

33 Hinkelammert, *Lo indispensable es inútil*, 81.

34 Hinkelammert, *Teología del mercado total*, 11.

35 See Hinkelammert, *Der Wachstumsprozess in der Sowjetwirtschaft*.

36 For the full story of Hinkelammert's ancestors' involvement with the Münster movement, see Nadal and Silnik, *Teología profana y pensamiento crítico*, 62–65.

37 Hinkelammert, *Lo indispensable es inútil*, 38.

38 For more on Hinkelammert's experience and research during this period, see Nadal and Silnik, *Teología profana y pensamiento crítico*, 104–9; and Hinkelammert, *Lo indispensable es inútil*, 39–42. For Hinkelammert's intellectual production in this period, see Hinkelammert, *Dialéctica del desarrollo desigual*; Hinkelammert, *El subdesarrollo latinoamericano*; and Hinkelammert, *Ideologías del desarrollo*.

39 Casos, "Fetichismo," 4n9; see also Hinkelammert, *Lo indispensable es inútil*, 141–42.

40 Nadal and Silnik, *Teología profana y pensamiento crítico*, 116–17. The volume comprises interviews with Hinkelammert, so the words cited are directly from him.

41 Hinkelammert, *Lo indispensable es inútil*, 42.

42 Nadal and Silnik, *Teología profana y pensamiento crítico*, 113.

43 Nadal and Silnik, *Teología profana y pensamiento crítico*, 124.

44 Hinkelammert, *Lo indispensable es inútil*, 42.

45 Hinkelammert, *Lo indispensable es inútil*, 42.

46 Hinkelammert, *Lo indispensable es inútil*, 46.

47 MacKenzie, *Engine, Not a Camera*, 16.

48 Nadal and Silnik, *Teología profana y pensamiento crítico*, 127.

49 Sohr, "Prologue," xx.

50 Soon after his departure from Chile, Hinkelammert started working on a book manuscript that would transform these notes into a reflection on the ideological roots of the coup. He could not find anyone to publish the manuscript, and so it remained unpublished until 1977. See Hinkelammert, *Ideologías del sometimiento*.

51 Hayek, "Extracts from an Interview."

52 Hayek, "Entrevista," *El Mercurio*, April 19, 1981, quoted in Hinkelammert, *La maldición*, 113.

53 Hinkelammert, *Ideological Weapons of Death*, 259.

54 Rieger, *No Rising Tide*, 24–25. M. Douglas Meeks's fundamental text *God the Economist* points in a similar direction and must be credited as an early and extremely articulate defense of the need for a theological critique of capitalism.

55 Hinkelammert, *Lo indispensable es inútil*, 84.

56 After his departure from Chile, Hinkelammert spent three years teaching in Germany. He returned to Latin America in 1976, first spending time in Honduras and later in San José, Costa Rica. At the end of 1976, together with Brazilian theologian Hugo Assmann and Chilean biblical scholar Pablo Richard, he founded the Departamento Ecuménico de Investigaciones (DEI; Ecumenical Department of Investigations). For a detailed account of this period in Hinkelammert's life, see Nadal and Silnik, *Teología profana y pensamiento crítico*, 58–59. To this day, the DEI is one of the most important centers of thought for liberation theology in Latin America. In his foreword to Hinkelammert's *The Ideological Weapons of Death*, Cornel West refers to the DEI as a "unique institutional setting" that "[shuns] the narrow confines of the intellectual division of labor in academic institutions." West, foreword, v.

   After more than thirty years of work in that institution, Hinkelammert cut his official ties to the DEI in 2007, following problems with the administration. Hinkelammert describes his departure with an acute sense of frustration and sadness: "I had to leave DEI in 2007 because several of my companions, who considered themselves liberation theologians, made my life impossible. I was condemned as a heretic in a true act of inquisition." Nadal and Silnik, *Teología profana y pensamiento crítico*, 178.

57 This vein of liberation theology is expanded by other Latin American authors like Hugo Assmann, Pablo Richard, Julio de Santa Ana, and, more recently, Jung Mo Sung—figures closely linked to Hinkelammert's work. For a review of this literature, see Sung, *Teologia e economia*. Since most of the work of these theologians has yet to be published in English, this vein within liberation theology—and Hinkelammert's work—remains virtually unknown to the English-speaking theological academy. In this setting Joerg Rieger is one of

the few theologians to engage in discussion with these authors and to expand their contributions to the discussion in theology and economics. See Rieger, *No Rising Tide*, 20–21, 81, 87.

58 Hinkelammert's conclusion to the book makes explicit that this connection between Christianity and Marxism does not mean that these traditions are one and the same. Rather, he argues that the traditions meet in their focus on "real life as the ultimate basis" of all reality. The specificity of the Marxist tradition, Hinkelammert argues, is the concept of "praxis that leads to transcendence within real life." As for Christianity, the pivotal element is "hope in the potentialities of praxis, going beyond what can be calculated to be humanly achievable." Hinkelammert, *Ideological Weapons of Death*, 273.

59 Hinkelammert, *Ideological Weapons of Death*, 3.

60 Hinkelammert, *Ideological Weapons of Death*, 3.

61 Marx's standard definition of commodity fetishism is this: "The mysterious character of the commodity-form consists therefore simply in the fact that the commodity reflects the social characteristics of men's own labour as objective characteristics of the products of labour themselves, as the socionatural properties of these things. . . . Through this substitution, the products of labour become commodities, sensuous things which are at the same time supra-sensible or social. . . . It is nothing but the definite social relation between men themselves which assumes here, for them, the fantastic form of a relation between things. . . . I call this the fetishism which attaches itself to the products of labour as soon as they are produced as commodities." Marx, *Capital I*, 164–65.

62 Hinkelammert, *Ideological Weapons of Death*, 3–4.

63 Hinkelammert, *Ideological Weapons of Death*, 4.

64 Hinkelammert, *Ideological Weapons of Death*, 4; see also Hinkelammert, *La maldición*, 144–55; and Hinkelammert, *El sujeto y la ley*, 505–16.

65 Hinkelammert, *Ideological Weapons of Death*, 11.

66 Hinkelammert, *Ideological Weapons of Death*, 20.

67 Hinkelammert, *Ideological Weapons of Death*, 52.

68 Hinkelammert, *Ideological Weapons of Death*, 54 (translation modified).

69 Hinkelammert, *Ideological Weapons of Death*, 54.

70 Hinkelammert, *Ideological Weapons of Death*, 127.

71 Hinkelammert, *Ideological Weapons of Death*, 127.

72 Hinkelammert, *Ideological Weapons of Death*, 131.

73 Hinkelammert, *Ideological Weapons of Death*, 141.

74 Hinkelammert, *Ideological Weapons of Death*, 186; see also 95–96, 213.

75 Hinkelammert, *Ideological Weapons of Death*, 184.

76 Hinkelammert, *Ideological Weapons of Death*, 215–16.

77 Hinkelammert, *Ideological Weapons of Death*, 4.

78 Hinkelammert, *Ideological Weapons of Death*, 27 (translation modified).

79 Hinkelammert, *Crítica de la razón utópica*, 9.

80 Hinkelammert, *Crítica de la razón utópica*, 9–10.
81 Hinkelammert, *Crítica de la razón utópica*, 18.
82 Hinkelammert, *Crítica de la razón utópica*, 23.
83 Hinkelammert, *Crítica de la razón utópica*, 30.
84 Rieger traces the same argument in Michael Novak's endorsement of capitalism. According to Novak, the incarnation of Christ means that Christians
accept the world as it is and that we cannot expect to bring about the reign
of heaven on earth. The logical conclusion, Rieger stresses, is that "god sanc-
tions the current embodiment of free-market economy." Rieger, *No Rising
Tide*, 6. See Novak, *Spirit of Democratic Capitalism*.
85 Hinkelammert, *Sacrificios humanos y sociedad occidental*, 161–62.
86 Hinkelammert's suspicions about Popper's philosophical work also stem
from the fact that he became the "court philosopher" of the national security
military governments in Latin America. See Hinkelammert, *Lo indispensable es inútil*, 142–43.
87 Hinkelammert, *Crítica de la razón utópica*, 134–35.
88 Hinkelammert, *Crítica de la razón utópica*, 134–35.
89 Hinkelammert, *Crítica de la razón utópica*, 278.
90 Hinkelammert, *Crítica de la razón utópica*, 135.
91 Hinkelammert, *Crítica de la razón utópica*, 138; see also 279.
92 Rieger, *No Rising Tide*, 13.
93 Rieger, *No Rising Tide*, 18.
94 Hayek, interview, *El Mercurio*, April 12, 1981, quoted in Hinkelammert,
Crítica de la razón utópica, 176.
95 Hinkelammert, *Crítica de la razón utópica*, 176.
96 Hayek, interview, *El Mercurio*, April 12, 1981, quoted in Hinkelammert,
Crítica de la razón utópica, 176.
97 Hinkelammert, *Crítica de la razón utópica*, 177.
98 Hinkelammert, *Lo indispensable es inútil*, 145–49.
99 Hinkelammert, *Sacrificios humanos y sociedad occidental*, 11–18. Contra
Sigmund Freud, Hinkelammert maintains that the story of the killing of
the father is only marginally important in comparison to the more decisive
myth of the sacrifice of an innocent figure such as Iphigenia.
100 See Hinkelammert and Assmann, *A idolatria do mercado*, 329; and Hinkelammert, *Sacrificios humanos y sociedad occidental*, 38.
101 Hinkelammert, *El sujeto y la ley*, 68.
102 Hinkelammert, *Sacrificios humanos y sociedad occidental*, 195; see also Hinkelammert, *El sujeto y la ley*, 73.
103 Hinkelammert, *Crítica de la razón utópica*, 288. Rieger has similarly described our predicament under neoliberalism by naming hope as a "scarce
commodity" during our time. Rieger, *No Rising Tide*, 149.
104 Hinkelammert, *Crítica de la razón utópica*, 295.
105 Hinkelammert, *Crítica de la razón utópica*, 296.
106 Hinkelammert, *Ideological Weapons of Death*, 4.

107 Hinkelammert, *Lo indispensable es inútil*, 128.

108 See Hinkelammert, *Ideological Weapons of Death*, 54.

109 Hinkelammert, *Ideological Weapons of Death*, 226–27.

110 Hinkelammert, *Ideological Weapons of Death*, 183.

111 Hinkelammert, *Ideological Weapons of Death*, 227.

112 Hinkelammert, *Ideological Weapons of Death*, 63.

113 Hinkelammert, *Ideological Weapons of Death*, 57, 59; see *Las armas ideológicas de la muerte*, 98.

114 Hinkelammert, *Lo indispensable es inútil*, 168.

115 Hinkelammert, *Cultura de esperanza*, 186.

116 Hinkelammert, *El sujeto y la ley*, 506; and Nadal and Silnik, *Teología profana y pensamiento crítico*, 59.

117 See Hinkelammert, *Crítica de la razón utópica*, 298, 380–86.

118 Hinkelammert, *Lo indispensable es inútil*, 177.

119 Hinkelammert, *La maldición*, 22.

FIVE. SIGHS OF THE TIMES

1 Alves, *Transparencies of Eternity*, 58.

2 Derrida, *Specters of Marx*, 59.

3 For a collection of Marx's theological memories, see Dussel, *Las metáforas teológicas de Marx*.

4 Marx, *Capital I*, 93.

5 To recall, these two definitions can be found in Gutiérrez, *Theology of Liberation*; and Gutiérrez, "Lenguaje teológico."

6 Quoted in Gutiérrez, "Lenguaje teológico," 141.

7 Gutiérrez, "Lenguaje teológico," 142.

8 See Barreto Júnior, "Rubem Alves."

9 Puleo, *Struggle Is One*, 189, 196–97.

10 Alves, *Suspiro dos oprimidos*, 64.

11 Cox, preface, vii. At the time Cox wrote his preface to Alves's book, the two did not know each other. They would later become good friends. See Junior, *É uma pena não viver*, 260–61.

12 For a contextualization of the importance of Alves's dissertation in the formative years of Latin American liberation theology, see Rivera-Pagán, "God the Liberator."

13 Alves, "Sobre deuses e caquis," 29.

14 The thesis would later be published and introduced by Alves to a Brazilian audience as Alves, *Teologia da libertação em suas origens*. For further information on the context of Brazilian Protestantism during the 1950s, particularly the influence of theologian Richard Shaull in Alves's theological education in Brazil, see Barreto Júnior, "Rubem Alves"; and Barreto Júnior, "Um convite a sonhar."

15 Alves, "Sobre deuses e caquis," 19.

16 Alves, "Sobre deuses e caquis," 22. Just months after that, in a stop at a bus station, military agents checked Alves's bags and found some books by the Brazilian educator Paulo Freire, a known "subversive" figure to the military regime. Fearing arrest, Alves used his former military credentials to avoid further interrogation. Junior, *É uma pena não viver*, 239–40.

17 Quoted in Junior, *É uma pena não viver*, 240.

18 Alves, *Theology of Human Hope*, 28.

19 Alves, *Theology of Human Hope*, 28–29.

20 Alves, *Theology of Human Hope*, 29.

21 This insight is more fully developed by Moltmann. See Moltmann, *Theology of Hope*. Moltmann sees the "making" of history in relation to that which indeed "discloses an eschatological future" (181).

22 Alves, *Theology of Human Hope*, 10.

23 Alves, *Theology of Human Hope*, 10.

24 Alves, *Theology of Human Hope*, 11.

25 Alves, *Theology of Human Hope*, 15.

26 Marx, *Capital I*, 928–30.

27 Alves, *Theology of Human Hope*, 36.

28 Alves, *Theology of Human Hope*, 43.

29 Alves, *Theology of Human Hope*, 45.

30 Alves, *Theology of Human Hope*, 57. While most Latin American liberationists wrote positively about Moltmann's *Theology of Hope*, this debate was often contentious. The exemplary debate of this controversy occurred between Moltmann and the Argentinian theologian José Míguez Bonino. See Bonino, *Doing Theology*; and Moltmann, "On Latin American Liberation Theology." For Bonino's later reflection on this conversation, see Bonino, "Reading Jürgen Moltmann."

31 Moltmann, *Theology of Hope*, 30.

32 Alves, *Theology of Human Hope*, 57.

33 Alves, *Theology of Human Hope*, 58.

34 Moltmann, *Theology of Hope*, 102.

35 Alves, *Theology of Human Hope*, 60.

36 Alves, *Theology of Human Hope*, 59.

37 Alves, *Theology of Human Hope*, 35–36.

38 Alves, *Theology of Human Hope*, 100.

39 Alves's *A Theology of Human Hope* was criticized by some of Reinhold Niebuhr's realist disciples in the United States, who accused him of being a utopian naïf. Alves responded by calling the realism of his critics the ideology of the establishment. Alves, "Christian Realism." For more on this debate, see Barreto Júnior, "Um convite a sonhar," 118–19.

40 Alves, *Variações*, 67.

41 Alves, *Variações*, 200.

42 Alves, *Tomorrow's Child*, 26.

43 Alves, *Tomorrow's Child*, 27.

44 Alves, *Tomorrow's Child*, 28–29.

45 Alves, *Tomorrow's Child*, 33.

46 Alves, *Tomorrow's Child*, 119.

47 Alves, *Theology of Human Hope*, 102.

48 Alves, *Theology of Human Hope*, 114.

49 Alves, *Theology of Human Hope*, 94.

50 Alves, *Theology of Human Hope*, 24, 28.

51 Alves, *Poet*, 74. See also Alves, *I Believe*, 171; and Alves, *Variações*.

52 Alves, *Poet*, 74.

53 Alves, *Theology of Human Hope*, 114.

54 Alves, *Theology of Human Hope*, 114–15. Alves does not take the suffering of the "slaves" as a virtue, remarking that the acceptance of suffering grants no access to a liberating hope. He insists that the complacency of the slave is yet another tragic result of structures of oppression.

55 Alves, *Variações*, 65.

56 Alves, *Tomorrow's Child*, 116.

57 Alves, *Variações*, 205.

58 Alves, *Variações*, 205.

59 Alves, *Variações*, 205.

60 Quoted in Junior, *É uma pena não viver*, 258.

61 Quoted in Alves, *Poet*, 137–38 (translation modified). See also Alves, *Variações*, 70–71.

62 Alves, *Variações*, 70.

63 Alves, *Variações*, 71.

64 Alves, *Variações*, 70.

65 See Alves, *Tomorrow's Child*, 116.

66 See Marx, *Capital I*, 93.

67 Alves, *Tomorrow's Child*, 194.

68 Alves, *Tomorrow's Child*, 194.

69 Alves, *Variações*, 65–66.

70 Alves, *Variações*, 66.

71 Alves, *Tomorrow's Child*, 201.

72 Alves, *Tomorrow's Child*, 200–201.

73 Alves, *Poet*, 139.

74 Alves, *Variações*, 193.

75 Alves, *Variações*, 196.

76 Quoted in Alves, *Poet*, 137.

77 See, for example, Alves, *Transparencies of Eternity*, 25.

78 Alves, *Theology of Human Hope*, 24, 28.

79 Derrida, "Of an Apocalyptic Tone."

80 Derrida, "Of an Apocalyptic Tone," 72.

81 Derrida, "Of an Apocalyptic Tone," 89.

82 Derrida, "Of an Apocalyptic Tone," 89.

83 Derrida, "Of an Apocalyptic Tone," 72.

84   See Alves, *Perguntaram-me se acredito em Deus*; and Lima Júnior, "Assim Beijava Benjamin." For a survey of Alves's different "phases," see Cervantes-Ortiz, "Theology of Human Joy."

85   The documentary is called *O sonho ecumênico* (The ecumenical dream) and was filmed by the Faculdade Unida de Vitória (Vitória Union School) in remembrance of the Protestant roots of the ecumenical and liberationist movements in Brazil during the 1940s and 1950s.

86   See, for example, Alves, *Perguntaram-me se acredito em Deus*.

87   Lima Júnior, "Pipas, piões e apostas," 65.

88   Lima Júnior, "Pipas, piões e apostas," 75–76.

89   Alves, *Tomorrow's Child*.

90   Barreto Júnior, "Um convite a sonhar," 122; see also Barreto Júnior, "Rubem Alves," 48.

91   This is exemplified in Alves's own relationship to his Protestant roots, which he often disavowed but had to recognize were ingrained in his thought and body. At the occasion of celebrations marking the 450th anniversary of John Calvin's birth, Alves spoke to a Geneva audience, confessing that "Protestantism is a part of my body . . . something which I love, something which I hate." He further stated that at points in his life he was ready to "vomit" his Protestantism out of him but realized he could not. And that is when he realized he could transform the bitter dreams he inherited from his Presbyterian formation into sweeter dreams. See Alves, "Invitation to Dream," 60.

92   Cervantes-Ortiz, "Theology of Human Joy," 11.

93   Derrida, "Of an Apocalyptic Tone," 89.

94   Alves, *Theology of Human Hope*, 166.

95   I borrow this formulation from Karmen MacKendrick's work about sound and accent. See MacKendrick, *Matter of Voice*.

96   Alves, *Theology of Human Hope*, 13.

97   Alves, *Theology of Human Hope*, 15.

98   Puleo, *Struggle Is One*, 191. The quotation comes from the author's interview with Alves.

99   Alves, *Poet*, 116.

100 Alves, *Variações*, 192–93. According to Barreto Júnior, "Alves's contributions as a theopoet reside in his contestation of ontological discourses about God." He continues, "In his move from theology to theopoetics he has affirmed that in order to know God one must forget God. In other words, we must 'let God be God.'" Barreto Júnior, "Rubem Alves," 63.

101 This is based on a possible reading of Derrida, *Specters of Marx*.

102 Alves, *Variações*, 202.

103 Quoted in Alves, *Tomorrow's Child*, 83.

104 Lima Júnior, "Assim Beijava Benjamin," 190. Lima Júnior's point has a biographical vein as he connects Alves's turn to poetics to the birth of his daughter Raquel, fourteen years after the birth of his youngest son. Alves in fact refers to this as a "conversion" experience for him. He states that he

realized then that he "would not spend another moment of my life writing academically." Puleo, *Struggle Is One*, 188.

105 See Alves, *I Believe*.
106 Alves, *Transparencies of Eternity*, 15.
107 Alves, *I Believe*, 30 (translation modified).
108 Alves, *I Believe*, 75.
109 Alves, *Poet*, 138.

SIX. FUGITIVE FUTURES

1 The gendered undertones of the destruction of Babylon, depicted by the book of Revelation as the "great whore," are impossibly misogynistic. In the ethical-liberationist reading of apocalypse, the patriarchal worldview represented by Revelation is cause for suspicion but also for probing how the text *functions* as a cultural artifact shaping the present moment. Feminist biblical scholars like Elisabeth Schüssler Fiorenza therefore prioritize the ethical pull Revelation may continue to exercise, sometimes even despite the text's glaring sexist and otherwise oppressive tropes. See Schüssler Fiorenza, *In Memory of Her*; and Schüssler Fiorenza, *Rhetoric and Ethic*. For a fine analysis of the gender tropes in Revelation as well as a case for its liberative and queer possibilities today, see Menéndez-Antuña, *Thinking Sex*. My guide through the gender trouble induced by Revelation is Keller, *Apocalypse Now and Then*, chap. 6.
2 Keller, *Apocalypse Now and Then*, xii, 276.
3 Winters, *Hope Draped in Black*.
4 See Moten, *Stolen Life*, 131; and Moten and Harney, *Undercommons*.
5 Keller, *Apocalypse Now and Then*, 4–5.
6 Keller, *Apocalypse Now and Then*, 10–11.
7 Keller, *Apocalypse Now and Then*, 8.
8 Keller, *Apocalypse Now and Then*, 87; see also 89–91. Keller later also suggests that apocalypse's ubiquity as the dominant mode of Western temporality—in both its reactionary and revolutionary embodiments—"serve[s] as a kind of epistemic *eschaton*, not unlike 'time' as a constitutive idea within the Kantian transcendental limit of reason" (90).
9 Keller, *Apocalypse Now and Then*, 276.
10 Keller, *Apocalypse Now and Then*, 2. Keller's attentiveness to apocalypse as an opening into the present is mobilized in her response to the crisis inflicted by the COVID-19 pandemic. See Keller and Thatamanil, "Is This an Apocalypse?"
11 Keller, *God and Power*, 85–87.
12 Keller, *Political Theology of the Earth*, 58.
13 Keller, *Political Theology of the Earth*, 113.
14 Keller, *Political Theology of the Earth*, 114.
15 Keller, *Political Theology of the Earth*, 59.

16 Keller, *Political Theology of the Earth*, 90.

17 Keller, *Apocalypse Now and Then*, 14.

18 Keller, *Apocalypse Now and Then*, 131.

19 Keller, *Apocalypse Now and Then*, 131.

20 It is always worth returning to this statement, which I have shared in my introduction: "In finance we worry about money and we worry about the future." Drake and Fabozzi, *Basics of Finance*, 1.

21 Keller, *Facing Apocalypse*, 113.

22 Keller, *Facing Apocalypse*, 114.

23 Keller, *Apocalypse Now and Then*, xii.

24 Keller, *Apocalypse Now and Then*, 134.

25 Keller, *Apocalypse Now and Then*, 134.

26 Keller, *Political Theology of the Earth*, 59. The term *ingather* is part of Keller's discussion of the Pauline text in 1 Corinthians 7:29: "The appointed time is short." The Greek term generally translated as "short," *sunestalemnos*, implies an ingathering, as if Paul were to say that "time is gathered together" or "contracted." Keller, *Political Theology of the Earth*, 2–3.

27 Keller and Moore, "Derridapocalypse," 204.

28 Keller, *Apocalypse Now and Then*, 30.

29 Keller, *Apocalypse Now and Then*, 134.

30 This formulation resonates deeply with Emmanuel Levinas's reflections in *Time and the Other*. For him, the future is yet another name for the Other. "The future," he states, "is what is in no way grasped. The exteriority of the future is totally different from spatial exteriority precisely through the fact that the future is absolutely surprising. . . . [T]he future is what is not grasped, what befalls us and lays hold of us. The other is the future. The very relationship with the other is the relationship with the future. It seems to me impossible to speak of time in a subject alone, or to speak of a purely personal duration." Levinas, *Time and the Other*, 76–77.

31 Keller, *Intercarnations*, 145.

32 Keller, *Apocalypse Now and Then*, 20.

33 Winters, *Hope Draped in Black*.

34 See K.-Y. Taylor, *Race for Profit*.

35 Racial capitalism, as conceived of by Cedric Robinson, challenges the Marxist understanding that capitalism represents a revolutionary moment that overcame feudalist modes of production and social relations. Capitalist development depended on slavery, imperial violence, and genocide. Robinson identifies how the formation of the modern proletariat, which Karl Marx deems as the historical necessary condition for the rise of capitalism, was a racialized and racializing process. Groups like the Irish and Jews were racialized subjects in the formation of the proletarian force igniting capitalism. Capitalist development, in this sense, has always been in sync with the deepening of racist regimes. See Robinson, *Black Marxism*.

36 See Wilderson, *Incognegro*; Wilderson, *Red, White and Black*; Wilderson, *Afropessimism*; Sexton, "Unbearable Blackness"; Hartman, *Scenes of Subjection*; and Moten, "Blackness and Nothingness."

37 Moten, "Blackness and Nothingness," 778.

38 For an account of these traditions and their differences from Afro-pessimism, see Sexton, "Affirmation in the Dark."

39 Sexton, "Affirmation in the Dark," 98.

40 Sexton, "Affirmation in the Dark," 101; see Fanon, *Black Skin, White Masks*.

41 Sexton, "Affirmation in the Dark," 102.

42 Warren, *Ontological Terror*, 2.

43 Warren, *Ontological Terror*, 9.

44 Warren, "Black Nihilism," 223.

45 Warren, "Black Nihilism," 243.

46 Warren, "Black Nihilism," 244; see also Warren, *Ontological Terror*.

47 Lloyd, "For What Are Whites to Hope?," 170.

48 Lloyd, "For What Are Whites to Hope?," 179.

49 Winters, *Hope Draped in Black*.

50 Winters, *Hope Draped in Black*, 6.

51 Winters, *Hope Draped in Black*, 6–7.

52 Winters bases his discussion in the engagements of Anne Cheng and Judith Butler with Freud's essay. See Cheng, *Melancholy of Race*; and Butler, *Precarious Life*.

53 Winters, *Hope Draped in Black*, 19.

54 Winters, *Hope Draped in Black*, 21.

55 Winters, *Hope Draped in Black*, 44; see also 85–90.

56 Winters, *Hope Draped in Black*, 50.

57 Winters, *Hope Draped in Black*, 62–63.

58 Winters, *Hope Draped in Black*, 251.

59 See Gutiérrez, *Theology of Liberation*, 168–77.

60 Brown, *Slave Life in Georgia*, 92.

61 Desmond, "American Capitalism Is Brutal."

62 Day, *Religious Resistance to Neoliberalism*, 4.

63 Day, *Religious Resistance to Neoliberalism*, 14.

64 Day, *Religious Resistance to Neoliberalism*, 137.

65 Day, *Religious Resistance to Neoliberalism*, 163.

66 This expression has been elaborated by Monica Coleman's womanist theology of salvation. See Coleman, *Making a Way*.

67 The image of the hush harbor has been explored theologically by Karen Baker-Fletcher. See Baker-Fletcher, "Erotic"; and Baker-Fletcher, "More than Suffering." In literature Toni Morrison's *Beloved* continues to be the most incisive rendering of the gatherings that take place in the hush harbor.

68 Moten, *Stolen Life*, 26–27.

69 Moten and Harney, *Undercommons*, 131.

70 Moten, *Stolen Life*, 131.

71 Moten and Harney, *Undercommons*, 42–43.

72 Moten, *Stolen Life*, 228.

73 My introduction detected that an emphasis on futurity has been framed as escapist by theologians committed to liberative praxis and theologies. While I do not deny the valence of these critiques, my work in this chapter has argued that future-talk does not imply a refusal to engage reality. The escape, as I construe it here, is less a refusal to engage reality and more a refusal to engage reality under its own constraints.

74 I thank Shelly Rambo for helping me craft this formulation.

75 Moten, *Stolen Life*, 228.

76 Moten, *Stolen Life*, 228. Elsewhere Moten suggests that "[the] desire to be free, manifest as flight or escape, as a fugitivity that may well prove to veer away even from freedom as its telos, is indexed to anoriginal lawlessness." Moten, *Stolen Life*, 15.

77 For Derrida, the intractable "tone" that speaks under the name of apocalypse is never "one" but rather a multiplicity of voices that "parasitize" any dominant voice. See Derrida, "Of an Apocalyptic Tone." I have offered a more detailed reading of this tantalizing essay in Maia, "Betrayed by Accent."

78 Keller, *Facing Apocalypse*, xiv–xv.

BIBLIOGRAPHY

Adkins, Lisa. *The Time of Money*. Currencies. Stanford, CA: Stanford University Press, 2018.

Allon, Fiona. "The Feminisation of Finance: Gender, Labour and the Limits of Inclusion." *Australian Feminist Studies* 29, no. 79 (2014): 12–30.

Allon, Fiona. "Speculating on Everyday Life: The Cultural Economy of the Quotidian." *Journal of Communication Inquiry* 34, no. 4 (October 2010): 366–81.

Alves, Rubem. "Christian Realism: Theology of the Establishment." *Christianity and Crisis* 33, no. 15 (September 7, 1973): 173–76.

Alves, Rubem. *I Believe in the Resurrection of the Body*. Translated by L. M. McCoy. Philadelphia: Fortress, 1986.

Alves, Rubem. "An Invitation to Dream." *Ecumenical Review* 39, no. 1 (January 1987): 59–62.

Alves, Rubem. *Perguntaram-me se acredito em Deus*. São Paulo: Editora Planeta do Brasil, 2007.

Alves, Rubem. *The Poet, the Warrior, the Prophet*. London: SCM Press, 1990.

Alves, Rubem. "Sobre deuses e caquis." *Comunicações do ISER (Instituto de Estudos de Religião)* 7, no. 32 (1988): 9–31.

Alves, Rubem. *Suspiro dos oprimidos*. São Paulo: Paulinas, 1984.

Alves, Rubem. *Teologia da libertação em suas origens: Uma interpretação teológica do significado da revolução no Brasil–1963*. Vitória, Brazil: IFTAV and Unisales, 2004.

Alves, Rubem. "A Theological Interpretation of the Meaning of the Revolution in Brazil." Master's thesis, Union Theological Seminary, New York, 1964.

Alves, Rubem. *A Theology of Human Hope*. Washington, DC: Corpus Books, 1969.

Alves, Rubem. *Tomorrow's Child: Imagination, Creativity, and the Rebirth of Culture.* New York: Harper and Row, 1972.

Alves, Rubem. "Towards a Theology of Liberation: An Exploration of the Encounter between the Languages of Humanistic Messianism and Messianic Humanism." PhD diss., Princeton Theological Seminary, 1968.

Alves, Rubem. *Transparencies of Eternity.* Translated by Jovelino Ramos and Joan Ramos. Miami, FL: Convivium, 2010.

Alves, Rubem. *Variações sobre a vida e a morte: A teologia e sua fala.* São Paulo: Paulinas, 1982.

Amadeo, Kimberly. "National Debt by Year: Compared to GDP, Recessions and Other Major Events." *About News,* n.d. https://www.thebalance.com /national-debt-by-year-compared-to-gdp-and-major-events-3306287.

Amato, Massimo, and Luca Fantacci. *The End of Finance.* Cambridge, UK: Polity, 2012.

Andrew, Edward. *The Genealogy of Values: The Aesthetic Economy of Nietzsche and Proust.* Lanham, MD: Rowman and Littlefield, 1995.

Ansell, David A. *The Death Gap: How Inequality Kills.* Chicago: University of Chicago Press, 2017.

Appadurai, Arjun. *Banking on Words: The Failure of Language in the Age of Derivative Finance.* Chicago: University of Chicago Press, 2016.

Appadurai, Arjun. "The Ghost in the Financial Machine." *Public Culture* 23, no. 3 (Fall 2011): 517–39.

Appadurai, Arjun. "The Wealth of Dividuals." In *Derivatives and the Wealth of Societies,* edited by Benjamin Lee and Randy Martin, 17–36. Chicago: University of Chicago Press, 2016.

Arnoldi, Jakob. "Derivatives: Virtual Values and Real Risks." *Theory, Culture and Society* 21, no. 6 (December 2004): 23–42.

Ascher, Ivan. *Portfolio Society: On the Capitalist Mode of Prediction.* New York: Zone Books, 2016.

Augustine. *Confessions.* Translated by Henry Chadwick. Oxford: Oxford University Press, 2008.

Ayache, Elie. *The Blank Swan: The End of Probability.* Chichester, UK: John Wiley and Sons, 2010.

Ayache, Elie. "On Black-Scholes." In *Derivatives and the Wealth of Societies,* edited by Benjamin Lee and Randy Martin, 240–51. Chicago: University of Chicago Press, 2016.

Baker-Fletcher, Karen. "The Erotic in Contemporary Black Women's Writings." In *Loving the Body: Black Religious Studies and the Erotic,* edited by Anthony B. Pinn and Dwight N. Hopkins, 199–215. New York: Palgrave Macmillan, 2006.

Baker-Fletcher, Karen. "More than Suffering: The Healing and Resurrecting Spirit of God." In *Womanist Theological Ethics: A Reader,* edited by Katie G. Cannon, Emilie Maureen Townes, and Angela D. Sims, 155–81. Louisville, KY: Westminster John Knox, 2011.

Baran, Paul A., and Paul M. Sweezy. *Monopoly Capital: An Essay on the American Economic and Social Order*. New York: Monthly Review Press, 1966.

Barreto Júnior, Raimundo César. "Um convite a sonhar: A influência de Richard Shaull na formação do pensamento de Rubem Alves, e sua relevância política." *Numen: Revista de Estudos e Pesquisa da Religião* 22, no. 2 (July 2019): 107–22.

Barreto Júnior, Raimundo César. "Rubem Alves and the Kaki Tree: The Trajectory of an Exile Thinker." *Perspectivas*, no. 13 (Spring 2016): 47–64. http://perspectivas.wpengine.com/wp-content/uploads/2016/02/P-E-R-S-P-E-C-T-I-V-A-S_Spring_2016.pdf.

Bell, Daniel. *The Cultural Contradictions of Capitalism*. 20th anniv. ed. New York: Basic Books, 1996.

Benítez, Hermes H. *Las muertes de Salvador Allende: Una investigación crítica de las principales versiones de sus ultimos momentos*. Santiago, Chile: RIL Editores, 2006.

Benjamin, Walter. "Capitalism as Religion." In *Selected Writings of Walter Benjamin*. Vol. 6. Edited by Michael W. Jennings and Marcus Bullock, 259–262. Translated by Chad Kautzer. Cambridge, MA: Belknap Press of Harvard University Press, 1996.

Benjamin, Walter. *Illuminations: Essays and Reflections*. Edited by Hannah Arendt. New York: Schocken Books, 2007.

Benjamin, Walter. *The Arcades Project*. Edited by Rolf Tiedemann. Translated by Howard Eiland and Kevin McLaughlin. Cambridge, MA: Harvard University Press, 1999.

Berlant, Lauren. *Cruel Optimism*. Durham, NC: Duke University Press, 2011.

Best, Beverley. "Postcolonialism and the Deconstructive Scenario: Representing Gayatri Spivak." *Environment and Planning D: Society and Space* 17, no. 4 (August 1999): 475–94.

Betcher, Sharon V. *Spirit and the Politics of Disablement*. Minneapolis, MN: Fortress, 2007.

Black, Fischer. "Noise." *Journal of Finance* 41, no. 3 (July 1986): 529–43.

Bloch, Ernst. *Thomas Münzer als Theologe der Revolution*. Bibliothek Suhrkamp 77. Frankfurt am Main: Suhrkamp, 1963.

Bonino, José Míguez. *Doing Theology in a Revolutionary Situation*. Confrontation Books. Philadelphia: Fortress, 1975.

Bonino, José Míguez. "Reading Jürgen Moltmann from Latin America." *Asbury Theological Journal* 55, no. 1 (Spring 2000): 105–14.

Borghi, Roberto, Fernando Sarti, and Marcos Cintra. "The 'Financialized' Structure of Automobile Corporations in the 2000s." *World Review of Political Economy* 4, no. 3 (Fall 2013): 387–409.

Bosworth, Barry, Gary Burtless, and Kan Zhang. *Later Retirement, Inequality in Old Age, and the Growing Gap in Longevity between the Rich and Poor*. Economic Studies at Brookings. Washington, DC: Brookings Institution, 2016. https://www.brookings.edu/wp-content/uploads/2016/02/BosworthBurtlessZhang_retirementinequalitylongevity_012815.pdf.

Brown, John. *Slave Life in Georgia: A Narrative of the Life, Sufferings, and Escape of John Brown, a Fugitive Slave.* Savannah, GA: Beehive, 1991.

Bustamante, Rodrigo. "Chile ante la 'verdad histórica' del suicidio de Allende." *BBC Mundo*, July 19, 2011. http://www.bbc.co.uk/mundo/noticias/2011/07/110719_allende_suicidio_ao.shtml.

Butler, Judith. *Precarious Life: The Powers of Mourning and Violence.* London: Verso, 2006.

Byles, John Barnard. *Byles on Bills of Exchange: The Law of Bills of Exchange, Promissory Notes, Bank Notes and Cheques.* 25th ed. London: Sweet and Maxwell, 1983.

Cahill, Damien, and Martijn Konings. *Neoliberalism.* Cambridge, UK: Polity, 2017.

Caldwell, Bruce, and Leonidas Montes. "Friedrich Hayek y sus dos visitas a Chile." *Estudios Públicos* 137 (Summer 2015): 87–132.

Callon, Michel, ed. *The Laws of the Markets.* Oxford: Blackwell, 1998.

Case, Anne, and Angus Deaton. "Rising Morbidity and Mortality in Midlife among White Non-Hispanic Americans in the 21st Century." *Proceedings of the National Academy of Sciences of the United States of America* 112, no. 49 (December 2015): 15078–83.

Casos, Alejandro. "Fetichismo, crítica de las utopías y teología de la liberación en Franz Hinkelammert." *Revista de Discusiones Filosóficas desde Acá* 6 (2008): 1–42. http://www.ideaz-institute.com/sp/CUADERNO6/C62.pdf.

CBS News. "Retirement Dreams Disappear with 401(k)s." April 17, 2009. http://www.cbsnews.com/news/retirement-dreams-disappear-with-401ks/.

Cervantes-Ortiz, Leopoldo. "A Theology of Human Joy: The Liberating-Poetic-Ludic Theology of Rubem Alves." *Perspectivas*, no. 13 (Spring 2016): 6–26. http://perspectivas.wpengine.com/wp-content/uploads/2016/02/P-E-R-S-P-E-C-T-I-V-A-S_Spring_2016.pdf.

Cheng, Anne Anlin. *The Melancholy of Race.* Oxford: Oxford University Press, 2001.

Chitty, Joseph. *A Practical Treatise on Bills of Exchange, Promissory Notes, and Bankers' Checks: Containing Forms of Affidavits of Debt in Actions Thereon, and of Declarations and Pleas in Such Actions, Adapted to the New Rules on Pleading: With All the Statutes and Decided Cases in Full, Relating to Bills and Notes the Bank of England and Bankers.* Vol. 1. London: S. Sweet, 1834.

Clinton, Angela. "Flexible Labor: Restructuring the American Work Force." *Monthly Labor Review* 120, no. 8 (August 1997): 3–27.

Coffey, Clare, Patricia Espinoza Revollo, Rowan Harvey, Max Lawson, Anam Parvez Butt, Kim Piaget, Diana Sarosi, and Julie Thekkudan. "Time to Care: Unpaid and Underpaid Care Work and the Global Inequality Crisis." Briefing paper, Oxfam International, January 2020. https://oxfamilibrary.openrepository.com/bitstream/handle/10546/620928/bp-time-to-care-inequality-200120-en.pdf.

Coleman, Monica A. *Making a Way out of No Way: A Womanist Theology.* Innovations. Minneapolis, MN: Fortress, 2008.

Cox, Harvey. Preface to *A Theology of Human Hope*, by Rubem Alves. Washington, DC: Corpus Books, 1969.

Dana-Farber Cancer Institute and Boston Children's Cancer and Blood Disorders Center. "Childhood Leukemia Patients from High-Poverty Areas More Likely to Suffer Early Relapse." February 23, 2016. https://www.dana-farber.org/newsroom/news-releases/2016/childhood-leukemia-patients-from-high-poverty-areas-more-likely-to-suffer-early-relapse/.

David, R. J., and J. W. Collins. "Layers of Inequality: Power, Policy, and Health." *American Journal of Public Health* 104, no. 1 (February 2014): s8–s10.

Day, Keri. *Religious Resistance to Neoliberalism: Womanist and Black Feminist Perspectives*. Black Religion, Womanist Thought, Social Justice. New York: Palgrave Macmillan, 2016.

De La Torre, Miguel A. *Embracing Hopelessness*. Minneapolis, MN: Fortress, 2017.

Deleuze, Gilles, and Félix Guattari. *Anti-Oedipus: Capitalism and Schizophrenia*. Translated by Robert Hurley, Helen R. Lane, and Mark Seem. New York: Viking, 1977.

De Man, Paul. *Allegories of Reading: Figural Language in Rousseau, Nietzsche, Rilke, and Proust*. New Haven, CT: Yale University Press, 1979.

Derrida, Jacques. *Given Time: I. Counterfeit Money*. Chicago: University of Chicago Press, 1992.

Derrida, Jacques. "Of an Apocalyptic Tone Recently Adopted in Philosophy." Translated by John P. Leavey Jr. *Semeia* 23 (1982): 63–97.

Derrida, Jacques. *Of Grammatology*. Translated by Gayatri Chakravorty Spivak. Corrected ed. Baltimore, MD: Johns Hopkins University Press, 1998.

Derrida, Jacques. *Specters of Marx: The State of the Debt, the Work of Mourning, and the New International*. Translated by Peggy Kamuf. New York: Routledge, 1994.

Desmond, Matthew. "American Capitalism Is Brutal. You Can Trace That to the Plantation." *New York Times Magazine*, August 14, 2019. https://www.nytimes.com/interactive/2019/08/14/magazine/slavery-capitalism.html.

Do Carmo, Marcelo, Mario Sacomano Neto, and Julio Cesar Donadone. "Financialization in the Automotive Industry: Shareholders, Managers, and Salaries." *Journal of Economic Issues* 53, no. 3 (2019): 841–62.

Dodd, Nigel. *The Social Life of Money*. Princeton, NJ: Princeton University Press, 2016.

Drake, Pamela Peterson, and Frank J. Fabozzi. *The Basics of Finance: An Introduction to Financial Markets, Business Finance, and Portfolio Management*. Hoboken, NJ: John Wiley and Sons, 2010.

Duhigg, Charles. "What Does Your Credit-Card Company Know about You?" *New York Times Magazine*, May 12, 2009. https://www.nytimes.com/2009/05/17/magazine/17credit-t.html.

Duménil, Gérard, and Dominique Lévy. *Capital Resurgent: Roots of the Neoliberal Revolution*. Translated by Derek Jeffers. Cambridge, MA: Harvard University Press, 2004.

Dussel, Enrique. *Las metáforas teológicas de Marx*. Estella, Spain: Verbo, 1993.

Dylag, Matthew. "The Negotiability of Promissory Notes and Bills of Exchange in the Time of Chief Justice Holt." *Journal of Legal History* 31, no. 2 (2010): 149–75.

Edelman, Lee. *No Future: Queer Theory and the Death Drive*. Durham, NC: Duke University Press, 2004.

Espín, Orlando. *Idol and Grace: On Traditioning and Subversive Hope*. Maryknoll, NY: Orbis Books, 2014.

Esposito, Elena. *The Future of Futures: The Time of Money in Financing and Society*. Translated by Elena Esposito and Andrew K. Whitehead. Cheltenham, UK: Edward Elgar, 2011.

Fabozzi, Frank J., and Franco Modigliani. *Capital Markets: Institutions and Instruments*. 4th ed. Upper Saddle River, NJ: Prentice Hall, 2009.

Faculdade Unida de Vitória. "O sonho ecumênico." Directed by Wanderley Pereira da Rosa. Recorded May 2012, uploaded August 25, 2017. YouTube video, 1:11:52. https://www.youtube.com/watch?v=dxLxbqsEdFM&t=11s.

Fanon, Frantz. *Black Skin, White Masks*. London: Pluto, 2008.

Firebaugh, Glenn, Francesco Acciai, Aggie J. Noah, Christopher Prather, and Claudia Nau. "Why Lifespans Are More Variable among Blacks than among Whites in the United States." *Demography* 51, no. 6 (December 2014): 2025–45.

Foster, John Bellamy. "The Age of Monopoly-Finance Capital." *Monthly Review* 61, no. 9 (February 1, 2010): 1–13.

Foucault, Michel. *The Birth of Biopolitics: Lectures at the Collège de France, 1978–1979*. New York: Picador, 2010.

Foucault, Michel. *The Order of Things: An Archaeology of the Human Sciences*. New York: Vintage, 1994.

Franklin, Benjamin. "Advice to a Young Tradesman, [21 July 1748]." In *Founders Online,* National Archives. https://founders.archives.gov/documents /Franklin/01-03-02-0130.

Friedman, Benjamin M. *The Moral Consequences of Economic Growth*. New York: Alfred A. Knopf, 2005.

Friedman, Milton. *Capitalism and Freedom*. With Rose D. Friedman. 40th anniv. ed. Chicago: University of Chicago Press, 2002.

Friedman, Milton. "The Need for Futures Markets in Currencies." CATO *Journal* 31, no. 3 (Fall 2011): 635–41.

Friedman, Milton. "Neo-liberalism and Its Prospects." *Farmand*, February 17, 1951. Collected Works of Milton Friedman Project records, Hoover Institution Archives. https://miltonfriedman.hoover.org/objects /57816.

Froud, Julie, Sukhdev Johal, Adam Leaver, and Karel Williams. *Financialization and Strategy: Narrative and Numbers*. New York: Routledge, 2006.

Galbraith, John Kenneth. *The Great Crash, 1929*. 50th anniv. ed. New York: Avon Books, 1980.

Giddens, Anthony. *Runaway World: How Globalisation Is Reshaping Our Lives.* London: Profile Books, 1999. Kindle.

Goodchild, Philip. "Exposing Mammon: Devotion to Money in a Market Society." *Dialog: A Journal of Theology* 52, no. 1 (March 2013): 47–57.

Goodchild, Philip. *Theology of Money.* Durham, NC: Duke University Press, 2009.

Graeber, David. *Debt: The First 5,000 Years.* Brooklyn, NY: Melville House, 2011.

Gutiérrez, Gustavo. *The God of Life.* Maryknoll, NY: Orbis Books, 1991.

Gutiérrez, Gustavo. *Las Casas: In Search of the Poor of Jesus Christ.* Maryknoll, NY: Orbis Books, 1993.

Gutiérrez, Gustavo. "Lenguaje teológico: Plenitud del silencio." *Revista Latino-americana de Teología* 13, no. 38 (May–August 1996): 141–62.

Gutiérrez, Gustavo. *The Power of the Poor in History.* Maryknoll, NY: Orbis Books, 1983.

Gutiérrez, Gustavo. *A Theology of Liberation: History, Politics, and Salvation.* Maryknoll, NY: Orbis Books, 1973.

Hamermesh, Daniel S. "The Timing of Work over Time." *Economic Journal* 109, no. 452 (January 1999): 37–66.

Hardoon, Deborah. "An Economy for the 99%: It's Time to Build a Human Economy That Benefits Everyone, Not Just the Privileged Few." Briefing paper, Oxfam International, January 16, 2017. https://www.oxfam.org/en /research/economy-99.

Hardoon, Deborah, Sophia Ayele, and Ricardo Fuentes-Nieva. "An Economy for the 1%: How Privilege and Power in the Economy Drive Extreme Inequality and How This Can Be Stopped." Briefing paper, Oxfam International, January 18, 2016. https://www.oxfam.org/en/research/economy-1.

Hartman, Saidiya V. *Scenes of Subjection: Terror, Slavery, and Self-Making in Nineteenth-Century America.* New York: Oxford University Press, 1997.

Harvey, David. "Afterthoughts on Piketty's Capital." Reading Marx's *Capital* with David Harvey, May 17, 2014. http://davidharvey.org/2014/05/afterthoughts -pikettys-capital/.

Harvey, David. *A Brief History of Neoliberalism.* Oxford: Oxford University Press, 2005.

Harvey, David. *A Companion to Marx's "Capital."* London: Verso, 2010.

Harvey, David. *The Enigma of Capital.* Oxford: Oxford University Press, 2010.

Hayek, Friedrich von. "Extracts from an Interview with Friedrich von Hayek." *El Mercurio*, April 12, 1981. Republished in *Punto do Vista Economico*, December 21, 2016, https://puntodevistaeconomico.com/2016/12/21/extracts-from -an-interview-with-friedrich-von-hayek-el-mercurio-chile-1981/.

Henderson, George. *Value in Marx: The Persistence of Value in a More-Than-Capitalist World.* Minneapolis: University of Minnesota Press, 2013.

Hillard, Derek. "History as a Dual Process: Nietzsche on Exchange and Power." *Nietzsche Studien: Internationales Jahrbuch für die Nietzsche-Forschung* 31 (2002): 40–56.

187

Hinkelammert, Franz J. *Las armas ideológicas de la muerte: El discernimiento de los fetiches: capitalismo y cristianismo*. San José, Costa Rica: EDUCA, 1977.

Hinkelammert, Franz J. *Crítica de la razón utópica*. Revised and expanded edition. Bilbao: Editorial Desclée, 2002.

Hinkelammert, Franz J. *Cultura de esperanza y sociedad sin exclusión*. San José, Costa Rica: Editorial DEI, 1995.

Hinkelammert, Franz J. *Dialéctica del desarrollo desigual*. Santiago, Chile: Ediciones Universitarias de Valparaíso, 1972.

Hinkelammert, Franz J. *Ideologías del desarrollo y dialéctica de la historia*. Buenos Aires: Paidós, 1970.

Hinkelammert, Franz J. *Ideologías del sometimiento*. San José, Costa Rica: EDUCA–DEI, 1977.

Hinkelammert, Franz J. *The Ideological Weapons of Death: A Theological Critique of Capitalism*. Translated by Phillip Berryman. Maryknoll, NY: Orbis Books, 1986.

Hinkelammert, Franz J. *Lo indispensable es inútil: Hacia una espiritualidad de la liberación*. San José, Costa Rica: Editorial Arlekín, 2012.

Hinkelammert, Franz J. *La maldición que pesa sobre la ley: Las raíces del pensamiento crítico en Pablo de Tarso*. San José, Costa Rica: Editorial Arlekín, 2010.

Hinkelammert, Franz J. *Sacrificios humanos y sociedad occidental: Lúcifer y la bestia*. San José, Costa Rica: Departamento Ecuménico de Investigaciones, 1991.

Hinkelammert, Franz J. *El subdesarrollo latinoamericano: Un caso de desarrollo capitalista*. Buenos Aires: Paidós, 1970.

Hinkelammert, Franz J. *El sujeto y la ley: El retorno del sujeto reprimido*. Heredia, Costa Rica: Editorial Universidad Nacional, 2003.

Hinkelammert, Franz J. *Teología del mercado total: Ensayos económico-teológicos*. La Paz: HISBOL, 1989.

Hinkelammert, Franz J. *Der Wachstumsprozess in der Sowjetwirtschaft: Eine Untersuchung der Produktionsstruktur, des Lenkungsprozesses und des Volkseinkommens*. Berlin: Osteuropa-Institut, 1961.

Hinkelammert, Franz J., and Hugo Assmann. *A idolatria do mercado: Ensaios sobre teologia e economia*. São Paulo: Vozes, 1989.

Hunt, P. J., and J. E. Kennedy. *Financial Derivatives in Theory and Practice*. Chichester, UK: Wiley, 2000.

Irwin, Neil, and Quoctrung Bui. "The Rich Live Longer Everywhere. For the Poor, Geography Matters." *New York Times*, April 11, 2016. https://www.nytimes.com/interactive/2016/04/11/upshot/for-the-poor-geography-is-life-and-death.html.

Jacobs, Jerry A., and Kathleen Gerson. *The Time Divide: Work, Family, and Gender Inequality*. Cambridge, MA: Harvard University Press, 2004.

Joseph, Miranda. *Debt to Society: Accounting for Life under Capitalism*. Minneapolis: University of Minnesota Press, 2014.

Junior, Gonçalo. *É uma pena não viver: Uma biografia de Rubem Alves*. São Paulo: Planeta do Brasil, 2015.

Kalleberg, Arne. "Evolving Employment Relations in the United States." In *Sourcebook of Labor Markets: Evolving Structures and Processes*, edited by Ivar Berg and Arne L. Kalleberg, 187–206. New York: Kluwer and Plenum, 2000.

Kalleberg, Arne L., Jeremy Reynolds, and Peter V. Marsden. "Externalizing Employment: Flexible Staffing Arrangements in US Organizations." *Social Science Research* 32, no. 4 (December 2003): 525–52.

Kantor, Jodi. "Working Anything but 9 to 5." *New York Times*, August 13, 2014. https://www.nytimes.com/interactive/2014/08/13/us/starbucks-workers -scheduling-hours.html.

Kaufmann, Walter. *Nietzsche: Philosopher, Psychologist, Antichrist*. Princeton, NJ: Princeton University Press, 1974.

Keller, Catherine. *Apocalypse Now and Then: A Feminist Guide to the End of the World*. 2nd ed. Minneapolis, MN: Augsburg Fortress, 2005.

Keller, Catherine. *Facing Apocalypse: Climate, Democracy, and Other Last Chances*. Maryknoll, NY: Orbis Books, 2021.

Keller, Catherine. *God and Power: Counter-Apocalyptic Journeys*. Minneapolis, MN: Fortress, 2005.

Keller, Catherine. *Intercarnations: Exercises in Theological Possibility*. New York: Fordham University Press, 2017.

Keller, Catherine. *Political Theology of the Earth: Our Planetary Emergency and the Struggle for a New Public*. New York: Columbia University Press, 2018.

Keller, Catherine, and Stephen Moore. "Derridapocalypse." In *Derrida and Religion: Other Testaments*, edited by Yvonne Sherwood and Kevin Hart, 189–208. New York: Routledge, 2005.

Keller, Catherine, and John J. Thatamanil. "Is This an Apocalypse? We Certainly Hope So—You Should Too." *ABC Religion and Ethics*, April 15, 2020. https:// www.abc.net.au/religion/catherine-keller-and-john-thatamanil-why-we -hope-this-is-an-apo/12151922?fbclid=IwAR3IcmdDb4pgJjO3OMaUhP4yfu WcCMz9aFjTRCAuoZxnIYYZHuX9VWaJplA.

Klein, Naomi. *The Shock Doctrine: The Rise of Disaster Capitalism*. London: Penguin, 2008.

Knight, Frank H. *Risk, Uncertainty and Profit*. Boston: Houghton Mifflin, 1921.

Konings, Martijn. *Capital and Time: For a New Critique of Neoliberal Reason*. Stanford, CA: Stanford University Press, 2018.

Kornbluh, Peter. *The Pinochet File: A Declassified Dossier on Atrocity and Accountability*. New York: New Press, 2004.

Koselleck, Reinhart. *Futures Past: On the Semantics of Historical Time*. Translated by Keith Tribe. New York: Columbia University Press, 2004.

Kotsko, Adam. *Neoliberalism's Demons: On the Political Theology of Late Capital*. Stanford, CA: Stanford University Press, 2018.

Krippner, Greta. *Capitalizing on Crisis: The Political Origins of the Rise of Finance*. Cambridge, MA: Harvard University Press, 2011.

Langley, Paul. *The Everyday Life of Global Finance: Saving and Borrowing in Anglo-America*. Oxford: Oxford University Press, 2008.

Lapavitsas, Costas. *Profiting without Producing: How Finance Exploits Us All*. London: Verso, 2013.

Las Casas, Bartolomé de. *Historia de las Indias*. Vol. 3. Caracas: Biblioteca Ayacucho, n.d.

Lasch, Christopher. *The True and Only Heaven: Progress and Its Critics*. New York: W. W. Norton, 1991.

Lazzarato, Maurizio. *Governing by Debt*. Translated by Joshua David Jordan. South Pasadena, CA: Semiotext(e), 2015.

Lazzarato, Maurizio. *The Making of the Indebted Man: An Essay on the Neoliberal Condition*. Translated by Joshua David Jordan. Los Angeles: Semiotext(e), 2012.

Lee, Benjamin. "Deriving the Derivative." *Signs and Society* 6, no. 1 (Winter 2018): 225–55.

Lee, Benjamin. "From Primitives to Derivatives." In *Derivatives and the Wealth of Societies*, edited by Benjamin Lee and Randy Martin, 82–139. Chicago: University of Chicago Press, 2016.

Lee, Benjamin. Introduction to *Derivatives and the Wealth of Societies*, edited by Benjamin Lee and Randy Martin, 1–14. Chicago: University of Chicago Press, 2016.

Lee, Benjamin, and Randy Martin. *Derivatives and the Wealth of Societies*. Chicago: University of Chicago Press, 2016.

Levinas, Emmanuel. *Time and the Other and Additional Essays*. Translated by Richard A. Cohen. Pittsburgh, PA: Duquesne University Press, 1987.

Lima Júnior, José. "Assim Beijava Benjamin." *Estudos de Religião* 31, no. 2 (May–August 2017): 181–203.

Lima Júnior, José. "Pipas, piões e apostas." *Numen: Revista de Estudos e Pesquisa da Religião* 22, no. 2 (July 2019): 64–84.

Linguet, Simon Nicolas Henri. *Théorie des Lois Civiles, ou, Principes Fondamentaux de la Société*. Vol. 2. London: n.p., 1767.

LiPuma, Edward. *The Social Life of Financial Derivatives: Markets, Risk, and Time*. Durham, NC: Duke University Press, 2017.

LiPuma, Edward, and Benjamin Lee. *Financial Derivatives and the Globalization of Risk*. Durham, NC: Duke University Press, 2004.

Lloyd, Vincent. "For What Are Whites to Hope?" *Political Theology: The Journal of Christian Socialism* 17, no. 2 (March 2016): 168–81.

Löwy, Michael. "Capitalism as Religion: Walter Benjamin and Max Weber." *Historical Materialism: Research in Critical Marxist Theory* 17, no. 1 (January 2009): 60–73.

Lysandrou, Photis. "Global Inequality, Wealth Concentration and the Subprime Crisis: A Marxian Commodity Theory Analysis." *Development and Change* 42, no. 1 (January 2011): 183–208.

MacKendrick, Karmen. *The Matter of Voice: Sensual Soundings*. New York: Fordham University Press, 2016.

MacKenzie, Donald. *An Engine, Not a Camera: How Financial Models Shape Markets*. Inside Technology. Cambridge, MA: MIT Press, 2006.

MacKenzie, Donald. *Material Markets: How Economic Agents Are Constructed*. Clarendon Lectures in Management Studies. Oxford: Oxford University Press, 2009.

MacKenzie, Donald, and Iain Hardie. "Assembling an Economic Actor: The Agencement of a Hedge Fund." *Sociological Review* 55, no. 1 (February 2007): 57–80.

MacKenzie, Donald A., Fabian Muniesa, and Lucia Siu, eds. *Do Economists Make Markets? On the Performativity of Economics*. Princeton, NJ: Princeton University Press, 2007.

Magdoff, Harry. "Problems of U.S. Capitalism." In *The Dynamics of U.S. Capitalism*, edited by Paul Sweezy and Harry Magdoff, 7–29. New York: Monthly Review Press, 1972.

Magdoff, Harry, and Paul M. Sweezy. "The Merger Movement: A Study in Power." In *The Dynamics of U.S. Capitalism*, edited by Paul Sweezy and Harry Magdoff, 68–87. New York: Monthly Review Press, 1972.

Magdoff, Harry, and Paul M. Sweezy. *Stagnation and the Financial Explosion*. New York: Monthly Review Press, 1987.

Maia, Filipe. "Betrayed by Accent: Theological Notes on a Racist Worldsound." In *Religion and Sustainability: Interreligious Resources, Interdisciplinary Responses*, edited by Rita Sherma and Purushottama Bilimoria. New York: Springer, forthcoming.

Marazzi, Christian. *The Violence of Financial Capitalism*. Translated by Kristina Lebedeva. South Pasadena, CA: Semiotext(e), 2011.

Marte, Jonnelle. "U.S. Household Debt Increased by $1 Trillion in 2021, the Most Since 2007." *Reuters*, February 8, 2022. https://www.reuters.com/business/us-household-debt-increased-by-1-trillion-2021-most-since-2007-2022-02-08/.

Martin, Randy. *Financialization of Daily Life*. Philadelphia: Temple University Press, 2002.

Martin, Randy. *Knowledge LTD: Toward a Social Logic of the Derivative*. Philadelphia: Temple University Press, 2015.

Marx, Karl. *Capital: A Critique of Political Economy*. Translated by Ben Fowkes. Vol. 1. New York: Penguin Books, 1990.

Marx, Karl. *Capital: A Critique of Political Economy*. Edited by Ernest Mandel. Translated by David Fernbach. Vol. 3. New York: Penguin Classics, 1993.

Marx, Karl. *Grundrisse: Foundations of the Critique of Political Economy*. Translated by Martin Nicolaus. New York: Penguin Books, 1993.

Marx, Karl. "A Contribution to the Critique of Hegel's Philosophy of Right: Introduction." In *Karl Marx: Early Writings*, 243–57. New York: Penguin Books, 1992.

Mauss, Marcel. *The Gift*. Translated by Jane Guyer. Expanded edition. Chicago: HAU Books, 2016.

McCarraher, Eugene. *The Enchantments of Mammon: How Capitalism Became the Religion of Modernity*. Cambridge, MA: Harvard University Press, 2019.

McClanahan, Annie. *Dead Pledges: Debt, Crisis, and Twenty-First-Century Culture*. Stanford, CA: Stanford University Press, 2018.

McClanahan, Annie. "Investing in the Future: Late Capitalism's End of History." *Journal of Cultural Economy* 6, no. 1 (2013): 78–93.

Meeks, M. Douglas. *God the Economist: The Doctrine of God and Political Economy*. Minneapolis, MN: Fortress, 1989.

Melamed, Leo. "Milton Friedman's 1971 Feasibility Paper." *CATO Journal* 31, no. 3 (Fall 2011): 633–34.

Menéndez-Antuña, Luis. *Thinking Sex with the Great Whore: Deviant Sexualities and Empire in the Book of Revelation*. New York: Routledge, 2018.

Mitchell Innes, Alfred. *Credit and State Theories of Money: The Contributions of A. Mitchell Innes*. Edited by L. Randall Wray. Cheltenham, UK: Edward Elgar, 2004.

Moltmann, Jürgen. "On Latin American Liberation Theology: An Open Letter to José Míguez Bonino." In *Liberation Theology: A Documentary History*, edited by Alfred Henelly, 195–204. Maryknoll, NY: Orbis Books, 1990.

Moltmann, Jürgen. *Theology of Hope: On the Ground and the Implications of a Christian Eschatology*. London: SCM Press, 1967.

Montez, J. K., and A. Zajacova. "Why Is Life Expectancy Declining among Low-Educated Women in the United States?" *American Journal of Public Health* 104, no. 10 (October 2014): e5–e7.

Morrison, Toni. *Beloved*. New York: Alfred A. Knopf, 2006.

Moten, Fred. "Blackness and Nothingness (Mysticism in the Flesh)." *South Atlantic Quarterly* 112, no. 4 (Fall 2013): 737–80.

Moten, Fred. *Stolen Life*. Durham, NC: Duke University Press, 2018.

Moten, Fred, and Stefano Harney. *The Undercommons: Fugitive Planning and Black Study*. New York: Minor Compositions, 2013.

Muñoz, José Esteban. *Cruising Utopia: The Then and There of Queer Futurity*. New York: New York University Press, 2009.

Nadal, Estela Fernández, and Gustavo Daniel Silnik. *Teología profana y pensamiento crítico: Conversaciones con Franz Hinkelammert*. Buenos Aires: CICCUS and CLACSO, 2012.

Nietzsche, Friedrich. *On the Genealogy of Morality*. Translated by Carol Diethe. Cambridge: Cambridge University Press, 2007.

Novak, Michael. *The Spirit of Democratic Capitalism*. New York: Simon and Schuster, 1982.

Oxfam International. "62 People Own Same as Half the World." Press release, Oxfam International, January 18, 2016. http://oxfamapps.org/media/prhow.

Piketty, Thomas. *Capital in the Twenty-First Century*. Translated by Arthur Goldhammer. Cambridge, MA: Harvard University Press, 2014.

Pinn, Anthony B. "Theology after Hope and the Projection of Futures." *American Journal of Theology and Philosophy* 40, no. 2 (May 2019): 24–47.

Prassl, Jeremias. *Humans as a Service: The Promise and Perils of Work in the Gig Economy*. Oxford: Oxford University Press, 2018.

Presser, Harriet B. "Employment in a 24/7 Economy: Challenges for the Family." In *Fighting for Time: Shifting Boundaries of Work and Social Life*, edited by Cynthia Fuchs Epstein and Arne L. Kalleberg, 46–76. New York: Russell Sage Foundation, 2004.

Presser, Harriet B. *Working in a 24/7 Economy: Challenges for American Families*. Albany, NY: Russell Sage Foundation, 2003.

Puleo, Mev. *The Struggle Is One: Voices and Visions of Liberation*. Albany: State University of New York, 1994.

Rambo, Shelly. *Resurrecting Wounds: Living in the Afterlife of Trauma*. Waco, TX: Baylor University Press, 2017.

Rambo, Shelly. *Spirit and Trauma: A Theology of Remaining*. Louisville, KY: Westminster John Knox, 2010.

Richard, Pablo, Severino Croatto, Frei Betto, Victorio Araya, Jorge Pixley, Jon Sobrino, Jiménez Limón, Franz J. Hinkelammert, Joan Casañas, and Hugo Assmann. *A luta dos deuses: Os ídolos da opressão e a busca do Deus libertador*. Translated by Álvaro Cunha. 2nd ed. São Paulo: Paulinas, 1985.

Rieger, Joerg. *No Rising Tide: Theology, Economics, and the Future*. Minneapolis, MN: Fortress, 2009.

Rieger, Joerg. "Why Class Matters in Religious Studies and Theology." In *Religion, Theology, and Class: Fresh Engagements after Long Silence*, edited by Joerg Rieger, 1–23. New York: Palgrave Macmillan, 2013.

Rieger, Joerg, and Rosemarie Henkel-Rieger. *Unified We Are a Force: How Faith and Labor Can Overcome America's Inequalities*. St. Louis, MO: Chalice, 2016.

Rivera-Pagán, Luis. "God the Liberator: Theology, History, and Politics." In *In Our Own Voices: Latino/a Renditions of Theology*, edited by Benjamin Valentin, 1–20. Maryknoll, NY: Orbis Books, 2010.

Robinson, Cedric J. *Black Marxism: The Making of the Black Radical Tradition*. Chapel Hill: University of North Carolina Press, 2000.

Rogers, James Steven. *The Early History of the Law of Bills and Notes: A Study of the Origins of Anglo-American Commercial Law*. Cambridge Studies in English Legal History. Cambridge: Cambridge University Press, 1995.

Ruyter, Alex de, and Martyn Brown. *The Gig Economy*. Newcastle upon Tyne: Agenda Publishing, 2019.

Schüssler Fiorenza, Elisabeth. *In Memory of Her: A Feminist Theological Reconstruction of Christian Origins*. New York: Crossroad, 1994.

Schüssler Fiorenza, Elisabeth. *Rhetoric and Ethic: The Politics of Biblical Studies*. Minneapolis, MN: Fortress, 1999.

Schwartz, Nelson D. "The Recovery Threw the Middle-Class Dream under a Benz." *New York Times*, September 12, 2018. https://www.nytimes.com/2018/09/12/business/middle-class-financial-crisis.html.

Sedgwick, Peter R. *Nietzsche's Economy: Modernity, Normativity and Futurity.* New York: Palgrave Macmillan, 2007.

Segundo, Juan Luis. *Our Idea of God.* A Theology for a New Humanity 3. Maryknoll, NY: Orbis Books, 1974.

Sexton, Jared. "Affirmation in the Dark: Racial Slavery and Philosophical Pessimism." *Comparatist* 43, no. 1 (October 2019): 90–111.

Sexton, Jared. "Unbearable Blackness." *Cultural Critique*, no. 90 (Spring 2015): 159–80.

Simmel, Georg. *The Philosophy of Money.* 3rd ed. London: Routledge, 2004.

Singh, Devin. *Divine Currency: The Theological Power of Money in the West.* Stanford, CA: Stanford University Press, 2018.

Singh, Devin. "Sovereign Debt." *Journal of Religious Ethics* 46, no. 2 (June 2018): 239–66.

Smith, Adam. *An Inquiry into the Nature and Causes of the Wealth of Nations.* Great Books of the Western World. London: Encyclopedia Britannica, 1952.

Smith, Adam. *Lectures on Jurisprudence.* The Glasgow Edition of the Works and Correspondence of Adam Smith. Indianapolis, IN: Liberty Classics, 1982.

Smith, Adam. *The Theory of Moral Sentiments.* The Glasgow Edition of the Works and Correspondence of Adam Smith. Indianapolis, IN: Liberty Classics, 1982.

Smith, Desmond. "The Wiring of Wall Street." *New York Times*, October 23, 1983. https://www.nytimes.com/1983/10/23/magazine/the-wiring-of-wall-street.html.

Smith, Susan J. "Owner-Occupation: At Home with a Hybrid of Money and Materials." *Environment and Planning A: Economy and Space* 40, no. 3 (March 2008): 520–35.

Sohr, Raúl. "Prologue: The Tragedy That Was Dressed Up as a Miracle." In *Neoliberalism's Fractured Showcase: Another Chile Is Possible*, edited by Ximena de la Barra, xix–xxiii. Critical Global Studies 27. Leiden: Brill, 2011.

Spivak, Gayatri Chakravorty. *An Aesthetic Education in the Era of Globalization.* Cambridge, MA: Harvard University Press, 2013.

Spivak, Gayatri Chakravorty. *A Critique of Postcolonial Reason: Toward a History of the Vanishing Present.* Cambridge, MA: Harvard University Press, 1999.

Spivak, Gayatri Chakravorty. "Ghostwriting." *Diacritics* 25, no. 2 (Summer 1995): 65–84.

Spivak, Gayatri Chakravorty. "An Interview with Gayatri Chakravorty Spivak." Interview by Sara Danius and Stefan Jonsson. *Boundary 2* 20, no. 2 (Summer 1993): 24–50.

Spivak, Gayatri Chakravorty. *Outside in the Teaching Machine.* London: Routledge, 1993.

Spivak, Gayatri Chakravorty. "Scattered Speculations on the Question of Value." *Diacritics* 15, no. 4 (Winter 1985): 73–93.

Spivak, Gayatri Chakravorty. "Speculations on Reading Marx: After Reading Derrida." In *Post-structuralism and the Question of History*, edited by Derek

Attridge, Geoffrey Bennington, and Robert Young, 30–62. Cambridge: Cambridge University Press, 1987.

Spivak, Gayatri Chakravorty. "Translator's Preface." In *Of Grammatology* by Jacques Derrida, ix–lxxxvii. Corrected ed. Baltimore, MD: Johns Hopkins University Press, 1998.

Sung, Jung Mo. *Desire, Market, Religion*. London: SCM Press, 2007.

Sung, Jung Mo. *Idolatria do dinheiro e direitos humanos: Uma crítica teológica do novo mito do capitalismo*. São Paulo: Paulus, 2018.

Sung, Jung Mo. *Teologia e economia: Repensando a teologia da libertação e utopias*. Rio de Janeiro: Vozes, 1994.

Tanner, Kathryn. *Christianity and the New Spirit of Capitalism*. New Haven, CT: Yale University Press, 2019.

Taylor, Keeanga-Yamahtta. *Race for Profit: How Banks and the Real Estate Industry Undermined Black Homeownership*. Chapel Hill: University of North Carolina Press, 2019.

Taylor, Mark C. *Erring: A Postmodern a/Theology*. Chicago: University of Chicago Press, 1984.

Trimble, Rufus James. "The Law Merchant and the Letter of Credit." *Harvard Law Review* 61, no. 6 (June 1948): 981–1008.

US Department of Treasury. "The Financial Crisis Response in Charts." 2012. https://www.treasury.gov/resource-center/data-chart-center/Documents /20120413_FinancialCrisisResponse.pdf.

Valdés, Juan Gabriel. *Pinochet's Economists: The Chicago School in Chile*. Historical Perspectives on Modern Economics. Cambridge: Cambridge University Press, 1995.

VanDerhei, Jack. "The Impact of the Recent Financial Crisis on 401(k) Account Balances." Issue brief, no. 326. Washington, DC: Employee Benefit Research Institute, February 2009.

Varoufakis, Yanis. "Egalitarianism's Latest Foe: A Critical Review of Thomas Piketty's *Capital in the Twenty-First Century*." *Real-World Economics Review*, no. 69 (2014). http://www.paecon.net/PAEReview/issue69/Varoufakis69 .pdf.

Verdugo, Patricia. *Salvador Allende: Cómo la Casa Blanca provocó su muerte*. Buenos Aires: Editorial El Ateneo, 2003.

Vogl, Joseph. *The Specter of Capital*. Stanford, CA: Stanford University Press, 2014.

Wariboko, Nimi. *Economics in Spirit and Truth: A Moral Philosophy of Finance*. New York: Palgrave Macmillan, 2014.

Wariboko, Nimi. *The Split Economy: Saint Paul Goes to Wall Street*. Albany: State University of New York, 2020.

Warren, Calvin L. "Black Nihilism and the Politics of Hope." CR: *The New Centennial Review* 15, no. 1 (Spring 2015): 215–48.

Warren, Calvin L. *Ontological Terror: Blackness, Nihilism, and Emancipation*. Durham, NC: Duke University Press, 2018.

195

Weber, Max. *The Protestant Ethic and the Spirit of Capitalism*. Translated by Talcott Parsons. London: Routledge, 2001.

Weber, Max. *The Protestant Ethic and the Spirit of Capitalism*. Translated by Stephen Kalberg. Revised ed. New York: Oxford University Press, 2010.

West, Cornel. Foreword to *The Ideological Weapons of Death: A Theological Critique of Capitalism*, by Franz J. Hinkelammert, v–vii. Maryknoll, NY: Orbis Books, 1986.

Westhoff, Patrick. *The Economics of Food: How Feeding and Fueling the Planet Affects Food Prices*. Upper Saddle River, NJ: Pearson, 2010.

Wilderson, Frank B. *Afropessimism*. New York: W. W. Norton, 2020.

Wilderson, Frank B. *Incognegro: A Memoir of Exile and Apartheid*. Cambridge, MA: South End, 2008.

Wilderson, Frank B. *Red, White and Black: Cinema and the Structure of U.S. Antagonisms*. Durham, NC: Duke University Press, 2010.

Winters, Joseph R. *Hope Draped in Black: Race, Melancholy, and the Agony of Progress*. Durham, NC: Duke University Press, 2016.

Wolman, William, and Anne Colamosca. *The Great 401(k) Hoax: Why Your Family's Financial Security Is at Risk, and What You Can Do about It*. Cambridge, MA: Basic Books, 2003.

Wortham, Simon Morgan. "What We Owe to Retroactivity: The Origin and Future of Debt." *Postmodern Culture* 23, no. 3 (May 2013). https://doi.org/10.1353/pmc.2013.0052.

INDEX

absences, 20, 99, 119; naming, 123–29
Adkins, Lisa, 45
"Advice to a Young Tradesman" (Franklin),
87–88, 166–67n2
aesthetic concerns, 124–26
Afro-pessimism, 138–39, 144
Allende, Salvador, 91, 167n25, 167–68n26
Allon, Fiona, 57
Alves, Rubem, 20, 110–29, 141, 172n11,
173n39; body as flesh of hope, 120–23;
and Brazilian military coup, 114–15,
121; "gut theology" of, 114–20; hope,
intrahistorical dimension of, 115, 117–18;
naming absences, 123–29; "poetico-
metaphorical overabundance" in works
of, 124, 127–29; Protestant roots of,
93–94, 175n91; religion-politics-play
triad, 124–25; theopoetics of, 113, 125,
175n100
Alves, Rubem, works of: "A Theological
Interpretation of the Meaning of the
Revolution in Brazil," 114; *A Theology
of Human Hope*, 10, 114, 120–23, 126,
151n45; *Tomorrow's Child*, 125; "Towards
a Theology of Liberation," 10, 114, 172n14
ambivalence, constructive, 133

anticipation, language of, 99, 101, 106–7
apocalypse, 14, 20, 128, 130–38, 176n8;
apocalyptic tone, 124, 179n77; counter-
apocalypse, 133–36, 147; habit of, 132–33,
135; justice, concern with, 131, 133, 137,
146–48; misogyny of script, 133, 176n1;
as now and then, 136–37, 147; as opening
to present, 136, 176n10; "third space" of,
132–33. *See also* edges
Appadurai, Arjun, 34, 37–38, 156n74
Arcades Project, The (Benjamin), 89
Arguedas, José María, 111
Arnoldi, Jakob, 33
Ascher, Ivan, 5, 63, 75–78
Augustine, 1, 62, 71, 84

Babylon narrative, 130–31, 135, 137, 147,
176n1
banking system, 19, 28, 37; Smith's account
of, 41, 46–48, 50
Bank of England, 42–43, 44, 157n7, 157n9
Baran, Paul, 26, 27
Barreto Júnior, Raimundo César, 125,
175n100
Barthes, Karl, 116
beauty, politics of, 126

as, 49, 64–66, 69–70; as social hedges, 77; unknowability as marketable, 33–34; value of, 64, 80. *See also* futures contracts

commodity fetishism, 89, 97–99, 106, 170n61

Communism and the Theologians (West), 114–15

competition, idealized, 102–3

Confessions (Augustine), 1, 62, 71, 84

conservative agenda, 11, 101–2, 117

constructive theology, 14–15, 131, 132–33

Cox, Harvey, 114, 172n11

credit, 157n4; expansion of, 28–29, 75; extension of, 27–29; money as, 42, 44, 87, 157n9, 158n15

creditor-debtor relation, 34, 41; future of debtor consumed by, 6, 51, 63, 76; guilt derived from, 53, 59, 88, 89, 108; space of promising and waiting, 54–55; violence of, 52–53, 161n63. *See also* debt; promissory notes

creditworthiness, 44, 87–88, 161n80; algorithmic calculations, 56, 75–76; credibility, 51, 75; gender hierarchies and racial stereotypes, 55–56

crises, financial: bailout of banks, 37; debt crisis of the 1980s, 29; financial crisis of 2007–2008, 4, 29, 74, 83–84

Crítica de la razón utópica (Hinkelammert), 86, 101–4

critical reflection, 10–11, 33, 85, 86–87, 111–12, 126

cruel optimism, 12, 151n54

Cruising Utopia (Muñoz), 15, 136

culpability, logic of, 59

Cultures of Finance Workgroup, 30–31, 34

currency markets, 31–33

Day, Keri, 142

death: premature, as material result of exploitation, 9, 70–71; sacrifice of individuals for economic purposes, 96–97, 100, 103–4

"death of despair," 74

Deaton, Angus, 74

debt, 158n20, 160n54; circulation of, 43–44; economies of, 8–9, 11, 17, 25–30, 54, 138; escape as tactic of temporal displacement, 132; financialized capitalism sustained by, 27–30, 76; forgiveness of, 53–54; gendered, 19, 42, 53, 55–56, 142, 177n35; haunting by, 20, 55, 60; higher education as pipeline to, 76–77; indebted subject, 8, 30, 41–42, 45, 54–56, 59–63, 76, 113, 132–33, 142, 162n99; material memory of, 45, 49, 51, 159n26; money as measure of, 42–43, 158n18; predatory inclusion, 41, 57–58, 138; punishment, threat of, 52–54, 59; racialized, 19, 41–42, 53, 55–56, 137–38, 142, 177n35; socialization of, 19, 26, 30, 51, 57, 59; submission, relations of, 37, 40, 59–61. *See also* creditor-debtor relation; financialized capitalism; promissory notes

Debt: The First 5,000 Years (Graeber), 42

deconstruction: of determinisms, 133, 135, 145; of value, 78, 80, 84

deferral, monetization of, 44–45

"defuturization," 116, 120

De La Torre, Miguel, 12–13, 151–52n61

demonic logic, 59

derivatives, 25, 30–35, 155n44, 155–56n52

Derrida, Jacques, 2, 63, 78, 80, 125, 136; apocalyptic tone, 124, 179n77

de Ruyter, Alex, 72

Desmond, Matthew, 142

determinism, 133–34, 136, 151n61

difference/differentiation, 78–81, 83; and apocalyptic thinking, 135–37

disability studies, 15–16

Dodd, Nigel, 43–44, 158n18

domestic space and time, 55, 57, 60, 73

Duménil, Gérard, 6

economic history, 26–27, 42–51, 157n4

economics: birth of in rupture of time, 48–49; bourgeois political economy, 64, 65; Chicago school of, 92; depoliticization of, 27; "heavenly future" promised by, 8; modern, 8, 48–50; as study of value, 49 economy: of Babylon, fall of, 130–31, 135, 137, 147; of debt, 8–9, 11, 17, 25–30, 54, 138; finance, split with, 3; future-devouring, 23–39; life-oriented, 100

"eco-social" relations, 135, 142–43

Edelman, Lee, 12

edges, 2–3, 107, 136–37; as escape route, 131–32; *eschatos*, 2, 146–47; financialized capitalism at site of, 23, 39; and fugitivity, 145–46; hedges, tension with, 3, 20, 85, 145; and love for future, 136; poetics of, 113, 126; of social body, 11, 111, 119; of working day, 72. *See also* apocalypse

Elie Ayache, 33

Embracing Hopelessness (De La Torre), 12–13

episteme, 160n42

erring, 11–12, 15

Erring (Taylor), 11–12, 15

escape: and apocalyptic tone, 124; from capitalism, as impossible, 21, 87–88, 105–7, 145; from debt, as impossible, 59; future-talk as tactic of, 20, 128–32, 138, 142–44. *See also* fugitivity

escapism, 131, 179n73; and denial of future-talk, 12–14, 152n64

eschatological imagination, Christian, 2, 106–8; body as flesh of hope, 120–23; "codes" of, 3; community, eschatological, 140; dismissal of, 11–14; historical grounding of, 114–15; hope in financial times, 7–11; oppressed body's desire for future, 119–20; resurrection, discourse of, 16, 99–100, 112, 120–23, 127; as a site of resistance, 1–2, 10, 86–87, 91; status quo sidestepped by, 107. *See also* liberation theologies

eschatology of liberation, 9–10, 11, 17–18, 20, 86, 105, 108, 112, 119, 122, 131–32, 144–46

eschaton, 2, 176n8

eschatos, 2, 146–47

Esposito, Elena, 4

Essay on Trade and Commerce, 68

ethos, 87

exchange relations, 46, 49, 52–53, 64–65, 80

exchange value, 64–66, 80–81

existentialism, 116, 143

expectations: consumed by exploitation of labor time, 6, 61, 63, 67, 68–70, 74–76, 145; monopolized by neoliberalism, 105; social distribution of, 5. *See also* hope

exploitation: expectations consumed by, 6, 61, 63, 68–70, 74–76, 145; gendered, 83–84; premature death as material result of, 9, 70–71

expropriation, 64, 69–71, 77, 85

Fabozzi, Frank, 3, 23

Facing Apocalypse (Keller), 135

Factory Act of 1850, 70

Fanon, Frantz, 139

fetishism. *See* commodity fetishism

financial discourse: futurology of, 33, 118–19, 132; hegemonic power over future-talk, 3, 10, 21, 77–78, 90; hopes shaped by, 7, 10–11, 21; spirit of capitalism in, 38. *See also* future-talk

financialization: as apocalypse habit, 135; conquest of the imagination by, 118–19; defined, 24–25; of everyday payments, 29–30; as gendered process, 57; of personal revenue, 29; social force of, 61; and surplus absorption problem, 27–28, 154n29. *See also* debt

financialized capitalism: debt as sustaining factor for, 29–30, 76; at edges of future-talk, 23, 39; escape from, 7, 11, 14, 20, 142–48; future consumed by, 6, 10–11, 25–26, 63, 76, 131–32; future determined by, 4–7; future-talk appropriated by, 3–5, 10, 77–78, 90; hope destroyed by, 6–7, 21, 105, 118–19; temporality of, 4, 25, 45, 83–84, 131–32. *See also* capitalism; debt; neoliberalism; prediction

financial system: imperial, 28–29, 158n20; temporalization of, 44–45

foreign currency, futures market in, 31

Foster, John Bellamy, 28

Foucault, Michel, 36–37, 48–49, 51, 54, 160n42, 164n77
Frankfurt school, 93, 97
Franklin, Benjamin, 87–88, 108, 166–67n2
free-market ideology, 90, 93, 95–96, 101–3
Freud, Sigmund, 140, 171n99
Friedman, Milton, 31, 32, 92, 150n25
fugitivity, 20, 138, 143–48, 179n76; desire for "outside," 144; fugitive futurity, 132, 143–47; future as ultimate fugitive, 145, 147. *See also* Black life; escape
future: actualizing of, 54; alternative, 86, 107; alternative, destruction of, 6, 105, 118–19; body's desire for, 119–20; as call to subjection, 38, 50; coconstituted by financial discourse, 35; collective, 4, 6, 23, 34, 38–39, 145, 147; colonization of, 6–7, 145; conquest of longings for, 118–19; constructing, 14–19; consumption of by capital, 6–11, 13, 18–19, 25–26, 38–39, 42, 45–26, 62–64, 68–71, 74, 76, 123–26, 131–34, 145, 153n8; debt as preemptive relation to, 37; and "eco-social" relations, 135, 142–43; exteriority of, 177n30; "fixed or determinable," 42; fugitive, 138, 143–48; future-devouring power, 24–26, 38–39, 60, 153n8; love for, 127–28, 136; "memory of the future," promise as, 52–53, 55; as "not—yet," 1–7, 11, 14–15, 17–21, 32, 61, 62, 71, 75, 84–87, 107–9, 112–13, 122–24, 126–28, 131–35, 137, 144–45, 148; "poetico-metaphorical overabundance" of, 124, 127–29; premature death, 9, 70–71; as "present absence," 108–9; sacrifice made in the name of, 87–89, 96, 103–4; as surprising, 8, 177n30; as ultimate fugitive, 145, 147; unknowability as marketable commodity, 33–34. *See also* hope; prediction
futures contracts, 3–5, 23, 30–35; agricultural backstory, 32; defined, 3, 23, 32. *See also* hedges
future-talk: absences, summoning of, 123–24, 126–29; anti-utopian rejection of, 101–2, 118; capitalist discourse as, 90; dismissal of, 11–14; as double entendre,

128–29; embodied mode of, 112, 121; as escape tactic, 11, 14, 20, 128–32, 138, 142–44; hegemonic power of financial discourse over, 3–5, 10, 21, 77–78, 90; idolatrous nature of capitalist, 87, 89–90, 96, 104; of the marginalized, 2–3, 9, 13; means of production of, 7, 20, 145; of neoliberalism, 40; oppression justified by, 9, 12–13, 90, 104; precarity of, 133; realistic, 117–18; sense of, 1–2; social production of, 7, 86, 99–100, 105, 108; tension between edges and hedges, 3, 20, 85, 145. *See also* financial discourse

Galbraith, John Kenneth, 26
Gerson, Kathleen, 72
Giddens, Anthony, 6
global economy, 19, 23, 135, 155n44; built on slavery, 142; Chile as watershed moment for, 92, 105; takeover of by financial sector, 3–4, 25–26, 32–34
God: and absences, 127; free market sanctioned by, 171n84; as God of the future, 116–17; *O futuro a Deus pertence* (the future belongs to God), 18; projection of human power onto, 97–98
Goethe, Johann Wolfgang von, 104
gold reserves, 41, 46–47, 51
gold standard, 31, 33
Goodchild, Philip, 8, 158n18
Graeber, David, 6, 28, 42, 157n4, 157n7, 158n15, 158n20, 161n63
Great Depression of the 1930s, 26
Grundrisse (Marx), 79
guilt, derived from debt relation, 53, 59, 88, 89, 108
Gutiérrez, Gustavo, 9, 10, 94, 111, 123, 141

Hamermesh, David, 72
Harney, Stefano, 144
Harriman, Mark W., 83
Harvey, David, 5, 64, 92–93
haunting, 127, 129; by debt, 20, 55, 60; of trauma, 16–17
Hayek, Friedrich von, 37, 92; language of sacrifice and death, 96–97, 100, 103

hedges, 3–5, 85; Christian eschatology applied to, 7–8; collective futures produced by, 4, 38–39, 145, 147; edges, tension with, 3, 20, 85, 145; financial, 3–5, 11, 23, 77; social, 77; and working day, 67. *See also* futures contracts

Hegelian thought, 79, 164n81, 165n92

Hinkelammert, Franz, 9, 20, 89–109, 118, 141, 169n50, 169n56, 169–70n57; Chilean coup and, 91, 93–97, 100; Christianity and Marxism, connection between, 97, 170n58; fetish, theory of, 89, 97–99, 106, 170n61; on idolatrous nature of capitalism, 89–90; intellectual formation of, 93–94; resurrection, view of, 99–100; on sacrifice of lives, 86, 103–4; "total market," 86, 95, 103–4; utopian thinking, critique of, 100–103, 105–8

Hinkelammert, Franz, works of: *Crítica de la razón utópica*, 86, 101–4; *The Ideological Weapons of Death*, 97–101, 169n56; *Sacrificios humanos y sociedad occidental*, 104

history, 114–18; economic, 26–27, 42–51, 157n4; as erring, 11–12, 15; eschatological imagination, grounding of, 114–15; intrahistorical dimension of hope, 115, 117–18; promissory notes, account of, 42–51, 157n4; remainders of, 16–17; sense given to, 107; and transcendence, 107, 115–16. *See also* apocalypse

Holy Saturday, space of, 16–17

hope: as acknowledgment of pain, 126; alternative senses of destroyed by financialized capitalism, 6–7, 21, 105, 118–19; alternative sources of, 11, 14–15, 86, 107; attention to "sighs of the oppressed creature," 10, 18; body as site of, 120–23; disabled bodies as affirmation of, 15–16; disparate levels of, 5; and easy guarantees, 12–13; for fall of imperialism, 130–31; in financial times, 7–11; grounded in material present, 106; hermeneutics of, 10, 111; intrahistorical dimension of, 115, 117–18; melancholic, 131, 133, 137–43; oppression justified by, 12–13;

as poietic, 124–25, 128–29; as political, 114; pseudo-hopes, 119; queering of, 15, 136; radical, 142–43; and resistance, 7, 15, 17; sacrificial, 90; as "scarce commodity," 171n103; shaped by financial discourse, 7, 10–11, 21; as social practice, 142–43; theology as critical reflection on, 10–11, 33, 85, 86–87, 111–12, 126; theology of, 114, 116, 136; as white supremacist tool, 139–40, 142; for a world of despair, 88. *See also* expectations; future

hopelessness, 6; white hope for, 139–40

Ideological Weapons of Death, The (Hinkelammert), 97–101, 169n56

idolatry, 87, 96–97, 118, 167n20; idolatrous nature of capitalism, 87, 89–90, 96, 104

imagination: economic, 20, 90, 103, 118–19; as form of critique, 126. *See also* eschatological imagination, Christian

imperial financial system, 28–29, 158n20; apocalyptic approach to, 130–31, 135

industrial sector, 5–6, 25–29, 43, 105; surplus absorption problem, 27–28, 154n29

inequality, 4–5, 19, 168n29; Chile, 96; of life expectancy, 73–74; temporal divide of working day, 72; twenty-first century as reprise of nineteenth-century western Europe, 23–24

"information," 36

ingathering, 136, 177n26

Innes, Alfred Mitchell, 42, 44

Instituto Latinoamericano de Doctrina y Estudios Sociales (ILADES), 94

"invisible hand," 92, 101, 108

Iphigenia, myth of, 104, 171n99

Jacobs, Jerry, 72

John of Patmos, 130, 135, 147

Joseph, Miranda, 27, 57

justice, 18, 20, 99, 108; apocalyptic concern with, 131, 133, 137, 146–48; beauty as necessary for, 126; denied by future-talk, 12–13, 105–7; and poiesis, 125

203

Marx, Karl, works of: *Capital,* 62–71, 75–76, 81, 111, 116; A Contribution to the Critique of Hegel's Philosophy of Right: Introduction," 110; *Grundrisse,* 79

Marxist theory, 26; credit extension, 27–29; surplus absorption problem, 27–28, 154n29

material conditions, 7, 19, 26, 41, 70, 162n99; of capitalist mode of production, 63–64, 66–67

material memory, of debt, 45, 49, 51, 159n26

McCarraher, Eugene, 151n42

McClanahan, Annie, 5, 55–56, 59, 161n80, 162n99, 166n112

Meeks, M. Douglas, 169n54

Melamed, Leo, 31

melancholic hope, 131, 133, 137–43

memory: mnemonic devices, 52–53, 55; "of the future," promise as, 52–53, 55; *saudade* as "longing remembrance," 127–28

mercantilist political economists, 46

messianic humanism, 119

"middle," 16–17

Middle Passage, 131, 137–39, 141–42

Modigliani, Franco, 3, 23

Moltmann, Jurgen, 114, 116–17, 136, 151n45, 151n61, 173n21, 173n30

money, 158n18, 159–60n41; as credit, 42, 44, 87, 157n9, 158n15; credit theory of, 42, 44, 45, 87; drawing and redrawing bank notes, 48; fictitious, 48–50; future as, 43; as measure of debt, 42–43; paper, 42, 44, 45, 46, 50–51; time as, 87–88

"Moneybags" character, 75–76

monopolies, corporate, 28

Monthly Review, 26, 28–29, 153n15

"moralist theology," 12

"moral values," used to promote neoliberalism, 97, 103

mortgage industry: dead pledges, mortgages as, 55–61; demonic logic of, 59; gender hierarchies and racial stereotypes, 55–56; home as liability, 60; predatory inclusion, 41, 57–58, 138;

social relations of mortgages, 34; subprime mortgages, 19, 29, 55, 57, 76; and the uncanny, 60

Moten, Fred, 20, 131, 138, 143–46, 179n76

Muñoz, José Esteban, 15, 17, 136

Munster, Anabaptist upheaval in, 93–94

National Survey of Families and Households, 73

Navarro, Jannette (barista), 24–25

"Need for Futures Markets in Currencies, The" (Friedman), 31

negation of the negation, 116, 126

neofascism, utopia appropriated by, 105–9

neoliberalism: anti-interventionist policies, 30, 95, 96, 100; anti-utopianism of, 100–101, 118; benevolent rhetoric of, 92–93; Chile as experiment in, 9, 92, 95, 105; competition, idealization of, 102–3; demonic logic of, 59; as economy of debt, 54; free-market ideology, 27, 90, 93, 95–96, 101–3; gold standard unpegged from dollar, 31; promise of future wealth, 40–41, 45, 51, 54, 60; rise of, 5–6, 150n25; socialization of debt under, 30, 59; speculative orientation of, 36–37; state terrorism linked with, 93; theological sensibility in, 95–97, 100; utopian thinking as captive to, 105–9, 136; utopian thought in, 102–3; womanist critiques of, 142. *See also* capitalism; financialized capitalism

New York Times 1619 Project, 142

Nietzsche, Friedrich, 19, 41, 51–53, 160n54, 160n58, 161n63

nihilism, Black, 139

Nixon, Richard, 31

"noise," 36

normalizing theologies, 15

Obama, Barack, 140

occupying means of prediction, 11, 20, 77–78, 85, 144, 146

Of Grammatology (Derrida), 80

promissory notes, 19, 40–62; as bonds, 44; British Parliament's definition, 42, 43; circulation of, 41, 43–44, 50–51, 53; defined, 42–43; double movement of, 45; historical account of, 42–51, 157n4; as legal tender, 44; negotiability of, 43; and promissory subject, 40, 46, 51–55; Smith's ambivalence toward, 41, 47–48; treated as money, 44. *See also* debt
prophecy, 9, 10, 121, 123, 134, 144, 147
protection, privatization of means of, 63, 75, 77
Protestant Ethic and the Spirit of Capitalism, The (Weber), 87–89
punishment, threat of, 52, 53–54, 59
Puritan Calvinists, 37

queer theory, 12–15, 17, 136, 176n1
queer time, 15, 136

racial capitalism, 138, 177n35
racialization of debt, 19, 41–42, 53, 55–56, 137–38, 142, 177n35
racism, anti-Black, 12, 58, 138–40
Rambo, Shelly, 16–17
Reagan, Ronald, 92
realism, 101–2, 107, 117–18, 173n39
redemption, 16–17, 44, 122
religion: Alves's religion-politics-play triad, 124–25; capitalism as secularized form of, 88–89, 167n16; Protestant anxiety linked with capitalism, 35, 37; as a reflection of material reality, 97. *See also* liberation theologies; theology
remainders, 16–17, 138, 140
representation, value as, 49, 79–81
reproduction, 67, 76, 106
reproductive futurism, 12
resistance: by Black people to financial capital, 142; eschatological imagination as a site of, 1–2, 10, 86–87, 91; fugitivity as, 131, 138, 143–48; hope as attitude of, 15; mournful, 126, 132, 137; to status quo, 3, 18, 100, 107, 111, 143
"responsibilization," 59
resurrection, 16, 99–100, 112, 120, 122–23, 127

Revelation, Book of, 130–31, 135, 137, 147, 176n1
Rieger, Joerg, 8, 97, 103, 169–70n57, 171n84
Robinson, Cedric, 138, 177n35
Roman Empire, 130

sacrifice, 86–87; atrocities as, 96; eating, dialectic of, 123; entrails of human misery, 121–22; Hayek's language of, 96–97, 100, 103; legitimation of, 104, 171n99; made in the name of the future, 87–89, 96, 103–4; market theological, 89; of poor, 89–90; "sacrificial hope," 90; Western logic of, 104
Sacrificios humanos y sociedad occidental (Hinkelammert), 104
salvation: Protestant anxiety about, 35, 37; sacrifice of others necessary for, 104
saudade, 127–28
"Scattered Speculations on the Question of Value" (Spivak), 78–84
School of the Americas, 91
self-interest, 48, 104, 159n29
sense, 1–3; of indebtedness, 53; made of imperialism, 131; made of suffering, 122; multiplicity of, 1–2, 125–26, 148; and relational ontology of time, 135–36
September 11, 1973 coup (Chile), 91–95, 100
September 11, 2001 attacks (United States), 91, 93
Sexton, Jared, 138–39
"sighs of the oppressed creature," 10, 18, 20, 110–11; naming absences, 123–29; prophetic and fleshly dimension of, 121; suffering, attention paid to, 112–13. *See also* oppression; suffering
signification, chain of, 80
"signs of the times," 19, 61, 97, 110–11, 122, 124
Singh, Devin, 44
slavery: financed by London money market, 142; as matrix of oppression, 138–39; Middle Passage, 131, 137–39, 141–42
Smith, Adam, 19, 46–51, 159n29, 159n37, 161n63; circulation vs. production, 66; divine providence in, 104; promissory notes, view of, 41, 46

Smith, Adam, works of: *Lectures on Juris-prudence*, 159n30; *The Wealth of Nations*, 47–48, 159n29

socialism, 91, 94, 101–2

socialization: of debt, 19, 26, 30, 51, 57, 59; of expropriation, 77; of labor, 99

social relations: and commodity fetishism, 97; "eco-social," 135, 142–43; exchange relations at core of, 53, 57; and future-talk, 99; of production, 19, 66–67, 97, 100; time as materially constituted through, 63; transformation in, 105, 107, 111. *See also* creditor-debtor relation

Sohr, Raúl, 92, 95, 168n29

Solomon, Peter, 83

spirit of capitalism, 8, 35, 37–38, 87–89, 96–97, 109

Spivak, Gayatri Chakravorty, 20, 78–84, 162–63n21, 163n27, 164n81, 165n86, 165nn91–92, 166n111; deconstructive approach of, 78, 80, 84; labor theory of value, view of, 64, 78–79, 82–83

status quo: conservation of, 37, 104, 118, 150n34; fragility of, 119; radical hope refusal to accept, 143; resistance to, 3, 18, 100, 107, 111, 143

student loan industry, 76–77, 164n77

student loans, 59

subject: entrepreneurial, 88; indebted, 8, 30, 41–42, 45, 54–56, 59–63, 76, 113, 132–33, 142, 162n99; promising, 19, 41, 52, 55, 59; promissory, 40, 46, 51–55. *See also* labor power

submission, relations of, 37, 40, 59–61

subprime mortgage industry, 19, 29, 55, 57, 76

suffering, 13, 106, 115–17, 174n54; attention paid to, 112–13; of body, 117, 120–23; as condition of possibility of hope, 119; hope triggered by, 117; pleasure of idol in, 90; sense made of by theology, 122; trauma, 16–17. *See also* "sighs of the op-pressed creature"

summons, 1–3, 11, 14, 112; of absences, 123–24, 126–29

surplus absorption problem, 27–28, 154n29

surplus labor, 67, 69–70

surplus value, 64, 67, 75, 80

Sweezy, Paul, 26, 27–28, 29, 154n29

Tanner, Kathryn, 8, 51, 150n34

Taylor, Keeanga-Yamahtta, 57–58, 138

Taylor, Mark C., 11–12, 13

temporal colonialism, 6

temporality, 160n48, 176n8; of capitalism, 6, 19–20, 55, 71, 90, 108; class power reinforces, 63; continuity of, 8, 119, 132, 150n34; death-dealing, 19–20; of financialized capitalism, 4, 25, 45, 83–84, 131–32; indefinite, 130–31; paradoxes of preemptive temporalities, 36–37; regime imposed on, 39; of trauma, 16–17. *See also* time

terrorism, state, linked with neoliberal-ism, 93

textuality of value, 78–84, 165n86

Thatcher, Margaret, 92, 119

"Theological Interpretation of the Mean-ing of the Revolution in Brazil, A" (Alves), 114

theology: constructive, 14–15, 131, 132–33; as critical reflection on hope, 10–11, 33, 85, 86–87, 111–12, 126; transcendental, 116

Theology of Hope (Moltmann), 114, 116–17, 136

Theology of Human Hope, A (Alves), 10, 114, 120–23, 126, 151n45

Theology of Liberation (Gutiérrez), 141

Theology of Money (Goodchild), 8

Third World: Alves as voice of, 114; labor of, 82–83

time: autochthonous laws of, 49–50; of capital and production, 49, 51; "chronic crisis over the clock," 5, 24, 71–74; com-puter management of, 82–83; constant and a variable quantity of, 67; diverse ways of construing, 2; economy of, 54; exercise of power over as profitable, 63; hauntology of, 127; materiality of, 82; as money, 87–88; normalization of, 119; organization of labor, 63; politics of, 133; as profit, 62, 70–71, 84–85; queer vs. straight, 15; relational dimension of,

time (continued)
135–37; rupture in experience of, 48–49;
spirit of, 88; value of, 62, 70–71, 82; wiring of Wall Street, 82–83. *See also* future;
temporality
"total market," 86, 95, 103–4
"Towards a Theology of Liberation"
(Alves), 10, 114, 172n14
transcendence, 101, 103, 165n86, 170n58,
176n8; fetishized vs. humanized, 106–7;
historical, 107, 115–16
trauma, 16–17
trust, 15, 42–43, 157n4

uncanny, the, 60, 144
uncertainty, 4; eliminated by prediction, 8;
of fugitivity, 20; liberationist maneuver,
7, 17; market economy generated by,
156n61; neoliberal orientation toward,
36–37; policing, 33–34; profitability of,
23, 25, 33–39; risk distinguished from,
35–36; as valuable, 155–56n52
undercommons, 144, 146–47
Unidad Popular (Popular Unity, Chile), 94
United States: debt of, 29; September 11,
2001 attacks, 91, 93; tensions in 1960s
and 1970s, 27
use value, 64–66, 68–69, 75, 80–81
utopian thinking: anti-utopianism of
neoliberalism, 100–101, 118; as captive to
neoliberalism, 105–9, 136; as dimension
of human rationality, 107–8; in free-
market ideology, 102–3; queer time, 15;
radical thread of, 135–36

Valéry, Paul, 110, 123
value: Bible and linen example, 65; as catachresis, 165n91; chain of, 79–84, 165n92;

of commodities, 64, 80; deconstruction
of, 78, 80, 84; as differential, 79–81, 83;
exchange value, 64–66, 80–81; labor
theory of, 49, 64, 69, 78–79, 82–83,
166n112; modern economics as study of,
49; as narrative starting point in Marx,
165–66n104; price confused with, 65; as
representation, 81; as socially necessary
labor-time, 64; surplus, 64, 67, 75, 80;
textuality of, 78–84, 165n86; of time, 62,
70–71, 82; use value, 64–66, 68–69, 75,
80–81
Vieira, António, 121, 122–23
violence: coded as sacrifice, 104; of
creditor-debtor relation, 52–53, 161n63.
See also sacrifice
Vogl, Joseph, 44–45

Wall street, wiring of, 82–83
Wariboko, Nimi, 3, 156n63
Warren, Calvin, 139, 144
Wealth of Nations, The (Smith), 47–48,
159n29
Weber, Max, 35, 37, 87–89, 156n74
"welfare state," 92, 93
West, Charles, 114–15
wholeness, projections of, 15–16
Winters, Joseph, 131, 137–38, 140–43
womanist critiques, 142
word processor, 82–83
working day, 49, 63, 67–71, 163n41; in age
of financialization, 71–74, 78; Factory
Act of 1850, 70; "natural" day compared
with, 68; nonstandard work schedules,
72–73; temporal divide, 72
worry, 4–5, 177n20
Wortham, Simon, 53
writing, labor power of, 80, 82–83